Suddenly
San Francisco

Suddenly
San Francisco

The Early Years of an Instant City
by Charles Lockwood

A California Living Book

FOR
PATRICK DANIELS
MARGARET W. WHITE
DAVID ROWINSKI

First Edition

Copyright © 1978
The San Francisco Examiner Division of The Hearst Corporation.
Special Projects, Suite 911, The Hearst Building,
Third and Market Streets, San Francisco, California 94103.

Printed in the United States of America.

ISBN 0-89395-003-3 (hardback)
ISBN 0-89395-004-1 (paperback)

Library of Congress Catalog Card Number 77-94873

7
INTRODUCTION

9
ACKNOWLEDGMENTS

11
CHAPTER ONE
Beginnings
Gold!
Boom Town
The Winter of 1849–50

27
CHAPTER TWO
The 49ers
Scarcity of Women
Prostitution
Gambling

39
CHAPTER THREE
Hard Work
Building the City
The Six Fires
Montgomery Street

53
CHAPTER FOUR
Hotels
Food and Drink

60
CHAPTER FIVE
Woman's Place
Worship
Schools
Rincon Hill/South Park
Feminism

75
CHAPTER SIX
Banking and Trade
Manufacturing
Real Estate

Public Transportation
Economic Slump of 1853
Growing Again
The Decline of Rincon Hill

93
CHAPTER SEVEN
Streetwalkers/Brothels
Games of Chance
Theater
Family Outings
Woodward's Gardens

115
CHAPTER EIGHT
Golden Gate Park
Cemeteries
Land's End/Cliff House
Enter the Tourist
Palace Hotel
Baldwin Hotel
Hotel and Apartment Living
Restaurants
Meiggs Wharf
Nob Hill
Chinatown

148
CHAPTER NINE
The Strains of City Life
Crime
Growth of the Neighborhoods
Victorians
Old Neighborhoods
Earthquake and Disaster

162
CHRONOLOGY

169
BIBLIOGRAPHY

172
INDEX

San Francisco has always been one of America's most colorful and most talked-about cities. One hundred years ago, people across the country were enthralled, and sometimes more than a little scandalized, with what was going on in San Francisco—the '49ers, who had struck it rich, idly tossing $20 gold pieces off the wharves into the Bay like country boys skipping flat stones across the surface of a pond—or the Big Four and the Bonanza Kings in competition over who would erect the grandest mansion on Nob Hill—or the colorfully mad Joshua Norton who proclaimed himself Emperor of the United States and Protector of Mexico and wandered the streets for twenty years in his shabby epauletted frock coat and plumed hat. And the story of the 1906 earthquake and fire has entered the national folklore.

San Francisco shows no signs of quieting down. The past twenty-five years have been just as exciting and closely observed by the rest of the nation as any period in the past. The Beatniks emerged and flourished here in the Fifties. The late Sixties saw the arrival of the flower children and the popularization of the drug culture, which culminated, at least from a media standpoint, in the 1967 Summer of Love in Haight-Ashbury. The big development of the Seventies is Gay Liberation and the increasing visibility of gay men and women in the city's economic and political life.

All these stories, both past and present, have become part of the city's legend. But one of the best stories about San Francisco has yet to be fully told—the story of how San Francisco, within a few decades of the Gold Rush, became a city—architecturally, economically, and socially.

Before the Gold Rush, San Francisco hardly qualified as a village, much less a city. "In 1847 we find her with a population of less than 400, with no commerce, no wealth, no power, and without a name, save as a small trading post and mission station," wrote one San Franciscan. The Gold Rush changed all that. By the end of 1849, there were 20,000 to 25,000 people in San Francisco, nearly all of them men. The 1852 state census counted 34,776 residents of San Francisco. By 1860 the city's population had jumped to 56,802.

Few American cities have equaled San Francisco's growth so quickly after their founding. Chicago was nineteenth-century America's best-known boom town, and by 1860 it surpassed San Francisco in population. But it was no instant city. When Chicago was incorporated as a town in 1833, its population was 350. Seventeen years later, its population had reached only 29,963. Its great surge in population came in the 1850s and 1860s, several decades after its settlement.

Nor can Washington, D.C. be considered an instant city. There wasn't even a village along the swampy banks of the Potomac River, south of Georgetown, until the United States Government decided to move there from Philadelphia. But Washington, D.C. was slow to grow in population and urban amenities, even though the Capitol, White House, and other federal buildings gave it the appearance of a city in some places. When the federal government moved there in 1800, the population in the present-day District of Columbia, excluding Georgetown, was a little over 3,000. In 1803 a city census counted 4,352 residents, and that number had risen to just 5,652 four years later. The city's population increased at a rate of about 500 people a year until 1840.

From the start, San Francisco had most of the amenities found in much-older and much-larger cities back East. Within two or three years of the Gold Rush, San Francisco had more than a dozen hotels, restaurants in all price ranges and of different nationalities, churches of every denomination, several theaters, a library, public and private schools, and several newspapers.

Because of the wealth pouring into the city from trade and from the mines, many San Franciscans lived well. No other city at the time had as many saloons, gambling dens, or courtesans, per person, as did San Francisco. Most men were quick to abandon the rough miner's garb of 1849 and 1850, and San Franciscans soon boasted that "New York dresses better than Paris, and

San Francisco better than New York." They knew how to eat and drink, too. Californians consumed twice as much coffee and sugar as East Coast folk and three times as much tea. They drank seven bottles of imported champagne for every one consumed in Boston.

But there were perils in this rapid growth. So many would-be gold miners flocked to San Francisco during the Gold Rush that food and housing were in short supply and their prices astronomical. Then, in 1850 and 1851, fires destroyed large parts of the town on six separate occasions. Some blocks burned down and were rebuilt two and three times before the rash of fires finally ceased. Builders had been in such a hurry and building supplies were so expensive that most of San Francisco had been put up cheaply and without much precaution against fire. The city government hadn't had the chance to organize a fire department or assure adequate water supplies for firefighting.

Moreover, San Francisco had grown up on an impractical spot for a city: a foggy, windswept peninsula, where water and trees were in short supply. San Franciscans remedied these problems or adapted to them, but they could do nothing about the danger of earthquake. The 1865 and 1868 earthquakes showed just how vulnerable the city was to destruction. Some frame buildings collapsed outright or ended up leaning on their neighbors, while the stone and brick facades of others tumbled into the streets in piles of rubble. Nothing was done to make buildings more solid or to ready the city for another earthquake. In 1906, earthquake and fire destroyed over half of the city, but another San Francisco—a second instant city—rose almost as quickly as the previous one had been destroyed.

This book covers the years from the 1849 Gold Rush to the 1906 earthquake. It tells how San Francisco became a city—how it erected its buildings, expanded into the surrounding countryside, paved its streets, and built the public transportation systems which enabled it to function. But beyond the inanimate objects, the buildings and real estate developments, this is the story of the men and women who built and lived in San Francisco, their work, their play, and the ways they found to adapt to the unusual and sometimes trying conditions they found here.

Charles Lockwood
San Francisco
1978

After I completed my second book, *Manhattan Moves Uptown*, early in 1976, I decided to make some changes in my life and moved from New York City to San Francisco. A grant from the Eva Gebhard-Gourgaud Foundation gave me the time to research and write this book. I am deeply indebted to the Foundation and its President, Robert Sincerbeaux, for their continuing support of my work.

I did nearly all my research in the Bancroft Library at the University of California at Berkeley and at the California Historical Society in San Francisco. The old photographs and engravings which illustrate the text come from the Bancroft Library, the California Historical Society, the Library of Congress, the Museum of the City of New York, the New-York Historical Society, and the San Francisco Public Library. Suzanne Gallup at the Bancroft Library and Gladys Hansen at the San Francisco Public Library were particularly helpful in locating suitable illustrations for me.

I must thank the John Simon Guggenheim Foundation for the Fellowship I was awarded in 1973–1974 to further my study of European visitors' impressions of America. The excerpts from their travel accounts provide indispensable insights into San Francisco of the 1850s and 1860s.

The Foundation for San Francisco's Architectural Heritage encouraged my work on this book from the beginning, and Robert Berner and Linda Jo Fitz were always ready with good advice and made certain resources of Heritage available to me as I prepared this book.

George Livermore followed the progress of my work and made several suggestions which became a part of the text. Lewis and Phyllis Sarasy were a great help to me during my first month in town. My good friends Lawrence R. Barker and Thomas Howard Tarantino aided this project by their continuing interest in my work. I am particularly grateful to James W. Harbison, Jr. for his moral support and good counsel in the past year.

Hal Silverman and Elaine Ratner took great pains to make this a carefully edited and attractive book.

My greatest personal appreciation goes to three people: Patrick Daniels, who first showed me San Francisco, Margaret W. White, whose kindness has meant so much to me while living here, and David Rowinski, whose encouragement and friendship helped me through some of the more trying parts of this book. I dedicate this book to them.

MAP
OF
SAN FRANCISCO
1854

When Captain John Montgomery and the troops from the *U.S.S. Portsmouth* seized San Francisco on July 9, 1846, it was a ragged-looking trading village on San Francisco Bay, with fifty adobe and frame buildings that stretched no more than several blocks in any direction. Its population was about 200. Another 100 people lived several miles south in a settlement near Mission Dolores, and a few dozen more lived near the Presidio. Men outnumbered women about two to one, and hardly anyone was more than forty years old.

San Francisco, as a name, did not even exist at the time. The village was called Yerba Buena, which means "good grass" in Spanish. The name came from the wild mint which grew all over the sand dunes in the vicinity of the village. Six months later, Washington Allen Bartlett, a Spanish-speaking lieutenant on the *Portsmouth* who had become the highest municipal official in town, changed the village's name to San Francisco, in honor of the Bay on which it was situated and the nearby Mission San Francisco de Assisi, or Mission Dolores. Bartlett lacked the authority, but he published his proclamation in the *California Star* anyway; and on January 30, 1847, the American military governor made the new name official.

That was just the first of many changes that would soon overwhelm this village where the greatest excitement had been the arrival of a trading ship or a "cavalcade of young paisanos, jingling in silver chains and finery, dashing into town, half a dozen abreast." By 1846 trade between San Francisco and the other villages around the Bay was increasing, and rising numbers of whalers and hide merchants' ships were anchoring in the sheltered Yerba Buena cove to rest and to take on fresh supplies. That year, the United States Government established a custom house, a Quartermaster's Store, and several buildings to quarter troops in San Francisco as part of its Mexican War efforts. In summer, a ship with 200 Mormons bound for Salt Lake arrived in San Francisco. Most of the Mormons decided to stay in the village, thereby doubling its population to 400.

By the beginning of 1848, San Francisco looked far different from the village that Captain Montgomery had seized two years earlier. Its population had risen to 1,000, and, for a place in the middle of nowhere, it had attracted a remarkably cosmopolitan population from every state in the Union and most countries of Europe and Latin America. More than 100 men were Indians, Hawaiians, or native-born blacks.

It boasted 200 buildings to accommodate its increased population, including two hotels, a church, a ten-pin alley, a billiard parlor, and thirty-five shanties. Merchants had erected several warehouses for their trade with Hawaii and the East Coast, and two wharves were under construction so that rowboats would no longer have to carry cargoes to the shore from ships anchored in the cove.

"The town was becoming one of some consequence and was assuming the pretentions and attractions of older, wealthier, and more populous communities," recalled the *Annals of San Francisco*, a book compiled in 1855 from articles in the *Alta California, California Sun,* and *Herald.* The town fathers saw a splendid future for their village and hired Jasper O'Farrell to draw a plan for a city of broad streets laid out in right angles. "There was much bustle, and even enthusiasm among the inhabitants, which promised a flattering future to the town," noted the *Annals.*

In May, 1848, this situation was "suddenly checked by means which, unpromising at first, ultimately led to the most extraordinary prosperity in the city." The *Annals,* of course, was referring to the Gold Rush. Several months earlier, on the morning of January 24th, James W. Marshall had found flecks of gold in the tailrace of John Sutter's mill on the American River, a branch of the Sacramento River. Marshall hurried to Sutter with his find, and once the two proved the shining particles were indeed gold, they decided to keep their discovery a secret.

But the news was soon out, and hundreds of Sutter's neighbors descended on his property with spades, shovels, even knives to dig up the earth and then wash it in pans, wooden bowls, baby cradles—anything that might bring out the gold. Word of the discovery spread throughout California. "Small parcels of the precious metal had also been forwarded to San Francisco, while visitors from the mines and some actual diggers arrived to tell the wonders of the region and the golden gains of those engaged in exploring and working it," reported the *Annals*. "In consequence of such representations, the inhabitants began gradually, in bands and singly, to desert their previous occupations and betake themselves to the American River."

By May at least 150 men had left San Francisco for the gold fields, and "every day since was adding to their numbers," according to the *Annals*. The authors of the *Annals*, newspapermen Frank Soule and James Nisbet and physician John H. Gihon, also hastened to the mines, and the town council did not meet from May to October, because so many members were there.

The Gold Rush was ruining San Francisco. It had been virtually abandoned, "like a place where plague reigns, forsaken by its old inhabitants, a melancholy solitude." Houses stood empty, and most shopkeepers had left town to sell their merchandise at 500 to 1,000 per cent mark-ups in the gold fields. On May 29th one of the town's newspapers, the *Californian,* ceased publication. The Editor wrote: "The whole country from San Francisco to Los Angeles, and from the sea shore to the base of the Sierra Nevada, resounds with the sordid cry of gold! Gold!! GOLD!!!—while the field is left half planted, the house half built, and every thing neglected but the manufacture of shovels and pick-axes." On June 14th, the *California Star* published its final issue, because it "could not be made by magic, and the labor of mechanism was as essential to its existence as to all other arts."

That summer and fall, San Francisco had become "almost a desert place," according to the *Annals*. But things were happening in the rest of the country that were going to change all that. In August, the New York *Herald* reported the discovery of gold. Other newspapers picked up the story, and the news quickly spread across the nation. At the same time, Richard B. Mason, the military governor of California, sent a messenger to Washington, D.C. with a report of the gold discovery and $3,000 in gold dust in a tea caddy. The messenger told everyone he met along the way the astounding news. By the time President James K. Polk reported the

discovery to Congress on December 5th, most of the country already knew what had happened, and thousands of young men had left their homes for California.

The ships carrying the would-be gold miners landed at San Francisco. But why San Francisco—rather than Sacramento on the Sacramento River or Stockton on the San Joaquin River, which were closer to the gold fields? The answer has to do with the transportation technology of the time. The Sacramento and San Joaquin rivers could not accommodate vessels that drew more than ten feet of water. That ruled out the ocean-going vessels which carried men and supplies to California. San Francisco offered the transportation break where men and cargo were loaded into smaller ships that could navigate the Sacramento and San Joaquin rivers.

In 1848 and 1849 there were more agreeable spots than San Francisco to land goods and men and to build a city from scratch. Yerba Buena cove was sheltered, but there were mud flats between the shore and the deep water where the ships anchored. And there was little level ground beyond the shoreline. Sand dunes dotted the town, and Nob, Rincon, Russian, and Telegraph hills stood in the way of its expansion on all sides. Water was scarce, and there were virtually no trees to provide timber and block the ocean winds which carried cold, wet fog and filled the air with grit and dust.

The flat Contra Costa shore, with its sunny weather and timber close by, was a more practical place for a city than San Francisco, as was the Benicia-Vallejo area at the north end of San Pablo Bay. But San Francisco attracted the ships' captains and grew into a city, because it already was the most populous place in the Bay Area and it offered functioning, if rudimentary, commercial facilities for merchants and ships arriving in California. These commercial advantages compensated for the topographic and climatic difficulties of the site. "Whatever advantages she may lack will soon be amply provided for by wealth and enterprise," remarked twenty-four-year-old Bayard Taylor, who was reporting the Gold Rush for Horace Greeley's New York *Daily Tribune*.

Bayard Taylor arrived in San Francisco on the ship *Panama* in mid-August of 1849 and, like all ocean-going travelers, his first

View of San Francisco in 1846—1847

Panoramic view, c. 1849

sight of the town was "the renowned harbor, crowded with the shipping of the world, mast behind mast and vessel behind vessel, the flags of all nations fluttering in the breeze!" Then Taylor caught his first glimpse of San Francisco. "Around the curving shore of the Bay and upon the sides of three hills which rise steeply from the water, the middle one receding so as to form a bold amphitheater, the town is planted and seems scarcely yet to have taken root, for tents, canvas, plank, mud, and adobe houses are mingled together with the least apparent attempt at order and durability."

While waiting to land, Taylor looked at the harbor again, more closely this time. Almost every visitor to San Francisco remarked that the Bay was "large enough to hold all the navies of the world" and that the sailing ships were anchored in Yerba Buena cove so thickly that they formed a "forest of masts." But there was something wrong in this impressive sight; many ships were riding the waves untended and abandoned. By the time Taylor arrived, an estimated 3,000 men had jumped ship and left 200 vessels stranded in the harbor, even though the penalty for desertion was six months at hard labor.

Soldiers and sailors were heading for the gold fields, too. The morning Taylor's ship dropped anchor, eighteen sailors from the U.S.S. Ohio had escaped in one of the ship's rowboats, under fire from all the Navy vessels anchored nearby. By the end of 1849, more than 600 ships had been abandoned in Yerba Buena cove.

Landing on shore was a problem, too. When Taylor arrived in August, there were only two rudimentary wharves in town, one built by William Squire Clarke at the foot of Broadway, known as Clarke's Point, and the other built by William A. Leidesdorff at the foot of Clay Street. These landing places were so crowded with ships taking on or discharging cargo that often there was no room left for ships to let off passengers. The ships' captains could not depend upon their own crews to land the passengers, according to Jessie Benton Fremont, wife of John C. Fremont, who arrived in the spring of 1849. "The crews who took boats ashore were pretty likely not to come back," she noted. For a fare of one or two dollars townspeople carried the passengers in rowboats from the ships to one of the wharves or to a spot where they might wade ashore.

The shore was not a welcome sight; it had become the local garbage dump. As far back as 1847 one U.S. Navy officer remarked that the shore was "strewn with heavy guns, carriages, piles of shot, ordinance stores, wagons, tents, and camp equipage." By 1849, the debris was empty boxes, old clothing and trunks, and spoiled or unwanted cargoes that were discarded by merchants and gold prospectors. The garbage decayed and became mixed with the mud. San Franciscans did not have to go down to the waterfront to see if the tide was out. They could smell it several blocks away.

Bayard Taylor reached the shore easily. A boat from one of the Navy vessels in the cove landed Taylor and his luggage on the Clarke's Point wharf. "We scrambled up through piles of luggage," he recalled, "and, among the crowd collected to witness our arrival, picked out two Mexicans to carry our trunks to a hotel." The men received two dollars apiece for carrying the luggage the several blocks to the Parker House, "a sum so immense in comparison to the service rendered," noted Taylor, "that there was no longer any doubt of our having actually landed in California."

The men who landed in San Francisco had read accounts of the place in their hometown newspapers or in guidebooks prepared for miners and settlers. But few were ready for the town's appearance or the day-to-day life in 1849. "Every newcomer in San Francisco is overtaken with a sense of complete bewilderment," declared Taylor. "The mind, however it may be prepared for an astonishing condition of affairs, cannot immediately push aside its old instincts of value and ideas of business, letting all past experiences go for naught and casting all its faculties for action, intercourse with its fellows, or advancement in any path of ambition into shapes which it never before imagined. As in the turn of the dissolving views, there is a period when it wears neither the old nor the new phase, but the vanishing images of the one and the growing perceptions of the other are blended in painful and misty confusion. One knows not whether he is awake or in some wonderful dream. Never have I had so much difficulty in establishing, satisfactorily to my own senses, the reality of what I saw and heard."

Every new arrival was amazed at how quickly San Francisco was growing and changing. "It's an odd place, unlike any other place in creation, and so should it be, for it is not created in the ordinary way, but hatched like chickens by artificial heat," observed one resident in 1849. Frederick Gerstacker, an adventuresome and perceptive young man who arrived that fall from Germany to dig gold, thought that the "old fairy tales . . . had been called into life again." The entire town "seemed to be raised from the ground as by magic," and it had happened so quickly that "there was scarcely anything left to remind one that it had once been a Spanish place."

Frame and brick buildings stood along Montgomery Street, which then ran along the shoreline, and around the Plaza, which had been renamed Portsmouth Square. But the entire town contained just "three or four regularly built houses" when Mrs. Fremont arrived that spring. As daughter of Missouri Senator Thomas Hart Benton and the wife of California's "Pathfinder," she was something of a celebrity, and several of the town's merchants treated her as graciously as they could until her husband arrived in San Francisco.

"I was taken out to one of these houses, which had been the residence of Leidesdorff, the Russian consul, who had recently died," she recalled in A Year of American Travel. "It was a time of wonderful contrasts. This was a well-built adobe house, one story high, with a good verandah about it, and a beautiful garden kept in old world order by a Scotch gardener. Luxuries of every kind were to be had, but there were wanting some necessaries. Fine carpets and fine furniture and a fine Broadwood piano, but no housemaid. The one room with a fireplace had been prepared for my sleeping room, and had French furniture and no end of mirrors, but lacked a fire. . . . There was no fuel proper; and little fagots of brushwood, broken up goods boxes and sodden ends of old ship timber were all that could be had."

William Leidesdorff, who had been born in the Virgin Islands of racially mixed parentage, had come to San Francisco in 1841 and become one of the town's leading merchants and real estate developers. Besides owning this fine home at Montgomery and California streets, he built one of the town's first hotels in 1846 at one corner of Portsmouth Square and one of the first warehouses at California and Leidesdorff streets. Before he died of "brain fever" in 1848, he had served as city treasurer and been a member of the first municipal council and school board.

His former home may have lacked such "necessaries" as a housemaid and proper firewood when Jessie Benton Fremont stayed there, but the merchants who were living there several to a room knew they were lucky to have even these crowded quarters. Rents for any type of building were astronomical at the height of the Gold Rush. Shacks with a pile of stones in the corner of one room as a fireplace went for $800 a month, and rents for shops and offices were even more inflated. Small stores, hastily thrown together, rented for $3,000 a month in advance. The two-story Parker House on Kearny Street facing Portsmouth Square collected $120,000 a year in rents, while the canvas tent next door, which sheltered a gambling saloon, went for $40,000 a year. Another building on Portsmouth Square, which was not much different from a six-horse stable back East, was the offices of Wright & Company, who paid $75,000 a year. One or two years earlier, the owners of these buildings considered themselves lucky to receive $10 to $20 a month.

Buildings were going up at the rate of 100 a month in 1849. But the demand for property of any kind was so great and so much gold was passing through San Francisco that rents remained at these levels into 1850. The high cost of labor and building materials also contributed to the prices. Laborers received $10 a day to push a wheelbarrow or clean up debris at a construction site, while skilled mechanics were paid $12 to $20 a day. Bricks cost $1 each, and lumber ran $400 to $500 a thousand feet. In 1849 it cost $15,000 to build a simple, one-story frame cottage.

Most men could not afford comfortable, home-like quarters. But here they displayed some of the ingenuity that turned San

Francisco from a Spanish village into an instant city. Many men lived in tents, which were "pitched in wild confusion" throughout the town, according to Frederick Gerstacker, "promiscuously turning their fronts towards any point of the compass, just as the whim of the moment suggested it to the architect." Other San Franciscans erected the framework for a one- or two-room shelter out of wood and used canvas for the walls and roof. Tents and canvas houses were practical, because it almost never rains in San Francisco in the summer and early fall.

Tents covered the slopes of Nob, Russian, and Telegraph hills, which were thought to be too steep for frame buildings. Between 1,000 and 2,000 tents were pitched in Happy Valley, just south of Market Street between First and Third streets, giving it the appearance of "half city, half camp." Furthermore, several hotels were nothing more than a "little muslin shed," according to Bayard Taylor, and the First Presbyterian Church worshiped for several months in a tent on Grant Avenue, between Pacific Street and Broadway, that formerly had been the marquee of a Massachusetts regiment. The Baptists gathered every Sunday in a rude frame building with a roof made from part of a ship's sail.

The clustered tents were a strange sight. "Houses, if we may call them by this name, were raised of the thinnest spars, covered with gay thin cotton," recalled Frederick Gerstacker, "but if the piece with blue flowers had not been sufficient, a red chequered strip was patched to it by means of large stitches, to fill up the space; after which a yellow pattern followed, which, having been procured in a larger quantity, completed the wall, the back, and the roof." At night, the lamps inside shone through the canvas walls and transformed the tents into "dwellings of solid light," according to Taylor. The sight of San Francisco from the deck of a ship anchored in the harbor was "unlike anything I ever beheld," he continued. "Seated on the slopes of its three hills, the tents pitched among the chaparral to the very summits, it gleams like an amphitheater of fire," while "here and there shine out brilliant points, from the decoy-lamps of the gaming houses."

Some men came prepared for San Francisco's housing crisis

and even landed with a canvas house or tent in their luggage. J. Sydam of New York City advertised his "California portable saloons, otherwise [known as] sectional framed tents" in James Wyld's *Guide to the Gold Country of California.* These so-called saloons were "one of the greatest improvements of the age," Sydam boasted. "Inconsistent, indeed, will be the man who will lie on the ground under the ordinary Tent when he can, for a trifle more, procure an article that affords all the comforts of the Hotel." That is exactly what Sydam had in mind for his canvas houses. "One of these saloons will conveniently lodge twenty persons (twelve on hammocks [and] eight on the ground.)" The canvas houses, in addition, were reputedly "perfectly dry and secured against the winds," yet "they are extremely light, compact, and portable; the whole apparatus weighing but 125 pounds" and "may be taken down or put up in two minutes."

But the tents and canvas houses offered little protection in the summer from the wind and airborne sand and dust. "There was dust on the counter, on the shelves, on the seats, on the decanters, and in them; on the tables, in the salt, on my beef steak and in my coffee," complained William Ryan about a restaurant located in a canvas shelter. And then there was the threat from donkeys, such as the one Taylor owned, who, it seemed, preferred canvas over grass or hay for eating. "Whenever he broke loose during the night, which was not seldom, it was generally followed in the morning by a visit from some emigrant, claiming damages for the amount of tent covering which had been chewed up," wrote Taylor.

Sometimes the donkey did not stop at tent canvas. "Once, indeed, a man who had indulged rather freely in bad brandy, at twenty-five cents a glass, wandered in the dark to a place where the donkey was tethered, lay down at his feet, and fell asleep. When he awoke in the morning, sobered by the coolness of his bed and foggy blankets, he found to his utter surprise and horror that the ravenous beast had not only devoured his cap but cropped nearly all the hair from one side of his head!"

Canvas-walled shelters were no good once the rainy season began in late October or early November. The rain passed through

Ships beached as buildings

the canvas and turned the ground beneath and around the tents into mud. Then there were the driving winds that often accompanied the rain. "It rained all night and blowed," complained 49'er David Cosad in his journal. "Sherman Kent and myself had to hold our tent to keep it from blowing down in the bay, and we got very wet and cold for we held it about three hours . . . the next morning most of the tents had blown down."

The 49'ers had to find a more practical solution to their housing problems. There were ships by the hundreds slowly rotting in the harbor. Some were turned into hotels. The floating hotels, however, were only a small help, because of the cost and the unreliability of getting a rowboat ride out to the ship. Furthermore, the ships were noisy and overcrowded. "A number of staterooms, containing six berths each," wrote Bayard Taylor, "ran around the sides of a large room, or cabin, where the lodgers restored to read, write, smoke, and drink at their leisure. The state-rooms were

An overcrowded lodging room

consequently filled with foul and unwholesome air, and the noises in the cabin prevented the passengers from sleeping, except between midnight and four o'clock."

Some ships were broken up for their lumber. The house now standing at 825 Francisco Street was built from materials salvaged from ships. But the most practical and the most picturesque use of the abandoned ships was turning them into buildings, either anchored alongside a dock or beached near the shore. The English brig *Euphemia,* which had sailed in the China trade, became the city's first prison in 1850, anchored off the Long Wharf. By that time, the *Apollo,* which had sailed from New York on January 16, 1849, with eighty-two passengers, was a saloon sitting high and dry on the Long Wharf. The *Panama* became a church, while the *General Harrison* was a warehouse at Clay and Battery streets. Giuseppe Bazzuro began to serve food of his native Genoa in a ship that had been beached at Davis and Pacific streets and thereby won the distinction of opening the first waterfront Italian restaurant in the city.

The best known ship-turned-building was the *Niantic,* a whaler whose passengers and crew heard about the Gold Rush when they stopped at Paita, Chile. Thousands of men had crossed the Isthmus of Panama and were anxiously waiting on the western side for transportation to California. The captain decided that taking on passengers was better than whaling, and the *Niantic* headed for Panama. Some men had waited in the sickly Panamanian climate for weeks and were frantic to leave it all behind and hurry on to the gold fields. "No price was deemed too high for a passage to the new El Dorado," recalled one San Franciscan. "Captain Cleveland stowed away as many as his vessel would hold, and forwarded $45,000 in gold coin to his owners, the amount of the passage money collected."

From there, things did not work out as smoothly as the captain had planned. The *Niantic* lost the favorable winds several hours out of Panama, and cholera, dysentery, and scurvy broke out among the passengers as the ship lay becalmed. When the *Niantic* finally reached San Francisco, the crew jumped ship and headed for the diggings along with the passengers. Captain Cleveland sold the *Niantic* to Gildmeister, De Fremesy & Company who used it as a warehouse on the northwest corner of Clay and Sansome streets. Several shacks were built on deck and rented out as sleeping quarters. On May 3, 1851, fire destroyed all but the ship's submerged hulk. That became part of the foundation of the Niantic Hotel, which stood on the site until 1872.

Derelict vessels were only a partial solution to the shortage of buildings. A ship's distinctive shape was suitable for only a few purposes, and it had to be used along the waterfront or not at all. A better answer to high construction costs in 1849 and 1850 was the pre-assembled buildings that were brought to San Francisco in pieces in ships' holds and erected with a minimum of labor.

The pre-fabricated buildings began to arrive along with the first hordes of gold seekers. Some were quite grand. "The only really private house," wrote Jessie Benton Fremont in the spring of 1849, "was one belonging to a young New Yorker, who had shipped it from home, house and furniture complete — a double two-story frame house, which, when in place, was said to have cost $90,000." But that house was large, a custom job, and included furniture. Simple cottages cost a few thousand dollars at most. By 1850 there were several hundred pre-fabricated buildings in San Francisco, including the Graham House, a hotel which had been "imported bodily from Baltimore," the Parker House, which was erected on Portsmouth Square in 1849, and Trinity Church, on Pine Street near Montgomery, a small frame structure shipped from Oregon.

The pre-fabricated buildings did not always go up according to their manufacturer's plan. The glass that came with the Parker House was the wrong dimensions, and, rather than reduce the size of the windows, the owners sent a ship to Hawaii for properly measured glass. Banker John Parrott, so the story goes, had to go to even greater lengths to complete the Parrott Block, an office building he started at California and Montgomery streets in 1851. The foundations were blue rubblestone from Goat Island, now Yerba Buena Island, but local quarries were so primitive that

PORTABLE IRON HOUSES, RUST PROOF.

THE GALVANIZED IRON HOUSES

CONSTRUCTED BY ME FOR CALIFORNIA,

HAVING met with so much approval, I am thus induced to call the attention of those going to California to an examination of them. The iron is grooved in such a manner that all parts of the house, roof, and sides, slide together, and a house 20 X 15 can be put up in less than a day. They are far cheaper than wood, are fire-proof, and much more comfortable than tents. A house of the above size can be shipped in two boxes, 9 feet long, 1 foot deep, and 2 feet wide, the freight on which would be about $18 to San Francisco. There will also be no trouble in removing from one part of the country to another, as the house can in a few hours be taken down and put up. They require no paint, *and will not rust*; while the surface being bright, the rays of the sun are reflected, so that they are much cooler than either tents or painted iron-houses. They can be made of any size that may be desired, varying in price, according to size and finish, from *One Hundred Dollars* and upwards.

Although more particularly calling the attention of parties going to California to these Houses, I would also bring them to the notice of those either residing in or trading with

SOUTH AMERICA AND THE WEST INDIES,

As being equally suitable to those climates. A specimen House of the above description can be seen by calling upon

PETER NAYLOR,
13 Stone Street, N. Y.

Peter Naylor's portable iron houses

Parrott sent to China for the granite for the building's walls. The granite was cut in China according to Parrott's specifications, but, when the blocks of stone arrived in San Francisco, the instructions for putting them all together were in Chinese. Parrott dispatched a boat to China to bring back stone masons who could decipher the Chinese characters and finish his building. Parrott, however, got a good deal for all his troubles. The Chinese masons received far less for their dawn-to-dusk days than did their American counterparts in San Francisco: one dollar a day, a quarter of a pound of fish, a half pound of rice, and an hour's lunch break.

Pre-fabricated buildings arrived from every city along the East Coast and from Great Britain, Germany, France, Belgium, China, Australia, and even Tasmania. But the Chinese appear to have been the busiest exporters of pre-assembled buildings. In 1849, "at least seventy-five houses had been imported from Canton and put up by Chinese carpenters," reported Bayard Taylor.

Sheet metal, for a time, was thought to be the best material for these structures. Peter Naylor sold "portable iron houses" at his factory in New York City. His advertisement in the back pages of Wyld's *Guide to the Gold Country of California* summed up all of galvanized sheet metal's advantages, real or imagined: "They are far cheaper than wood, are fire-proof, and much more comfortable than tents. . . . They require no paint, *and will not rust;* while the surface being bright, the rays of the sun are reflected, so that they are much cooler than either tents or painted iron houses. . . . The iron is grooved in such a manner that all parts of the house, roof, and sides, slide together, and a house twenty-by-fifteen can be put up in less than a day. . . . A house of the above size can be shipped in two boxes, nine feet long, one foot deep, and two feet wide, the freight on which would be about $18 to San Francisco. . . . They can be made of any size that may be desired, varying in price, according to size and finish, from $100 and upwards."

Naylor's houses were attractive, for one- and two-room shacks, but were not popular in San Francisco. Perhaps people could not reconcile themselves to the idea of shining, unpainted metal walls. E. T. Bellhouse of Manchester and John Walker of London offered pre-assembled buildings of corrugated iron, which were generally painted a dark brown. In 1849, the *Illustrated London News* showed one of John Walker's buildings, a warehouse seventy-five feet long, forty feet wide, and two stories tall, with a front porch that was covered by the overhang of an odd-looking, convex-shaped iron roof. It cost £600, or roughly $3,000.

Several dozen of these British-made structures were assembled along the waterfront as countinghouses and warehouses. One became the city's most fashionable restaurant for a time, the Iron House, on Montgomery Street, between Jackson and Pacific streets. Daniel Wadsworth Coit, a representative of the Rothschild family, was a staunch supporter of pre-assembled technology and erected several British-made sheet metal warehouses on the hills near the shore. But the ground beneath Coit's warehouses gave way, and the buildings and their valuable contents landed at the bottom of the hill in a twisted heap.

That event summed up San Francisco's experience with sheet metal buildings. J. D. Borthwick, an Englishman who arrived for the Gold Rush in 1849 and later wrote up his experiences in *Three Years in California,* thought that the brown-painted buildings were "the most unsightly things possible," and most San Franciscans agreed with him. Besides that, the buildings weren't as practical as their inventors claimed. The metal walls offered little or no insulation from the weather; the buildings were unbearably hot in summer and damp and cold during the wet San Francisco winters.

The iron buildings, furthermore, were no match for the fires that swept the city in 1850 and 1851. Twenty-eight-year-old Heinrich Schliemann, later the famed archeologist, was in San Francisco for one fire in 1851, and he reported that the iron buildings "got red-hot, then white-hot, and fell together like cardhouses." Quite a few people lost their lives in 1851, because they believed that the warehouses were fireproof, as their manufacturers claimed, and decided to wait out the flames indoors. When the buildings became intolerably hot from the nearby blaze, the men rushed to the doors to escape, but, according to the *Annals,* "they found, O horror! that the metal shutters and doors had

Iron buildings, northwest corner of Jackson and Battery streets, 1905

expanded by the heat, and could not be opened! So, in these huge, sealed furnaces, several perished miserably."

That was the end of iron for pre-assembled buildings in San Francisco. Besides, by 1851, local sawmills were producing lumber at prices which made iron buildings an extravagance and, furthermore, wages had fallen to levels which made regular construction more economical than pre-assembled buildings. Wood had already proved the most practical material during the 1849–1850 heyday of pre-fabricated buildings. It offered protection against heat and cold and could be altered as later needs dictated. In 1849, the New York *Evening Post* visited Messrs. Spann and Company's "model portable house," made of wood, and reported that "the parts may readily be put together by any person, however unaccustomed to mechanics—no plane or saw being wanted in its erection." Messrs. Spann were shipping 100 pre-assembled cottages to San Francisco on the next steamer, and they had drawn plans for handsomely ornamented four- and five-story-tall commercial buildings that "would not even disgrace [New York's] Broadway," applauded the *Evening Post*.

But nothing came of Messrs. Spann's lofty plans. The most popular pre-assembled frame structures were the two- and three-room pitched roof cottages. San Franciscans purchased several thousand of these houses, with the invariable white and green trim paint jobs, shutters, and ornamental scroll work around the roofline and door that reminded them of their homes back East. But there the resemblance to life back East ended. San Francisco lacked even the basic requirements of a modern city: the paved streets, the gas lighting, the ample supply of fresh water.

San Francisco did have a grid street plan to guide its rapid growth, thanks to the foresight of the city fathers in 1847. But many streets existed only as lines on a surveyor's map. In 1849, Sacramento Street, above Grant Avenue, was a "deep ravine," which was so "impassable during the rainy season . . . that parties living near Stockton Street had to go by way of Clay Street to get to their homes," recalled one newspaper.

Whatever good humored tolerance San Franciscans had for

their rutted dirt streets vanished with the onset of the rainy season late in 1849. Fifty inches of rain reputedly fell in the city that winter. Not a single street was paved or planked, and sidewalks were few and far between. The rains and the constant pedestrian and wagon traffic quickly turned the streets into muddy morasses. "One could not walk any distance without getting at least ankle-deep," complained Bayard Taylor, "and although the thermometer rarely sank below 50°, it was impossible to stand still for even a short time without a deathlike chill taking hold of the feet." "Yet we must pick our way!" exclaimed another 49'er, William S. Jewett. "Pick, jump, stride and totter and we got somewhat in something that no doubt looks very like a street on a map but it was not recognizable in its natural form although they called it 'Broadway,' " and "it proved so to us for . . . all succeeded in getting stuck."

The winter of 1849–1850

Hauling goods around town by wagon was all but impossible that winter. The heavily laden wagons just sank into the mud and, according to B. E. Lloyd in his *Lights and Shades of San Francisco*, "one mule team, wagon and all, entirely disappeared beneath the quicksand and was never recovered, while many times men would become mired, and could be rescued from their extreme peril only by prompt and vigorous aid from their fellows." Sometimes a man stumbled and fell in the street at night, and he was too drunk or sick to extricate himself from the mud. In January and February of 1850, the bodies of three men were discovered in the mud along Montgomery Street.

The answer to muddy streets was to cover them with planking. But wood was running $400 to $500 per thousand feet that winter and buildings were in such demand that sidewalks and planked streets had to wait until the next year. During the "mud plague" of 1849–1850, "anything and everything was used to bridge the walks and crossings," recalled B. E. Lloyd. "Brushwood and the limbs of trees from the surrounding hills were cut and carted to the softest places; but these were not sufficient to stand the constant travel, and gave only temporary relief. Boxes, bags of rice and beans, caddies of tobacco, barrels of stale provisions, sacks of coffee, and everything possessing solidity, that was valuable, were used to build secure footing."

Some Montgomery Street merchants made foot paths out of boxes and barrels, and all day long a line of people made their way down the street single file, one step at a time. In other places, the pedestrians gingerly walked on piles of bottles and broken glass. "Empty bottles were as plentiful as bricks — and a large city might have been built with them," observed J. D. Borthwick.

Getting through the hazardous streets sometimes wasn't the only difficult part of the journey home. The city established street grades in 1850, but some San Franciscans did not want to waste time or money leveling their lots and bringing their homes down to street level. The results were often strange looking and more than a little annoying. Lydia Rowell Prevaux wrote her mother-in-law that she "had to come up a ladder twenty feet high" to get into her home. "We drew up our wood and water with a rope. . . . We are not troubled with callers or a desire to go out or rather down."

With no designated garbage dumps in town, San Franciscans threw more than empty bottles into streets. "Allow me to name some nuisances that exist which are very annoying and exceedingly dangerous to the public," wrote one drayman to a newspaper, "viz: the throwing of glass bottles, iron hoops, tin lard cans, tin cheese boxes, tin egg cans, wooden hoops with nails in them, besides any quantity of nails and all sorts of old rubbish, into the streets." Indoor plumbing and sewers were nonexistent, and San Franciscans emptied their chamberpots into the streets every morning.

Some refuse — the scraps of food, discarded clothing, and household wastes — disappeared into the mud. The rains carried other filth down the east-to-west streets and into the Bay or at least into a "vast mass of putrid substances" along the waterfront "from whence proceeded the most unwholesome and offensive smells." But during the dry summer months, the garbage stayed where it was thrown, while "the heat gradually dries them up."

San Francisco was a paradise for rats, admitted the *Annals*. "Rats — huge, fat, lazy things, prowled about at pleasure, and fed on the dainty garbage," while "the pedestrian at night, stumbling along the uneven pavements, and through streets that were only a series of quagmires, would occasionally tread on the loathsome, bloated, squeaking creatures, and start back in disgust and horror, muttering a curse or two at such a villainously unclean town."

The city was so filthy that San Franciscans were infested with fleas. More than one visitor announced that the town was "famous for three things — rats, fleas, and empty bottles." J. D. Borthwick recalled: "It was quite a common thing to see a gentleman suddenly pull up the sleeve of his coat, or the leg of his trousers, and smile in triumph when he caught his little tormentor. After a few weeks' residence in San Francisco, one became naturally very expert at this sort of thing."

Cholera, not surprisingly, ravaged San Francisco in 1850 and again in 1851 and 1852, killing close to 100 people a week at the height of each year's epidemic. The dead were often dumped along the shore to be carried out to sea by the tides. But considering the appalling sanitary conditions and the shortage of doctors, it's a wonder that health conditions weren't even worse those first few years after the Gold Rush.

The list of inconveniences suffered by the first San Franciscans goes on. Water from springs and wells in the city was scarce and often polluted. Barrels of fresh water, brought across the Bay from Sausalito, were sold from wagons or stationary tanks at 5 cents to 12 cents a pail. Public transportation was unknown, and a man owned a horse or got around town on foot. Gas was not available, and, therefore, homes and streets were without gas light. Worst of all, San Francisco was isolated from the rest of the country. Letters from a wife or a business partner back home took weeks, if not months, to reach California.

The isolation and loneliness was the most difficult problem facing San Franciscans in 1849. The water shortages, lack of indoor plumbing, even the bad housing, as awful as they sound now, were not that great an imposition for the 49'ers. Men came to San Francisco for the chance to make a lot of money, and they were forewarned about the difficult living conditions. Besides, things weren't that much better on the farms and frontier back East in those days. The men from large Eastern cities did not have that much to complain about either. New Yorkers had just gotten running water, indoor plumbing, and practical gas lighting for the first time in the mid-1840s, and pigs, rather than rats, roamed the muddy streets scavenging for garbage.

San Franciscans thought that their city was something very special from the beginning. Almost immediately they began to glorify the hardships of the first winter and their foresight in coming to San Francisco. Even the *Annals,* which was published in 1855, looked back on the hardships of 1849 and 1850 as the good old days.

The first thing everyone noticed on their arrival in San Francisco in 1849 was the absence of women. "Think of a city of thirty thousand inhabitants peopled by men alone! The like of this was never seen before," exclaimed Bayard Taylor. It was quite an unusual group of men that had come to San Francisco, too. Frederick Gerstacker declared: "Strange as the houses might appear to us on our first entering the town, we almost forgot them for the men." The 49'ers had come from all corners of the world. "The every-day aspect of the plaza [Portsmouth Square] and streets was of the most curious and interesting kind," declared the Annals. "There were hordes of long pig-tailed, blear-eyed, rank-smelling Chinese, with their yellow faces and blue garbs; single dandy black fellows, of nearly as bad an odor, who strutted as only the Negro can strut, in holiday clothes and clean white shirt; hideously tattooed New Zealanders; Feejee sailors; and even the secluded Japanese, short, thick, clumsy, ever-bowing, jacketed fellows."

That was only the beginning of the Annals' stereotyped descriptions of the men who had flocked to San Francisco. The 49'ers also included "the people of the many races of Hindoo land; Russians with furs and sables; a stray, turbaned, stately Turk or two, and occasionally a half naked shivering Indian; multitudes of the Spanish race from every country of the Americas, partly pure, partly crossed with red blood—Chileans, Peruvians, and Mexicans, all with different shades of the same swarthy complexion, black-eyed and well-featured, proud of their beards and moustaches, their grease, dirt, and eternal gaudy serapes or darker cloaks." The Spaniards were "more dignified, polite, and pompous than even their old colonial brethren," while the Englishmen were "fat, conceited, comfortable" and "pretended to compete in shrewdness with the subtle Yankee." The Germans, Italians, and Frenchmen all were "gay, easy-principled, philosophical . . . their faces covered with hair, and with strange habiliments on their persons, and among whom might be particularly remarked a number of thick-lipped, hook-nosed, ox-eyed, cunning, oily Jews."

Messrs. Soule, Gihon, and Nisbet, the authors of the Annals, saw nothing wrong with these descriptions of the men at the diggings and in San Francisco. Maybe they thought it would be amusing for their American readers. Anyone who was at all familiar with San Francisco in 1849 knew quite well that the Chinese and native-born Blacks were not the only 49'ers who sometimes smelled bad. Sanitation facilities were so primitive that year that almost everyone went unwashed for days at a time. But the characterizations in the Annals do reflect the racism and prejudices against foreigners of some San Franciscans at the time.

Americans were particularly upset at the thought of foreigners making money in the gold fields. U.S. Army General Persifer Smith, while en route to California in 1849 to become military governor, announced that only citizens should be allowed to dig for gold. That did not happen, but, on April 13, 1850, the State Legislature did pass a law requiring all miners who were not native-born American citizens to pay a tax of $20 a month. The State Legislature did not stop there. Soon after, it prohibited the testimony of Blacks and Indians in court, thereby limiting their rights to protect their lives and property. In 1854 the State Supreme Court extended this act to the Chinese.

San Francisco city laws closed jobs like draying or driving hackney coaches to aliens. Thugs robbed and beat up Chinese and even Latin American immigrants on the streets, and mobs occasionally looted and burned their homes and shops. But bigoted Californians were not about to exclude foreigners and Blacks from every aspect of life in San Francisco. J. D. Borthwick recalled that "in the mines the Americans seemed to exhibit more tolerance of Negro blood than usual in the states—not that Negroes were allowed to sit at tables with white men or considered to be all on an equality, but, owing partly to the exigencies of the unsettled state of society . . . Negroes were permitted to lose their money in the gambling rooms."

Most foreigners considered Americans' behavior stereotypical of the region of the country where they had lived before coming to California. Pringle Shaw wrote about Americans for his readers

Opposite, Four 49'ers

back home in England with the same tone as the *Annals* described foreigners. "Your b'hoy of New York is a gay rollicking fellow," observed Shaw, "half of them are dentists—dressy if he can afford it, and much addicted to heavy betting and sherry cobblers. . . . He has much less originality than his eastern brother, in language and physiognomy, but is far in advance of him in his ideas of manifest destiny, braggadocia, and filibusterism."

"The Kentuckians, Pennsylvanians and the Buck-eyes," wrote Shaw, "are a thriving prudent race . . . and are among the most industrious and well-doing of American citizens." But the Southerners "are far—very far, in the rearward, in comparison with those named, in almost all the essentials that constitute refinement and enlightenment." Shaw thought that the "first families" of the South "possess all the haughtiness of the little German prince, minus urbanity and respect to the laws of their country," while the Southern farmers, "despite their bootless boast of free citizenship" were as ignorant and dishonest as Russian peasants.

The Americans, like the Europeans and Asians, lived and socialized with men from their home towns. Boarding houses and hotels took names like the New England House, the Manhattan Hotel, and New Orleans House. In 1850 one man who had previously lived in Boston wrote: "I lodge . . . with a number of other Boston people. Holden and Reddington of E[ast] Boston live next door so that we have a regular Massachusetts neighborhood." Another 49'er, who had come from Rochester, New York, remarked that his boarding house "is the regular Rochester Headquarters and there is from ten to fifteen Rochester men here all the while. So that I hear from every Mail from Rochester . . . and Lewis Kenyon takes two Rochester papers which he brings right here so that I have the general news."

When men brought their families to San Francisco and lived in private homes a few years later, the geographical cliquishness of 1849 and 1850 persisted. Happy Valley, a middle class neighborhood near Second and Howard streets, was "inhabited chiefly by New England people," according to one resident, while nearby

Rincon Hill, with the "families of sea captains and shipping merchants," had the "flavor of Nantucket and Martha's Vineyard." Southern families favored Green and Vallejo streets, above Kearny Street.

In 1849 a man's nationality was not immediately apparent to the casual observer, because almost everyone wore the same rough-looking miner's garb. Only the Chinese and Blacks, with

A miner

their obvious racial differences, stood out in a crowd. One 49'er recalled that everybody wore "a heavy woolen shirt, trousers held up by a sash or belt around the waist, and the legs inserted in a pair of high-legged boots. A slouch hat covered the head." Most men stopped shaving, and their beards gave them the "rough, rugged, savage" look which suited their clothing.

A group of these "stalwart, bearded men, most of whom are in the early prime of life, fine, healthy, handsome fellows, . . . make a *tout ensemble* that is very awful to contemplate," observed the *Annals*. But most 49'ers looked that way out of necessity rather than any desire for show. L. M. Schaeffer explained why he looked the way he did when he returned to San Francisco from the diggings in 1849: "My clothes were stored on board a vessel lying in the stream; those I had on were not only well worn, but, like Joseph's coat, of varied colors. But as I had not yet secured a permanent lodging-house, and was not engaged in any business, I did not care how I looked, or what kind of a figure I presented for in truth, I was not singular in this respect."

Everyone's clothes were dirty, too. That is "the greatest privation that a bachelor is in this country exposed to," Wyld's *Guide* warned would-be immigrants to California. Laundresses charged $5–$8 to wash and press a dozen shirts and, even then, "you have to court them besides," complained Wyld. Some men discarded their shirts when they became dirty; it was just as cheap to buy new ones. Others sent their dirty shirts to Hawaii and China. "A vessel just in from Canton brought two hundred and fifty dozen, which had been sent out a few months before," wrote Bayard Taylor in 1850, while "another from the Sandwich Islands [Hawaii] brought one hundred dozen, and the practice was becoming general."

Sending your shirts to a Chinese laundry that was actually in China may have been something to write home about, but it was no answer to the dirty clothes problem. By mid-1849, Mexican and Indian women were washing clothes out by the Presidio along the Fresh Pond, which soon became known as Washerwoman's Lagoon. They were doing so well that several dozen men set up laundries there too. Washing clothes may not have been tra-

ditionally a man's job, but it paid two or three times as much as pushing a wheelbarrow or unloading ships' cargoes.

The washerwomen settled on one edge of the lagoon, and the washermen took over the other side. The men "went into the business on a large scale, having their tents for ironing, their large kettles for boiling the clothes, and their fluted washboards along the edge of the water," wrote the ever-curious Bayard Taylor. "It was an amusing sight to see a great, burly, long-bearded fellow kneeling on the ground, with sleeves rolled up to the elbows, and rubbing a shirt on the board with such violence that the suds flew and the buttons, if there were any, must soon snap off. Their clearstarching and ironing were still more ludicrous, but, notwithstanding, they succeeded fully as well as the women, and were rapidly growing rich from the profits of their business."

Other men discovered ingenious ways to support themselves. During the winter of 1849–1850, quick-witted L. M. Schaeffer found that "my success enabled me to live much more comfortably than I had anticipated. I was known as a doctor, collector, agent and messenger; made mattresses out of common muslin and stuffed them with shavings, peddled cigars, patent medicines and notions; and what was thought an accomplishment at home now became the source of my pecuniary profit—I mean performing on the flute."

Some men made one-time killings from items of little or no value back home. Bayard Taylor arrived in San Francisco with another New Yorker who brought along 1,500 copies of New York newspapers in his baggage. As soon as he landed he began hawking his months-old newspapers in the streets. He disposed of all 1,500 at $1 apiece in two hours. "Hearing of this I bethought me of about a dozen papers which I had used to fill up crevices in packing my valise," wrote Taylor. "There was a newspaper merchant at the corner of the City Hotel, and to him I proposed the sale of them, asking him to name a price. 'I shall want to make a good profit on the retail price,' said he, 'and can't give more than ten dollars for the lot.' I was satisfied with the wholesale price, which was a gain of just four thousand per cent!"

Washerwoman's Lagoon

Albert Benard de Russailh, a young Frenchman who came to San Francisco in 1851 at the age of thirty-two to seek his fortune and to forget an unhappy romance, made a "great profit" from toothpicks, "a wholly worthless" article back home. De Russailh sold brushes, gloves, perfumes, and small articles of clothing from a table made of several boards resting on sawhorses that he set up on the Long Wharf, at the foot of Commercial Street. He had brought two cartons of toothpicks along with him as gifts for friends and for his own use, and one morning he laid out several boxes on his table. An amazing thing happened. "They had scarcely left the box when a grave gentleman paused before my shop and began to examine my merchandise. He picked up . . . a few other things, . . . but laid them down again, and he seemed about to walk away, when his eye happened to light on the toothpicks. He picked up a pack, held it up, and said, 'How much?'

"I was quite taken aback," recalled de Russailh, "for I had no idea what to charge. It had never occurred to me that anyone would buy them, and I had rather planned to give them away. But I remembered suddenly that in California nothing is given away; everything is sold. With as serious an expression as I could command, I replied, 'Half a dollar, sir.'

"He gave me a long look. 'It is not possible,' he said finally. 'That is very little.'

"At first, I thought he was joking. Then I feared that he would fly into a rage. I smiled and was about to say politely, 'There is nothing for you, sir.' But he quietly gathered up four packs, handed me $2, nodded pleasantly, and moved away."

The next day, de Russailh brought along several more packs of toothpicks, and they, too, sold almost immediately. That night, he split all the remaining packs of twenty-four toothpicks into packs of twelve. "The plan was excellent," he declared, and "in less than a week they had all gone for 50 cents a pack. I could hardly restrain my laughter whenever a man paid me half a dollar for only twelve. If I had a 1,500-ton ship loaded to the gunwale with toothpicks, my fortune would have been made . . . but, unluckily, I had only 496 packs."

Not all the 49'ers were so resourceful in supporting themselves or adjusting to life in San Francisco. Although Bayard Taylor estimated that between two thirds and three quarters of the new arrivals were "active, hopeful, and industrious," he reported that "the remaining portion see everything 'through a glass, darkly.' " Some men, he thought, had run out of energy during the exhausting journey to San Francisco, while others were completely bewildered by the unfamiliar values and lifestyles. But it was blasted hopes that probably hurt the most men. "Many men had come to the country with their expectations raised to an unwarrantable pitch, imagining that the mere fact of emigration to California would insure them a rapid fortune," observed J. D. Borthwick. "But when they came to experience the severe competition in every branch of trade, their hopes were gradually destroyed by the difficulties of the reality."

Another 49'er, Hinton R. Helper, a Carolinian who later achieved national notoriety with *The Impending Crisis,* a criticism of Southern slavery, described disappointed men "passing to and fro with haggard visages and head declined, muttering to themselves." Some men lost themselves in liquor, and J. D. Borthwick reported seeing "here and there . . . a drunken man lying groveling in the mud, enjoying himself as uninterruptedly as if he were merely a hog." Other men decided that taking their own lives was the only way out of their misery, and San Francisco quickly acquired its reputation for having more than its share of suicides.

One reason for the unhappiness was the virtual absence of women in San Francisco in 1849 and 1850. Estimates vary as to the number of women living in San Francisco in 1849. The *Annals* reported that 700 of the 34,000 people who landed in the city that year were women. But not every woman who arrived in San Francisco stayed there, and probably no more than a few hundred were living in the city in 1849.

Of these few hundred women, only a handful were "ladies." Jessie Benton Fremont, herself unquestionably a lady, told the story of a New York merchant who shipped an entire house and its furnishings to San Francisco early in 1849 so that his wife would come along with him. "At a party given to welcome her," recalled Jessie Fremont, "the whole force of San Francisco society came out, the ladies sixteen in number." Most gentlemen-turned-49'ers left their wives at home. San Francisco was considered too unsettled and rough for genteel womenfolk, and the houses and servants that made for a proper Victorian home were virtually unobtainable at any price.

Faced with the prospect of no female company of any sort for months at a time, the 49'ers discarded their back-East breeding and did not care if a woman was a lady or not. J. A. Drinkhouse recalled just how scarce women were when he landed in December, 1849. "When our vessel came into the harbor, we were boarded by half a dozen or more boats, and they all inquired if there were any women on board; they would give them two or three hundred dollars to sit behind a gambling table or fill some similar position."

Men afforded extraordinary courtesies to the few women in town. "You have no idea how few women we have here," lawyer John McCraken wrote to his sister, "and if one makes her appearance in the street, all stop, stand, and look. The latest fashion is to carry them in the arms (the streets are incredibly muddy). This we see every day." A baby was an even greater "curiosity," according to B. E. Lloyd. "Brawny, stalwart men, with shaggy beards and unshorn locks, would press forward to get to touch the tiny soft hand, and some would even snatch the child from its mother's arms, and toss it up, or kiss it, in an ecstasy of joy."

San Franciscans not only missed the company of women; they also believed, as Wyld's *Guide* noted, that "the society . . . without woman, is like an edifice built on sand. Woman, to society, is like cement to the building of stone. The society here has no such cement; its elements float to and fro on the excited, turbulent, hurried life of California immigrants."

San Franciscans talked about hiring ships to bring unmarried women from the East Coast to California. One woman back in New York actually tried to do it. In February, 1849, Eliza Farnham, a former matron at Sing Sing prison, decried the shortage of proper young ladies out West in a letter to the New York *Daily Tribune.*

The newspaper published the letter, and soon Mrs. Farnham was planning to take a boatload of young women to San Francisco, with the blessing of such New York celebrities as preacher Henry Ward Beecher, poet and publisher William Cullen Bryant, and the *Daily Tribune*'s editor, Horace Greeley. Mrs. Farnham chartered the *Angelique,* planned an April 15, 1850 sailing, and started advertising for young women who were morally fit and had the $250 passage money.

San Franciscans rejoiced at news of Mrs. Farnham's plans, particularly when they learned that 200 women had signed up for the voyage. But the excitement soon turned to bitter disappointment. Mrs. Farnham was a woman of the highest moral standards, and she was not about to bring just any young woman to San Francisco with her. Besides, the $250 passage was a lot of money. Only three other women besides Mrs. Farnham set sail on the *Angelique,* two of them already married. When the *Angelique* finally reached San Francisco, Mrs. Farnham was not on board, and

Women for California

that was perhaps best for her. She had been anything but a model passenger on the voyage out of New York. When the *Angelique* dropped anchor at Valparaiso, the captain tricked her into going ashore on a mission of mercy. Then the *Angelique* sailed off, leaving her to find another ship to San Francisco.

Most of the women who made it to San Francisco in 1849 and 1850 were anything but the virtuous ladies that Mrs. Farnham had planned to bring. For the most part, they were saloon girls and prostitutes who had come to San Francisco, like the menfolk, to better themselves and make a lot of money. In the first few months after the discovery of gold, these women mainly came from Mexico and South America. They boarded the ships carrying the 49'ers around the Horn as they stopped for repairs or provisions along the west coast of Mexico and South America.

These women did not have money for a ticket, but that didn't stop them from getting to San Francisco. "They did not pay passage on the ships," wrote Captain José Fernandez, "but when they reached San Francisco, the captains sold them to the highest bidder. There were men who, as soon as any ship arrived from Mexican ports with a load of women, took two or three small boats, or a launch, went on board the ship, paid to the captain the passage of ten or twelve unfortunates and took them immediately to their cantinas, where the newcomers were forced to prostitute themselves for half a year, during which the proprietors took the bulk of their earnings."

The Latin American whores looked the part. Colonel James J. Ayres recalled seeing one of these women "dressed from head to foot in loud colors with face 'painted an inch thick.' Her outfit and tonsure both proclaimed her calling." Despite attempts at an elegant appearance, these Latin American women lived and worked out of a miserable collection of tents, known as "Little Chile" or "Chilecito" on the southern slope of Telegraph Hill, bounded by Montgomery, Pacific, Jackson, and Kearny streets. "Their dwellings were dens of infamy, where drunkeness and whoredom, gambling, swindling, cursing and brawling were constantly going on," reported the *Annals*. But that did not stop the

Hooking a victim

49'ers from hiking through the sand dunes that separated Little Chile from Portsmouth Square. They were the only available women in town at the time, and things got so busy that half a dozen women entertained their customers inside a single tent simultaneously, while a line of impatient men waited outside.

By the middle of 1849, the Latin American women had lost their monopoly on the local prostitution trade. News of the Gold Rush had spread to New York and Europe, and every ship that carried would-be miners to San Francisco also brought women out to seek their fortunes. These women were busy at work long before the ships reached California. The voyage from Great Britain to San Francisco could take six months, and the men soon tired of reading and gambling to pass the time. Albert Benard de Russailh's journal tells just how the crew and passengers of his ship, the *Joseph*, passed the many months of their voyage. The tall, blond, and always-laughing Mlle. Meyer, whose conversation was anything but ladylike, spent long hours with the steward in his cabin. Mme. Chalis had attracted the eye of the captain, while the second officer preferred Mme. Lucienne, who called herself an actress. Mme. Falco, who passed as Mlle. Meyer's middle-aged sister, bestowed her affections on a young student.

De Russailh considered his journal a private thing, and he wrote these selections for his own amusement. But another 49'er, J. Lamson, on board the *James W. Paige* out of Maine, could not resist sharing his journal with other passengers. Lamson had found a captive audience for his long-hidden journalistic talents, and soon he was recklessly showing everyone the excerpts which told about the affair the captain was having with a woman who was going to San Francisco to meet her husband. The captain demanded that Lamson destroy his diary, but the passengers forced him to back down and even urged the young man to publish the journal once he reached San Francisco.

Prostitution in San Francisco grew more sophisticated with the arrival of every ship from the East Coast and Europe. These women were professionals. They knew how to dress, practiced a certain subtlety in their art, and, as housing conditions improved in 1850, they set up handsome brothels. But San Franciscans paid dearly for their company. Albert Benard de Russailh, apparently planning to use a few parts of his journal as the basis for a guidebook for French immigrants to California, carefully explained the costs of things in San Francisco, including the prices for "women of easy virtue."

"To sit with you near the bar or at the card table, a girl charges one ounce ($16) an evening. She has to do nothing save honor the table with her presence. This holds true for the girls selling cigars. . . . For anything more you have to pay a fabulous amount. Nearly all these women at home were streetwalkers of the cheapest sort. But out here, for only a few minutes, they ask a hundred times as much as they were used to getting in Paris. A whole night costs from $200 to $400. You may find this incredible," he declared, "yet some women are quoted at even higher prices."

Only a few prostitutes worked the saloons or prowled the streets by day as well as night in search of customers. Most worked out of their own rooms or one of the brothels. "Occasionally you find one who hides her real business and pretends to be a dressmaker or a milliner," reported de Russailh, "but most of them are quite shameless, often scrawling their names and reception hours in big letters on their doors."

In 1849 and 1850 brothels were among the most comfortable and home-like places in town. Sometimes the madams held balls for their clientele. "See yonder house. Its curtains are of the purest white lace embroidered, and crimson damask. Go in," declared the *Annals*. "It is a *soiree* night. The 'lady' of the establishment has sent most polite invitations, got up on the finest and most beautifully embossed note paper, to all the principal gentlemen of the city, including collector of the port, mayor, aldermen, judges of the county, and members of the legislature. A splendid band of music is in attendance. Away over the Turkey or Brussels carpet whirls the politician with some sparkling beauty, as fair as frail; and the judge joins in and enjoys the dance in company with the beautiful but lost beings whom, to-morrow, he may send to the house of correction."

Around midnight the dancing ended, and everyone headed for the supper table. "Every thing within the bounds of the market and the skill of the cook and confectioner is before you," noted the *Annals*. These evenings were always a success. "Every thing is conducted with the utmost propriety. Not an unbecoming word is heard, not an objectionable action seen." The madam did her best to please steady customers and, at the same time, sell them $10 and $12 bottles of champagne. The gentlemen guests were more than happy to attend the brothel balls, which compared favorably with parties they attended back home and offered much-missed female company. Most 49'ers spent nearly all their leisure time with other men and, out of desperation, ended up dancing with each other in the saloons and gambling dens.

Because of the shortage of women, the saloon girls and whores did pretty well as they pleased. They imported the finest clothing and jewelry with their fabulous earnings and often strolled down Montgomery Street in the middle of the day, not caring if their finery dragged in the dust, as they nodded at their many gentlemen acquaintances. The *Annals* reported that San Franciscans often saw "several together of the same class, mounted on spirited horses, and dashing furiously by, dressed in long riding skirts, or what was quite as common, in male attire."

These women felt free to frequent the same saloons and gambling rooms as their male clientele. "Abandoned women visit these places openly," observed one 49'er. "I saw one the other evening sitting quietly at the monte-table, dressed in white pants, blue coat, and cloth cap, curls dangling over her cheeks, cigar in her mouth and a glass of punch at her side. She handled a pile of doubloons with her blue kid gloved hands, and bet most boldly."

On January 11, 1848, the city council tried to stop gambling with stringent laws. One resolution even authorized constables "to seize for the benefit of the town all the money found on a gambling table where cards are played." The law was so obviously ridiculous that the city council repealed it at the next meeting. But had the law remained on the books and actually been enforced, declared the *Annals,* "the town in a single night would have become wealthy," because "gambling was a peculiar feature of San Francisco at this time. It was *the* amusement—*the* grand occupation of many classes—apparently the life and soul of the place."

Everyone gambled in 1849 and 1850, from the day laborer to the judges and merchants, and, as a result, visitors like J. D. Borthwick noticed that "in California the word gambler is not used in exactly the same abstract sense as with us. An individual might spend all his time, and gain his living, in betting at public gaming-tables, but that would not entitle him to the distinctive appellation of a gambler. It would only be said of him that he gambled."

The gambling saloons of 1848 and 1849 were large tents with dirt floors, and the tables usually were several planks laid across two sawhorses. The men sat on empty barrels or shipping crates more often than on chairs. The favorite games were monte, faro, roulette, rondo, rouge et noir, and twenty-one. The usual stakes, according to the *Annals,* were fifty cents to $5, but sometimes a "rich gamester . . . getting desperate" or a "half tipsy miner . . . just come from the diggings with a handsome 'pile' " provided some

real excitement. These men bet thousands of dollars, as if they were only several, and sometimes $25,000 rode on the turn of a single card.

Gambling was so popular and so profitable that the gambling dens were among the first comfortable and permanent buildings erected in San Francisco. By 1850 there were several hundred gambling establishments scattered throughout the city, and they had completely taken over the eastern edge of Portsmouth Square and most of the northern and southern sides. Places like the El Dorado, the Bella Union, and the California were busy soon after they opened at 9 a.m., and at night men crowded the tables three or four deep, "every one vieing with his neighbors for the privilege of reaching the board, and staking his money as fast as the wheel and ball could be rolled or the card turned."

With crowds that large and action that fast, the several dollars that most men wagered in each game rapidly accumulated into enormous sums. The gaming tables were piled high with gold and silver coins and bags of gold dust. Inevitably, some men cheated. Hinton R. Helper described two men who signaled each other about other players' hands. "One of them is a lank, cadaverous fellow, with a repulsive expression of low cunning, full of hypocrisy and deceit, taciturn in disposition, unengaging in manners, who was formerly a Baptist preacher in Connecticut. The other has a vinous, fat, and jolly countenance, is open faced, enjoys a joke, is lively . . . is affable and courteous to strangers, talks a great deal, as might be expected, since, before he came to California, he was considered one of the most promising young lawyers in Mississippi."

Most gamblers, however, were honest men. The professionals who rented a permanent place at a table usually left their winnings behind unguarded when they got up to take a break. San Francisco was a violent and vice-ridden town in 1849, but money was "exposed in such a way as would be thought madness in any other part of the world," according to J. D. Borthwick. Maybe gold was so abundant that year and prices so high that money had lost its ordinary hold over men. The 49'ers who did strike it rich enjoyed

Two miners

their new-found wealth with an enthusiasm not seen in other parts of the country. Rufus Lockwood threw $20 gold pieces from the end of Meiggs Wharf into San Francisco Bay just like a country boy skipping flat stones across the surface of a pond. John Henry Brown, the manager of the City Hotel, recalled how one fun-seeking nouveau riche auctioneer "rode up to the barroom window (which was very large) and said he was going to ride through. I informed him that if he did so it would be a very dear ride. He asked how much it would cost him. I made the figures rather high, thinking it would keep him from coming through. The price was $500. The words were hardly out of my mouth when he threw a bag of dust through the window to me and said, 'Weigh out your $500, and take enough out for a basket of wine,' and before I could pick up the bag he and his horse were through the window into the barroom."

Men crowded the gambling saloons looking for more than the chance of winning money. Some enjoyed the excitement of watching others win and lose. Others were looking for friendly, comfortable surroundings in which to pass their free time. Who wanted to sit in a canvas tent that was damp with fog and filled with gritty dust and sand when he could go to a warm and music-filled gambling den decorated with crystal chandeliers, gilt, paintings, and fine furniture from back home?

Drinking was the only pastime that rivaled prostitution and gambling. In 1849 and 1850 bars were usually part of a gambling establishment. At one gambling den J. D. Borthwick visited, the bar was "a long polished mahogany or marble counter, at which two or three smart young men officiated, having behind them long rows of ornamental bottles, containing all the numerous ingredients necessary for concocting one hundred and one different 'drinks' which were called for. This was also the most elaborately decorated part of the room, the wall being completely covered with mirrors and gilding, and further ornamented with china vases, bouquets of flowers, and gold clocks."

Most men did not know what to make of openly flourishing prostitution, gambling, and drinking when they arrived in San

Francisco. But the 49'ers readily adapted to the situation. They were without family or permanent homes to restrain them, and San Francisco was isolated from the rest of America. "A man's actions and conduct were totally unrestrained by the ordinary conventionalities of civilized life," declared J. D. Borthwick, and "so long as he did not interfere with the rights of others, he could follow his own course for good or for evil, with utmost freedom."

Victorian America could not consider, much less tolerate, such a free way of life. As reports of life in San Francisco were published back East, the city gained a reputation as "a sink of iniquity" and worse. Some men worried where this social freedom might lead. "Among so many temptations to err, thrust prominently in one's way, without any social restraint to counteract them," warned J. D. Borthwick, "it was not surprising that many men were too weak for such a trial and, to use an expressive though not very elegant phrase, went to the devil." Without social limitations, he continued, "the human nature of ordinary life appeared in a bald and naked state, and the natural bad passions of men, with all the vices and depravities of civilization, were indulged with the same freedom which characterizes the life of a wild savage."

The prevailing Victorian ethic valued proper appearances above all things. Prostitution, gambling, and drinking did not, by themselves, give San Francisco a bad name. Similar pleasures, or vices, flourished in all the East Coast cities. But they were generally hidden and certainly never acknowledged by polite society. The Annals knew that back East "the criminal, the fool, and the voluptuary are not allowed to boast, directly or indirectly, of their bad, base, or foolish deeds, as is so often done in California."

Messrs. Soule, Gihon, and Nisbet worried like J. D. Borthwick about what could happen in a town without the usual social restraints, still recognized that San Franciscans had "one virtue — though perhaps a negative one" in their free and easy behavior. "They are not hypocrites, who pretend to high qualities, which they do not possess. In great cities of the old world, or it may be even in those of the pseudo-righteous New England States, there may be quite as much crime and vice committed as in San Francisco, only the customs of the former places throw a decent shade over the grosser, viler aspects."

While genteel folk in the rest of the country were scandalized by reports of open gambling and brothel balls—or secretly wishing they were there, the 49'ers were hard at work trying to make their fortunes and to build a city in the middle of the wilderness.

Though San Franciscans toiled as hard as they played, the city never gained a reputation for hard work. Journal-keeping visitors and newspaper correspondents would rather search out and report San Franciscans' unusual daily lives and pleasures than report the long hours most men spent in the countinghouse or pushing a wheelbarrow. But the *Annals* did not gloss over the truth. "San Francisco is a place for work—real, useful, *hard* work. If any man can give *that*—it may sometimes be with the head, but oftener with the hand, he is sure, not merely of subsistence, but of a competence, and indeed a fortune in the long run. If lazy, or incapable of such work, the sooner the useless thing takes his departure, the better for himself and the place."

Actually, a preoccupation with work and money led to some of the city's genuine moral faults. Too many men were solely motivated by greed, thought James Wyld. They "have no souls" and "are but a grand automaton, whose springs Mammon alone makes vibrate." "It was one intense scramble for dollars," wrote J. D. Borthwick, and "the man who got most was the best man—how he got them had nothing to do with it."

The get-rich-quick ideal was so pervasive that "refinement and convenience had to give room, at least for the time, to money-making," reported *Frank Leslie's New Family Magazine.* Many men worked twelve and fourteen hours a day because there was not much else to do. Once a man tired of gambling or whoring at night, he could sit around his uncomfortable and usually overcrowded quarters. Or he could work a few more hours.

James Wyld believed that the arrival of women and families in San Francisco would reduce men's greed and dishonesty, just as he thought that the "fair ones" would improve the moral tone of the town. But most 49'ers did not plan to stay in San Francisco or at the diggings for more than a year or two. Fewer than one man out of a hundred in 1849 intended to settle permanently in California, according to Frederick Gerstacker. "All of them have come only to make a fortune, and having made it, to return as quickly as possible to the United States, or wherever else they may have come from."

Even the church favored men's hopes for quick fortunes. On December 1, 1850, the Reverend Charles A. Farley, pastor and organizer of the First Unitarian Church in San Francisco, declared in his Sunday sermon that "the seeking for gold is as legitimate and laudable an object as the seeking for anything else. It is, in fact, the indispensable condition upon which I will not say our bread depends, but upon which depends the civilization and Christianization of the world."

Reverend Farley took up the question of sin in San Francisco, and he admitted that things were just as bad as many Americans feared. "But *here,* it is open, unmasked—makes no apologies and asks none," he declared. He asked Americans to understand San Francisco's unusual situation. Many men had come from countries whose customs were different from those in America, and everyone in town was "animated primarily, it must be confessed, by one passion, and that a passion for money." But he expected that "passion" would save most men from evil. "Time here is money, and they are a great deal too busy to spend much time at Vanity Fair, or to make common cause with the devil."

San Francisco's rapid growth, Farley believed, was proof of the 49'ers' inherent righteousness. "It is not idleness nor vice which has converted a wilderness with almost miraculous rapidity into thriving cities and towns. . . . It is not idleness nor vice which throngs these streets with a wide-awake multitude, which has put up these warehouses, and built these wharves, and graded and planked these streets."

"There is no place in the world that has undergone, and is still undergoing, such rapid changes as the city of San Francisco," reported the *Illustrated London News* in July, 1850. In 1848, before the discovery of gold, San Francisco's population was about 11,000 people. By the beginning of 1849, that figure had risen to 2,000, and by the end of 1849, to nearly 25,000. By the time J. D.

Opposite, Montgomery Street, 1851

Borthwick arrived in 1851, "hardly a vestige remained of the original village," and "everything bore evidence of newness."

Many of the men who arrived in San Francisco in 1849 or 1850 went off to the diggings at once and returned to the city months later. Bayard Taylor was out of town for four months and, upon his return, he exclaimed: "Of all the marvellous phases of history of the Present, the growth of San Francisco is the one which will most tax the belief of the Future. . . . When I landed there, a little more than four months before, I found a scattering town of tents and canvas houses, with a show of frame buildings on one or two streets, and a population of about six thousand. Now, on my last visit, I saw around me an actual metropolis, displaying street after street of well-built edifices. . . . Then the town was limited to the curve of the bay fronting the anchorage and bottoms of the hills. Now it stretched to the topmost heights, and followed the shore around point after point."

"A street scene on a rainy night"

By 1850 San Franciscans were busy planking the streets. No one wanted a repeat of the winter of 1849–1850. When Frederick Gerstacker returned to San Francisco after several months at the diggings, he declared that "what more than anything gave to the town a comfortable and cleanly appearance was the condition of the streets." That summer the city had planked seventeen streets, some for as many as eight or ten blocks. Montgomery Street, for example, was now graded and planked between California Street and Broadway. The east-to-west streets, such as California and Sacramento, were generally planked from the waterfront to Stockton Street or Grant Avenue, where the steepness of Nob Hill temporarily halted development in that direction. Gerstacker proudly noted that "not only the footpaths but even the carriage-roads [are] being completely paved with a flooring of strong planks, and lined with gutters, so that, in the heaviest rain, the San Franciscans might walk from one end of their city to the other, over comparatively dry and clean ground."

The hills had always been one of San Francisco's most distinctive and picturesque features, but they were an obstacle to the city's growth. There was almost no flat land between Nob Hill and the water's edge along Montgomery Street. Trade, the activity which would mean lasting prosperity for San Francisco once the gold mines were exhausted, needed plenty of flat space for its counting-houses and warehouses. Horses could not pull loaded wagons from warehouse to warehouse or from ship to warehouse up and down the steep hills.

San Francisco decided to make more level land by filling in Yerba Buena cove. The idea itself was not rash, but the way the 49'ers went about it was. Factories back East sold steam-powered shovels, which moved earth in large quantities. But San Francisco did not want to wait the year it would take to order and receive the engines, which were nicknamed "steam paddies" (because they could dig as much dirt as a team of Irish laborers). So they ordered the steam paddies and, while they waited, began to fill in the cove with anything they could find—sand and dirt excavated from cellars and street openings, spoiled or unwanted merchandise, and

Opposite, Street planking in progress on Battery Street

even the town's garbage. By the time the steam paddies arrived early in 1851, the landfill already extended to Front Street, three blocks beyond the original shoreline.

The steam paddies quickly leveled the sand hills that dotted the city. Huge shovels dumped the sand into boxcars which rolled down to the waterfront along iron rails in the middle of the streets. When they reached the harbor, the cars were emptied and hauled back to the steam paddies by mules. After one man committed suicide by jumping beneath a sand car on its way to the harbor and another lost a leg in an accident, the Board of Aldermen passed the

so-called "Leg Preserving Ordinance," which put a six-mile-per-hour speed limit on sand cars.

Not waiting for the landfill work to reach their underwater lots, some businessmen built warehouses on piles. They knew that their property would be dry land in a year or two. A kind of "go ahead" fever also infected the town's builders. They were not going to dawdle over a construction job. The sooner they finished one project the sooner they could start another. But labor was still scarce in 1850. Wages had remained at the high 1849 levels, while materials had dropped to as little as one-sixth of the previous year's

The "steam paddy" in operation; Eighth and Harrison streets

costs. The builders got around the high cost of labor by finishing jobs as quickly as they could. One builder constructed a brick warehouse, several stories tall, in just thirty days.

San Francisco soon began suffering the consequences of too much speed in building the city. The frame warehouses, built on piles over the water or on the wharves themselves, shook and rattled with every passing wagon. The brick warehouses were not much steadier. On April 12, 1854, a portion of the U.S. Bonded Warehouse at Battery and Union streets collapsed without warning, and the *Annals* reported that "this was only one of several accidents of a like nature which happened about this time." The trouble was "the generally inferior character of building materials used in San Francisco" and the "shifting and treacherous nature" of the building sites. Many buildings below Montgomery Street had already settled unequally, and "many fine houses have been, or will soon be, totally ruined," complained the *Annals.*

Some people feared that the garbage used for the Yerba Buena cove landfill was a menace to public health. "The climate of this city, taken above Montgomery Street, is probably unequaled for salubrity by any other on the earth," wrote Dr. J. B. Phinney in a letter published in the *Pioneer* in 1854, "but below Montgomery, as is well known, the atmosphere is impregnated with the malaria or miasma arising from the great quantity of decaying vegetable matter. . . . As far as my experience goes, not only do the sudden deaths almost invariably occur in the lower portions of the city, but by far the greater majority of all the deaths; and when they do not occur there, the causes of the disease can generally be traced to sleeping or working at night and early morning, below the old water line." Dr. Phinney reported that a few men had died almost immediately after lying down on this man-made land to sleep. Nothing could be done to remedy the bad quality of the landfill, but Dr. Phinney had some advice: "I will never allow a patient to sleep below Montgomery Street if I can possibly avoid it."

Most San Franciscans were too busy making money and building their city to worry about Dr. Phinney's warnings or the occasional warehouses that fell down. Millions of dollars in gold passed through the city every month, and by 1850 San Francisco was the equal of Philadelphia in trade. San Francisco's population had jumped from 1,000 in 1848 to between 20,000 and 25,000 in 1850. "Its growth appears to be magic," declared James Wyld. "There is nothing similar on records; one may say without exaggeration that it has been inaugurated in one moment by some superhuman power, or sprung like one of those ambulating towns do spring the day before a fair. In fact, it looks very much like one of those cities only built for a day. Its houses built of planks and cotton sheetings cannot last but a day."

Wyld's remarks were prophetic. No less than six fires destroyed large parts of San Francisco between late 1849 and the middle of 1851. On December 24, 1849, fire broke out at Dennison's Exchange, a hotel on the east side of Portsmouth Square. The hotel burned quickly, because many of the walls and ceilings were painted canvas. The flames quickly engulfed that side of the Square and part of Washington Street down to Montgomery Street. The city had no fire company yet, so residents fought this fire by pulling down the buildings in the path of the fire or blowing them up. The next morning, San Francisco organized its first volunteer fire company. And builders were already beginning new structures before the ashes of the old ones were cold.

The fire caused more than $1,000,000 damage. But almost all signs of the conflagration had disappeared within a few weeks. "The place was covered as densely as before with houses of every kind," said the *Annals.* The builders, however, had not learned anything from the fire. The new buildings, "like those that had just been destroyed, and like nearly all around, were chiefly composed of wood and canvas, and presented fresh fuel to the great coming conflagrations."

The second fire broke out six months later in almost exactly the same spot as the first one. The United States Exchange, another hotel on the east side of Portsmouth Square, caught fire at 4 a.m. on May 4, 1850. By noon, the three blocks north and west of the Square were smoking ruins. The volunteer fire companies were not ready, and again San Franciscans were forced to stop the flames by destroying the buildings in their path. More than $4,000,000 in property was destroyed.

Again the work of rebuilding started before the last flames were out, and, within a few weeks, the *Annals* reported that "the whole burned space was covered with new buildings, and looked as if no fire had ever been there." The second fire was almost certainly the work of arsonists, as were an estimated 31.6 per cent of the fires that broke out in San Francisco between 1851 and 1856, according to the *Alta*. The police arrested several men on suspicion of arson, but there was no trial and they were set free.

The Board of Aldermen recognized the folly of rebuilding the same blocks again and again and ordered fines for men who did not help fight fires or move goods out of the way of the flames. Furthermore, every householder had to keep six buckets filled with water on the premises at all times. Another ordinance authorized the digging of artesian wells and reservoirs so that there would be ample water to fight fires.

But scarcely had the city recovered from the second fire when the third one broke out at 8 a.m. on June 14, 1850, in a bakery behind the Merchants' Hotel on Montgomery Street, between Sacramento and Clay streets. There were strong winds that day, and, within hours, everything was ablaze from Clay to California streets and from Kearny Street to the waterfront.

Several volunteer fire companies were ready this time, but the blaze was so fierce that "a fire engine was no more use than an old maid's teapot," in the words of Captain George Coffin, whose ship, the *Alhambra,* was anchored in Yerba Buena cove. Captain Coffin watched merchants frantically trying to rescue merchandise from their warehouses, then went down to the Clay Street wharf to be near his ship. About 500 other men had crowded that wharf to wait out the fire. Soon the flames reached the waterfront and cut them off from the rest of the city. "We had nothing to do but gaze at the devouring monster," wrote Coffin, "who at every blast of the hurricane came surging down the wharf in clouds of smoke and cinders, obliging us to lie flat on our faces."

The flames engulfed the nearby Army Quartermasters ware-house, which contained 5,000 loaded muskets, among other things. The roar of the fire was so loud that Coffin could not hear the muskets going off, but the "rapid and constant succession of flashes showed they were being discharged. Our escape was owing to the fact that these muskets were fitted in perpendicular racks so that the shells were thrown upward." Next, the flames engulfed several warehouses at the foot of the wharf. Within an hour they were all ashes, except for a million board feet of stacked lumber in their yards. "The scene was sublime when these pyramids of lumber got well on fire," wrote Coffin. "They continued burning for several days, and when everything else was swept away, they stood like fiery giants, with innumerable arms and tongues of flames, constantly spitting out flashes and cinders, and the knots and slivers snapped and cracked, sounding as if all the firecrackers in China were being let off at once."

Frank Marryat, a British journalist who described his California visit in *Mountains and Molehills,* arrived in San Francisco aboard a Panama steamer at the height of the fire. He watched the flames from the safety of the ship and went ashore the next day. He found "nothing particularly impressive in the scene," because the fire had made "a clean sweep" of the frame and sheet metal buildings in the area. About the only things left standing on most blocks were two- and three-story brick chimneys. But Marryat did enjoy looking at what the fire's intense heat had done to ordinary metal objects. "Gun-barrels were twisted and knotted like snakes; there were tons of nails welded together by the heat, standing in the shape of the kegs which had contained them; small lakes of molten glass all the colors of the rainbow." Although the third fire was the most destructive one yet, Marryat reported that "there was little time wasted in lamentation . . . and in forty-eight hours after the fire the whole district resounded to the busy din of workmen."

San Franciscans did not have to wait long for the next fire. It broke out about 4 a.m. on September 17, 1850, in the Philadelphia House on the north side of Jackson Street between Kearny Street and Grant Avenue. This fire, the fourth, destroyed most of the area bounded by Montgomery, Washington, Grant, and Pacific.

1849 fire engine

The losses did not pass $1,000,000, because most of the buildings were one-story frame shacks. The fire turned out to be a blessing in disguise for everyone, even the owners of the destroyed buildings. By quickly clearing a large well-located area of substandard buildings, it was the nineteenth-century equivalent of urban renewal. Merchants and real estate investors could erect larger and more durable masonry buildings on the site without the trouble of buying and demolishing every shack and shanty in the area. The burnt district was more desirable for trade than before the fire, and even the men whose buildings had burned down made money from the rising real estate values.

Somehow San Francisco got through the rest of 1850 and part of 1851 without another major fire. But everyone was apprehensive about the ever-present danger, and "the sound of the first stroke of a fire-bell was enough to clear church or theater, or drowsy bed, in an instant," according to the *Annals*. In 1851, the Reverend Samuel H. Wiley declared that the entire city could burn down in a single night, "and yet every man was acquiring with such rapidity that all hoped to complete a fortune ere such a disaster should occur." Most men tried to figure out ways to get through the next blaze without losing everything they owned.

Attorney John McCrakan kept his law books in boxes on his bookshelves so that he could run into his office and rescue them quickly. Merchant J. D. Farrell tied a scow beneath his store, which stood on piles over the water. Other merchants stored their merchandise at the edge of town, while William Weston rented space "in three different quarters of the city, in order to lessen the chance of losing all at one fire."

Weston's precautions did no good. The fifth fire, which broke out on May 4, 1851, destroyed all his property. This fire broke out on the first anniversary of the third one, and it was no accident. All San Francisco expected trouble that day. "Threats had been made, it was said, that it was to be signalized by a similar spectacle," according to the *Annals*. And despite the precautions of the police, San Franciscans did not have to wait long after sunset for the anniversary celebration to begin. The fire broke out in a paint store on the south side of Portsmouth Square and, thanks to a stiff northwest wind, the entire block was in flames within minutes.

This was the fastest-moving and most destructive fire of them all. Some merchants, according to the *Annals*, "removed their stocks of goods four or five times, and had them overtaken and destroyed by the flames at last." Some men went temporarily insane, rushing headlong into the flames, while others wept and talked nonsense as they wandered glassy-eyed through the streets. Every few minutes the earth shook, as barrels of gunpowder exploded. The fifth fire destroyed more buildings than all the previous ones combined. The next morning, more than eighteen square blocks lay in ashes. Three-quarters of the town was gone. The damage was $12,000,000.

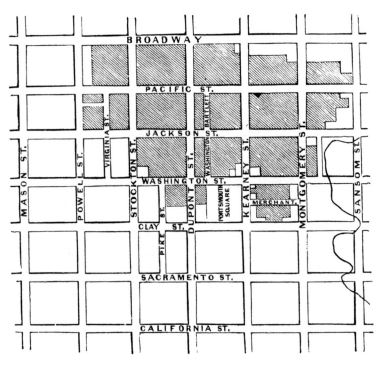

The burned district from the June 22, 1851 fire.

Some San Franciscans wondered if the city would ever recover from the disaster. It was "a terrible blow upon the city," said the *Annals*. "Its progress seemed stopped, its prosperity paralyzed." But the spirit of quick rebuilding came to the rescue again, and just ten days later 300 buildings had been completed or nearly completed in the burnt district.

Even as the rebuilding got underway, people worried what would happen on June 14th, the anniversary of the fourth fire. Rumors had it that the rowdies who had just burned down most of the town were ready to do it again. But June 14th passed uneventfully. The entire town was on the lookout, and the fire fiends were laying low. They waited until June 22nd to set a fire in an empty house at Pacific and Powell streets, then the outskirts of the city. Firemen arrived on the scene quickly enough to contain the blaze to just a few buildings, but there was no water in the area, and "the element had its will." Onlookers stood by helplessly as the fire devoured fifteen blocks roughly bounded by Sansome and Mason streets, Washington Street and Broadway.

For once the flames had spared most of the mercantile district along Montgomery Street and the waterfront. But hundreds of people lost their homes. Some decided they had had enough of San Francisco and moved to inland towns or left California for the East Coast or Australia. The sixth fire also destroyed the last relics of San Francisco's pre-Gold Rush days, with the single exception of Robert A. Parker's adobe building on Grant Avenue, erected as a store in 1847 or 1848. "This has stood through all the fires, and it is hoped that it may remain for years as a relic of the past," wrote the *Alta*. But the building was torn down the next year, and several larger houses were built on the site.

On May 22, 1852, the Board of Aldermen passed the first of several ordinances "providing for more perfect security of property from fire." This law fixed a "fire district" bounded by Union, Powell, Post, Second, and Folsom streets. Within these limits, open fires in streets or vacant lots were forbidden, and men working in stables or other places where "combustibles" like hay were stored had to use lanterns for light rather than candles or open

San Francisco firemen

lamps. All tents and buildings with canvas walls or ceilings had to be taken down. The Board of Aldermen appointed several "fire wardens" to enforce the law. A later ordinance, passed on July 6, 1853, enabled the wardens to remove any wooden signs or canvas awnings which might endanger the building on which they hung in the event of fire nearby.

After the sixth fire, San Francisco also revamped its volunteer fire companies along the lines of those in New York City. By the end of 1852 the city had fourteen engine companies, three hook and ladder companies, and a group of boys who ran ahead of the engines at night lighting the street with torches. A fire watch scanned the city twenty-four hours a day from the top of City Hall.

The Board of Aldermen paid the salary for a fire chief and his assistants. But the firemen received no wages, and even had to pay for their uniforms, engines, and fire fighting equipment. The firehouses, which the volunteers erected with some financial assistance from the city, were among the best-looking buildings in town. Although a few companies took names like Vigilant or

Monumental engine house, Brenham Place, 1856

Young America, most chose names that reflected the home towns of their members. By the mid-1850s, there were the Empire, Manhattan, Knickerbocker, Pennsylvania, Monumental [Baltimore], and Crescent [New Orleans] companies.

Joining a volunteer company in the 1850s conferred the same distinction as membership in a fashionable club offered men in later decades. The companies tried to outdo each other in the grandeur of their firehouses, the cut of their uniforms, and the speed with which they arrived at the scene of a fire. The volunteer firemen even had their own day, February 22, for a parade through the city to show off their engines and equipment. "The chief interest, however, of the exhibition," observed the *Annals,* "lay in the appearance of the *men* themselves. These were of every class in the community, and were a fine athletic set of fellows."

The firemen were heroes to San Franciscans who had watched their city nearly burn down six times. "At the awful peal of the alarm-bell, no matter at what hour or place, or how occupied, the fireman rushed to his post, to drag and work his pet engine where most needed," observed the *Annals.* "At busy noon, he threw aside his cash-book and ledger; in the evening, he abruptly left the theatre, or other place of amusement; at midnight, he started from sleep, and only half-dressed, leaped and ran to his appointed quarters. A few minutes later, and the whole city might be in a blaze! This thought gave speed to his heels and strength to his arms. Scarcely had the first heavy strokes of the alarm bell ceased to vibrate on the panic-stricken ear, when were heard the lighter, cheerful peals of the bells of the engines, as they were wheeled from their houses and hurried rapidly through the streets."

The Board of Aldermen made sure that the men would have an ample supply of water near the scene of any fire. No one wanted a repeat of the sixth fire, where the engines reached the blaze in time but had no water to put it out. Hydrants were unknown in the early 1850s because San Francisco did not yet have a water system with reservoirs and mains beneath the streets. Instead the city dug fifteen cisterns around town, each of which held 14,800 to 30,000 gallons. Actually the cisterns were nothing more than square wooden boxes, made of tar-soaked planks with caulked seams and flat wood covers, sunk ten to fifteen feet in the ground. By 1856 the number of cisterns in service increased to thirty-six.

Building codes required all new construction to be fire resistant. A December 6, 1852 law forbade the erection of any frame structures within densely built-up portions of town after July 1, 1853. Existing frame buildings could remain standing but could not be altered, enlarged, or moved to another lot within these limits. The roofs of all new buildings had to be slate, tile, or similar fire-resistant material.

Passing the laws was easy; enforcing them proved to be another thing. In 1855 the *Alta* criticized the wardens for doing nothing about the "vast number of stove funnels passing through wooden tenements," which made "the buildings liable to take fire at any moment by a spark or two lodged in a dry spot." Frame buildings continued to be built within the district where they were forbidden.

The volunteer firemen's work was apparently more difficult than it needed to be. The streets in some parts of town were so badly rutted that several companies announced in October, 1855 that they would no longer "roll their machines below Davis Street, on any occasion of fire, until the streets were repaired." By then many companies were less prepared to fight fires than they had been two or three years earlier. Half the cisterns were empty or in bad repair in the late 1850s, and most of the firemen's hose was defective or worn out. The Howard Engine Company even suffered the indignity of being evicted from its firehouse.

Careless planning further hampered fire fighting efforts. Fourteen of the city's sixteen companies were located within the area bounded by Broadway, Bush, Stockton, and Front streets. Of the two companies outside that district, one was south of Market Street and the other was in the countryside near the Mission Dolores. The area so well served by the fourteen companies was the most densely populated part of the city, but the buildings there were more solidly erected and adhered to the fire codes more closely than those elsewhere in the city. When a building caught fire outside the

Opposite, The Call building, southeast corner of Clay and Montgomery streets, 1859

favored section, it usually burned to the ground, because the firemen simply could not reach it in time.

In 1856 fire broke out at the slaughterhouse near California and Larkin streets. The nearest fire companies were on the other side of Nob Hill. One company managed to drag its engine up the California Street hill, but they were so exhausted by that effort that the machine got away from them on the way down the hill. The engine was badly damaged, and several men nearly injured. And all the suffering was in vain; the slaughterhouse had burned down in the time it took to answer the alarm.

San Franciscans began to erect substantial fire-retardant buildings even before the Board of Aldermen passed the fire codes. More and more men saw San Francisco as their home, and they knew that the city and their property would never be safe if canvas and wood remained the favorite building materials. In 1851 and 1852 some merchants built stores and warehouses with brick walls, sometimes two or three feet thick, slate roofs, and double sets of iron shutters protecting the doors and windows from fire and burglars. Some warehouses had a water tank on the roof to flood the premises in event of fire.

These warehouses would have been out of the question a year or two earlier when San Francisco imported nearly all its building materials at great cost. But by 1851 several local brickworks had opened near the clay deposits where Mission Creek emptied into the Bay. "California-made bricks are certainly inferior to well-burned English or United States bricks," admitted the *Annals*, "yet they are considerably cheaper, and when painted or in some way protected from the weather serve their purpose very well." Iron foundries, lumber mills, and even a stone yard opened in Happy Valley, the area just south of Market Street which had been a tent city in 1849 and 1850 but was now rapidly changing into an industrial location.

The finest buildings in town rose along Montgomery Street, which emerged as the business center of San Francisco in 1849. Bayard Taylor was amazed at the "marvellous change" Montgomery Street had undergone during one of his trips away from the city. "All the open spaces were built up, the canvas houses replaced by ample three-story buildings, an exchange with lofty skylight fronted the water, and for the space of half a mile the throng of men of all classes, characters, and nations, with carts and animals, equaled Wall Street before three o'clock."

The Montgomery Street Taylor knew almost completely disappeared in the fires of 1850 and 1851. But the new buildings which rose after each fire were grander than the ones they replaced. By 1854 Montgomery Street was lined with "substantial" and "beautiful" buildings. The *Annals* credited the Parrott Block with being the first of this "superior class of private edifices." The granite blocks for this building, you may recall, arrived from China with the instructions for their assembly written in Chinese, and John Parrott had to send a ship to China to bring back stonemasons to complete the work.

The $140,000 Parrott Block, which stood at the northwest corner of Montgomery and California streets, was finished in December, 1852. In the next year nearly twenty office blocks were completed on or near Montgomery Street at a cost of more than $2,000,000. The grandest and most-talked-about of these was the Montgomery Block, located on the south side of Montgomery Street between Washington and Merchant streets. People had laughed at Henry W. Halleck's plans for the building and predicted that it would be known as Halleck's Folly. San Francisco, they thought, was not ready for a four-story building with nearly 150 offices. Where would Halleck find tenants for all those offices and the fourteen ground-floor stores?

But the laughter turned to praise for Halleck's courage and vision as the building neared completion and filled up with tenants. The Montgomery Block symbolized San Francisco's rising wealth and the pride its residents felt for their city. "This building is the largest and most tastefully finished on the Pacific Coast," reported LeCount and Strong's 1854 *Directory*. What's more, the Montgomery Block compared favorably with buildings San Franciscans had known back East. "Its extent, solidity, and architectural beauty would attract attention in any city of the Union,"

Opposite, The Montgomery Block

continued the 1854 *Directory*. Architect G. P. Cummings employed the newly fashionable Italianate style, and the Montgomery Block included such stylish touches as bronzed iron front doors framed by stone columns (supposedly modeled on those at Diocletian's Baths in Rome), prominent lintels and sills for all the windows, and an overhanging cornice at the roofline "upon which all the taste and skill of the architect have been exhausted."

Architect Cummings made the Montgomery Block comfortable and durable as well as good looking. Each office had the novelty of gas light and fireplace grates to take the chill out of rainy or foggy days. An artesian well in the center courtyard provided water on each floor. Every window had iron shutters against fire or thieves, and all the walls were solid brick, resting on piles and "carefully anchored and tied." San Franciscans were already worried about making their buildings earthquake resistant.

But Montgomery Block did not remain the grandest building in town for long. An even bigger spender than Henry W. Halleck had come to San Francisco—namely the United States Government. The custom house had burned down in the fire of May 4, 1851, and there were no other public buildings in town suitable for such an important facility. After all, the federal government collected more revenue from import duties than any other source. In 1852, the cornerstone was laid for a combined custom house and post office on the west side of Battery Street, between Washington and Jackson streets. By the time it was finished in October, 1855,

the United States Government had spent more than $850,000 on the three-story Greek Revival style building. But the money was well spent. The new custom house was the finest building west of St. Louis and gave proof of the federal government's respect for San Francisco's commercial might.

By 1851 San Francisco was already fourth in the nation in the value of its foreign trade, after New York, New Orleans, and Boston. Practically overnight San Francisco became the "freight handler" for the West Coast. Nearly all the goods sent from the East Coast and the rest of the world to any spot on the West Coast passed through San Francisco and, conversely, so did most of the West Coast shipments going elsewhere. Between April 1, 1847, and April 1, 1848, the last full year before the Gold Rush, eighty-four ships dropped anchor at San Francisco. In 1855 that number increased to 1,250. The tonnage entering San Francisco jumped from 50,000 in 1848 to 550,000 in 1853.

For the first few years after the Gold Rush, ships returned almost empty to their home ports. Gold didn't take up much space, and the captains took on ballast for the return voyage, often rock from Telegraph Hill, which ended up as street pavement in cities all over the world. But California was producing more than gold and rock for export by the mid-1850s. Some 49'ers again took up the farming they had dropped to come to San Francisco, and in 1855 California exported several million dollars worth of flour, wheat, barley, and oats.

By 1851 or 1852, Montgomery Street was the favorite location for merchants' counting houses, banks and insurance companies, and auction houses. But it was not yet exclusively a street of finance and trade. "Montgomery was the chief business street, fashionable promenade, and shopping-place rolled into one," one newspaper said.

Eleven of the city's 160 hotels stood along Montgomery Street in the mid-1850's, mostly in the vicinity of Market Street. More than 75 others were located a block away on Kearny Street or on the streets leading to the waterfront. Some were left from the Gold Rush era. The St. Francis, which opened in 1849, had been "the fashionable house of the day," according to the *Annals*. This first St. Francis "completely threw into the shade all former establishments," wrote Bayard Taylor. "The rooms were furnished with comfort and even luxury, and the tables lacked few of the essentials of good living, according to a 'home' taste." Room and board ran $150 a month, but that was "unusually cheap" for 1849; the Ward House, which Taylor thought not nearly as desirable, charged $250 a month.

The St. Francis was not as fancy as it sounds, except by the standards of the 49'ers. The ungainly building was a dozen prefabricated cottages thrown together and stacked one on top of the other. The interior walls were "the thinnest sort of board partitions, without either lath or plaster, and consequently but little privacy could be enjoyed by the lodgers," according to the *Annals*. "These by whispering too loudly, or talking too plain, frequently and unconsciously gave their neighbors intimations of facts which it was not intended, and, indeed, which it was quite improper should be known abroad. Hence, the house soon became as remarkable for stories of laughable incidents, and even tales of scandal, as for its ridiculous aristocratic pretentions." Somehow the St. Francis escaped destruction in the six fires of 1849–1851, but it burned on the morning of October 22, 1853. By then, it had been eclipsed by several other hotels.

The "first really substantial and elegant hotel of the city," declared the *Annals*, was the Union, a four-story brick building, which opened in 1851 on the east side of Kearny Street, between Clay and Washington streets. Its rivals were the Oriental, a three-story wood structure at Battery and Bush, the Rassette House at Sansome and Bush, and Jones' at Sansome and California. Any of these hotels, declared the *Annals* proudly, "was constructed, arranged, furnished, and conducted as well as any similar establishment at that time in the United States."

But as we have already seen, the *Annals* cannot always be trusted for complete accuracy. The public rooms in these hotels were indeed impressive looking. "Good hotels were not wanting," reported J. D. Borthwick, "but they were ridiculously extravagant places . . . furnished and decorated in a style of most barbaric splendour, being filled with the costliest French furniture, and a profusion of immense mirrors, gorgeous gilding, magnificent chandeliers, and gold and china ornaments, conveying an idea of luxurious refinement which contrasted strangely with the appearance and occupations of the people by whom they were frequented."

But things were considerably simpler once the guests climbed the stairs to their rooms. Hotel rooms were scarce in 1851 and

St. Francis Hotel

Portsmouth House, c. 1852

1852, and six or eight men often slept together, as they had in 1849. Alexandre Holinski, a Lithuanian traveler who wrote in French, was fortunate to get a room to himself at the stylish Jones Hotel in 1851. But the room measured just eight feet by twelve feet. It contained a bed, porcelain toilet articles, a table, two chairs, a chest of drawers, and a small mirror. The walls were papered, and the floor carpeted, partly for comfort and partly to hide the cracks between the floor boards.

Holinski did not complain about San Francisco's hotels; he was lucky to have a room to himself. But other travelers did not suffer their inconveniences silently. Traveler Charles G. Plummer wrote "of lodging I cannot say much in favor." Sir Henry Vere Huntley, an Englishman who spent much of his time in California complaining, was particularly upset at the size of the hotel towels, fourteen inches square.

Almost everybody, however, agreed that the hotel dining rooms served good food and plenty of it, even in the difficult times of 1849 and 1850. John Henry Brown, who ran the City Hotel, recalled: "I found it very difficult to keep up the boarding department . . . and would have failed entirely had it not been for the fact that I was personally acquainted with the captains of vessels, and consequently had an opportunity of procuring from them a portion of what they had for the use of their ships." Every time a ship sailed for Oregon, Brown ordered butter, ham, bacon, eggs. An old man named Herman brought him fresh vegetables such as cabbages, lettuce, carrots, and turnips. "These he brought daily; I had to pay him fifteen to twenty dollars per day," wrote Brown. "Another item of considerable expense to me was the hiring of two hunters and a whale boat to go off up the creeks after game; they would make two trips per week and were usually very successful." Brown estimated that if he had purchased all these provisions at the city markets, the hotel would have lost $100 a day in the dining room. And even with all his efforts finding food at reasonable prices, Brown wrote: "Had it not been for the large amount of wine that was generally consumed at the dinner table, I could never have stood the losses made in the boarding department."

BILL OF FARE.

WARD HOUSE, RUSSEL & MYERS, Proprietors.

THURSDAY, DECEMBER 27, 1849.

Soup.

Ox Tail..$1 00

Fish.

Baked Trout, White and Anchovy Sauce.........................$1 50

Roast.

Beef.....................$1 00 | Mutton, do. $1 00
Lamb, stuffed.............. 1 00 | Pork, Apple Sauce........... 1 25

Boiled.

Leg of Mutton, Caper Sauce.... $1 25 | Corned Beef and Cabbage...... $1 25
Ham $1 00

Entrees.

Curried Sausages, a mie........$1 00 | Tenderloin Lamb, Green Peas... $1 25
Beef, stewed with Onions...... 1 25 | Venison, Port Wine Sauce...... 1 50
Stewed Kidney, Sauce de Champagne... $1 25

Extras.

Fresh California Eggs, each $1 00

Game.

Curlew, roast or boiled, to order.............................$3 00

Vegetables.

Sweet Potatoes, baked.........$ 50 | Irish Potatoes, mashed........$ 50
Irish do. boiled .... 50 | Cabbage................. 50
Squash................. $ 50

Pastry.

Bread Pudding.............$ 75 | Rum Omelette.............$2 00
Mince Pie................ 75 | Jelly do. 2 00
Apple Pie................ 75 | Cheese................. 50
Brandy Peach .... 2 00 | Stewed Prunes 75

Wines.

Champagne..................$5 00 | Claret..................$2 00
do. half bottles........ 2 00 | Champagne Cider........... 2 00
Pale Sherry.............. 3 00 | Porter................. 2 00
Old Madeira.............. 4 00 | Ale.................. 2 00
Old Port, half bottles........ 1 75 | Brandy, per bottle......... 2 00

BREAKFAST—From half-past 7 to 11, A. M.
DINNER—From half-past 1 to 6, P. M.
TEA—From half-past 6 to 12.

Monson and Valentine, Book and Job Printers.

Ward House bill of fare, December 27, 1849

Gathering sea bird eggs at the Farallones

But hotel managers like Brown weren't the only ones going to great lengths to find good food. Eggs were a rarity in 1849—$1 each if they were available. So San Franciscans sailed out to the Farallones Islands, thirty-two miles west of the Golden Gate, and collected sea bird eggs by the hundreds. Climbing around the barren, windswept islands was hard work, but it was better than the job of sorting the fresh eggs from the rotten ones back on the mainland. Hen eggs were readily available by the early 1850s, but cheap restaurants and Chinese grocers bought the Farallones eggs until the United States Government banned all egg gathering in 1897.

By 1851 finding good provisions in the public markets was no longer a problem. "The epicure might traverse the globe, and have no finer living than what this city yielded; the glutton would here find both eye and palate satisfied," enthused the *Annals*. Most visitors to San Francisco in the early 1850s had not expected to find such abundance. "The market was well supplied with every description of game—venison, elk, antelope, grizzly bear, and an infinite variety of wild fowl," noted J. D. Borthwick. "The harbour abounded with fish, and the Sacramento River was full of splendid salmon, equal in flavour to those of the Scottish rivers. . . . The wild geese and ducks were extremely numerous all round the shores of the bay, and many men, chiefly English and French, who would have scorned the idea of selling their game at home, here turned their sporting abilities to good account and made their guns a source of handsome profit. A Frenchman with whom I was acquainted killed fifteen hundred dollars' worth of game in two weeks."

Other 49'ers were farming by the Presidio or the Mission Dolores. Their farms supplied the city with milk, eggs, and fresh vegetables. "In 1849, the announcement of a real cabbage at dinner would have set half the population frantic with strangely stirred appetites," declared the *Annals*. "Now, the many cultivated spots named daily furnished numerous loaded carts of all kinds of fresh vegetables to the city markets. Potatoes were no longer a rarity; turnips could be had for money—and at a moderate price, too."

By 1854, just five years after the "hardship and semi-starvation of 1849," the city boasted five large public markets; the New World at Commercial and Leidesdorff streets, the United States fronting on Washington and Merchant streets between Montgomery and Sansome, the Pacific on Commercial Street between Leidesdorff and Sansome, the Clay on Clay Street between Montgomery and Sansome, and the Eagle between Leidesdorff and Sansome streets. There were more than sixty "private markets" or grocery stores, some named after the street on which they were located and others called the Philadelphia Market, Knickerbocker Market, or the Fanieul Hall Market in honor of the proprietor's home town.

The restaurants, likewise, had improved from the days when they were housed in canvas tents and served sand to their customers along with the beefsteak and coffee. San Francisco had more than its share of restaurants, because there were so many single men and visitors staying for a year or two who did not have homes. By 1854 there were sixty-eight restaurants and "coffee saloons" plus many more hotels, boarding houses, saloons, and refreshment stands serving food.

Most restaurants served simple fare, often family style, at one or two large tables and at reasonable prices. The days of $1 eggs and $3 beefsteaks had disappeared by 1850. The Dime House along the waterfront, for instance, charged ten cents for each dish. Another popular spot was the dining room at Robert B. Woodward's What Cheer House hotel on Pike Street, between Washington and Clay. The lunches and dinners at the What Cheer House were so good that men who worked nearby took their meals there, too.

By then, there were also restaurants with pretensions to *haute cuisine* and a fashionable setting: Delmonico's, Sutter's, the Irving, Jackson's, Franklin's, and the Lafayette where a meal with wine ran $5 to $10. Most San Franciscans were delighted that their several-year-old city had reached such a level of refinement so quickly, but less chauvinistic visitors were not as impressed with the food in these places. One morning in 1851 journalist Frank Marryat ate at Jackson's, located at California and Montgomery streets. "Here are a hundred small tables nearly all occupied; I secure one and peruse the bill of fare. I could have wished for fresh eggs, but these were marked at two shillings each and . . . I considered economy a duty. 'Fricassée de Lapin,' that sounded well, so I ordered it; I didn't tell the waiter, when he brought it, that it was not rabbit but gray squirrel, but I knew it from the experience I had had in the anatomy of that sagacious animal."

While not all meals were what they claimed to be, San Francisco's restaurants did offer food of every imaginable nationality. The strangest restaurants for American tastes were the Chinese. By 1850, 800 Chinese men lived in the city, mostly along Sacramento Street near Kearny and Grant. A year earlier, they had opened a number of restaurants, which J. D. Borthwick believed "belong to the best of the town." But he was put off by the appearance of the "dried fish, dried ducks, and other very nasty

looking Chinese vegetables" displayed in the windows of the restaurants and grocery stores. "A particularly nasty smell pervaded this locality," wrote Borthwick, who must have overlooked the raw sewage and animal innards lying around the streets in other parts of town. But he did add that "it was generally believed that rats were not so numerous here as elsewhere."

French restaurants were the most popular in town. A few like the Lafayette or Jackson's were run by "elegantly dressed *dames du compotoir* with all the arrangements . . . in the Parisian style," according to J. D. Borthwick. Although Hinton R. Helper thought the names of ordinary places like *Trois Freres* and the *Cafe de Paris* "rather ambitious," he considered them superior to most American-run restaurants. After visiting the *Cafe du Commerce*, Helper wrote: "A better dinner can be procured here than in an American house, because the French are better cooks, cleaner in their culinary arrangements and preparations, more polite and attentive to their guests, and less accustomed to adulterating their provisions."

Nearly 5,000 Frenchmen lived in San Francisco by 1854, and some parts of town resembled France down to the architecture of the buildings and the signs in the shop windows. The French

Gold Rush restaurant

community had two newspapers, a theater—the Adelphi, and even a gambling house—the Polka. The menfolk organized their own volunteer fire company, the Lafayette, with a firehouse on Stockton Street between Pacific and Broadway. The Americans welcomed the French immigrants and did not think of them as foreigners, according to Pierre Charles de Saint-Amant, a French government agent. The only problem with Frenchmen, declared the *Annals*, was "the wild glorification . . . to every thing connected with their beautiful France."

The French were too tactful to say what they thought of the city's American-run restaurants. But Englishman J. D. Borthwick liked the American places and wrote that some were just as good as the town's best French restaurants. Like several other foreign visitors, he pointed out the regional varieties of American food. For instance, there were places "where those who delighted in corn-bread, buckwheat cakes, pickles, grease, molasses, apple-sauce, and pumpkin pie could gratify their taste to the fullest extent."

The saloons, likewise, had increased in number and comfort in the few years since 1849. San Franciscans had not given up their love of drink. "Very many also continue the habit of occasionally taking a daily 'drink' or two; while most of the inhabitants take many more 'drinks' than they would perhaps care to confess to a rigidly sober acquaintance," declared the *Annals*. Hinton R. Helper estimated that 12,000 to 15,000 of the State's 250,000 people worked in the liquor trade and that the annual consumption was 5,000,000 gallons, or twenty gallons for every man, woman, and child in California. He also reported that San Francisco had four grog shops for every street intersection. That estimate might not be far off. In 1853 the *Christian Advocate*, a newspaper published in San Francisco, counted 573 places in the city selling liquor.

Saloons were good business, and their proprietors spent freely to lure customers from their competitors. At some saloons the typical free lunch of crackers and cheese turned into real meals of "bear meat and cold salmon or salad and cheese." At night,

"dashing females" sometimes served men their drinks and small meals of game and oysters. "Such were employed at high wages to decoy and entertain customers . . . who were attracted to these saloons more by a graceful figure and charming face, than the viands to be procured," noted the *Annals*. Other establishments hung paintings and engravings on the walls, "some of them of the size of life, representing nude women in every imaginable position of obscenity and indecency," fumed the sensitive Helper.

Maybe he would have been happier patronizing one of the temperance hotels or restaurants. Hillman's Temperance Hotel stood at 80–82 Davis Street. L. M. Schaeffer stayed at Smith's Temperance House. He liked his room but wrote home that the dining room food was awful. One temperance restaurant, Winn's Fountain Head, which opened in July, 1851, at 78–80 Commercial Street, served excellent meals. By 1854, M. L. Winn opened branches at Montgomery and Washington streets and on Clay Street between Battery and Sansome. Winn's temperance principles had little to do with his success. For one thing, San Franciscans appreciated fine food, and for another, Winn had wisely installed the city's first soda fountain.

Temperance principles did not get far in San Francisco. The

Winn's Branch

Board of Aldermen passed laws closing saloons after midnight and all day Sunday, but they were rarely enforced. The town's population was almost entirely men in the early 1850s, and they enjoyed their drinking, gambling, and whoring. They also enjoyed the luxurious barber shops. One of the high points of British journalist Frank Marryat's 1851 stay was a shampoo, shave, and bootblacking one morning. "I enter a shaving-saloon . . . [and] seating myself in an easy chair of velvet, and placing my legs on an easy chair, also of velvet, I become drowsy under the influence of the fingers and thumbs of the operator, as they are passed over my skull, as if with a view to making a phrenological chart.

"Next I am conducted to a marble washstand and a tap of cold water is turned on me." Marryat thought that he had washed his hair thoroughly earlier that morning, "but it appears not, judging from the color of the water. My head is dried by hard labor, then is wetted again by a shower of eau de Cologne and water, thrown at me when least expected.

" 'Will I be shaved, sir?' Of course I will! 'Take a seat.' I sink into the velvet chair, and contemplate my dirty boots, that for days have not known blacking, but have known mud, as they contrast with the crimson pile velvet on which they rest. The back of the chair is raised by means of a screw, until my head is in the proper position for operation. First I have hot water on my chin, and a finger and thumb (generally the property of a colored gentleman) feels for my beard in a dreamy way with a view to softening the stubble. Then comes the lather, and shave the first, and I am about to get up, when I am stopped by more lather, and shave the second; this is conducted in a slow methodical manner, the finger and thumb wandering about in search of any stray hairs, like gleaners after the harvest."

Then Marryat decided to do something about his muddy boots, and he headed for a "bootblacking saloon" run by several Frenchmen. "I seat myself on a comfortable fauteuil, two Gauls are at my feet, each Gaul has two brushes, and such a friction is commenced that my feet are being shampooed as much as my head was. The morning paper has been handed to me, and I have scarcely settled down to the lead article when 'V'la, M'sieur' announces that all is over. What a change! I pay the money with pleasure, one shilling, not before I am brushed though."

Muddy boots and red velvet foot stools typified San Francisco in the early 1850s. The town was getting more comfortable and modern with every passing day, but there was still plenty of squalor and primitive conditions. The wild-eyed and ill-kempt miners shared the plank sidewalks of Montgomery Street with merchants and bankers dressed in broadcloth coats and white shirts. Frame shacks, which were already ramshackle when they were thrown together in 1849 or 1850, stood next to impressive brick warehouses and shops displaying tempting merchandise behind their sparkling plate glass windows. But everyone in town, poor and well-to-do alike, still did without running water, indoor plumbing, and gas lighting.

Most men just accepted these dichotomies of life in San Francisco. Rather than complain about the town's failings, they pointed to the fortunes they were making, the handsome new buildings going up everywhere, and the rising real estate values as proof that San Francisco was becoming a great city in every sense of the word. Everyone was particularly proud of how quickly San Francisco had become a city. "We have seen her, but a few years since, only a barren waste of sand-hills—a paltry village—a thriving little town—a budding city of canvas, then of wood, and next a great metropolis of brick," enthused the *Annals*. "Nothing seems impossible in the progress of San Francisco. Her future will be far more glorious than even the present. As the lover expatiates rapturously upon his mistress, whose perfections, though nature may have been bountiful, he chiefly himself creates, so do the San Franciscans speak of their beloved city, whose magnificence is principally the work of their own hands."

San Franciscans had every reason to be proud of their city and its growth. The mining camp and Gold Rush port eras had ended in 1851, and San Francisco had the wealth, population, and sophisticated vices of any Eastern city. But it was still an incomplete city, without real homes and without women and families.

A year before the Gold Rush, women constituted one-third of San Francisco's population. But when thousands of men swarmed to California in search of riches, women became just a tiny portion of the city's population. And only a handful of these were "virtuous ladies." As Albert Benard de Russailh dryly observed: "There are some honest women in San Francisco, but not many."

The situation was not much better in 1850. Men still stopped and stared at the occasional ladies who passed on the plank sidewalks. "Respectable" women were even scarcer in the inland gold fields and mining towns. One Sacramento woman wrote in her diary: "Every man thought every woman in that day a beauty. Even I have had men come forty miles over the mountains, just to look at me, and I never was called a handsome woman, in my best days,

even by my most ardent admirers." The 49'ers were so starved for female companionship that they gave presents to any women they knew, even married ones, just to have the opportunity to pass some time with them during the brief social call. Sarah Royce, a young woman who arrived in San Francisco with her husband and two-year-old daughter in January, 1850, "blushed to discover, by conversations held in my presence, that there were instances of women watching each other, jealously, each afraid the other would get more or richer presents than herself." The upright Sarah Royce did not intend to accept any presents from any men, no matter how honorable their intentions. "I have since seen some sad falls into positive vice of those whose downward course appeared in these and similar practices."

The scarcity of women in San Francisco eased somewhat the following year. On February 4, 1851, the *Alta* happily reported that "each succeeding steamer is bringing to California the wives and families of many of our merchants and mechanics who have preceded them and built for them a home amongst us." On June 27, the newspaper declared that "during the last few months there has been a most marked increase of the gentler sex into our city," while James G. Eastland wrote: "Instead of a woman being regarded as a natural curiosity, of which every man would stop to look, they are now seen in almost as great a number as they would anywhere else, and their influence is felt in Society."

Eastland was a wishful thinker. San Francisco was still an overwhelmingly male city, but it was beginning to change. In 1851, merchants and professional men began replacing the rough-looking miners' garb that they had worn in 1849 and 1850 with the fine clothing of their East Coast counterparts. "The fashions of San Francisco are very materially improved from last year," wrote Robert Lammot early in 1851. "Patent leather boots and beaver hats are quite as common this winter as were 'cow hide extensions' and felt tiles, last." Dressing well for the ladies was easier than it had been a year or two earlier. Quite a few shops now stocked such clothing, and keeping all of it clean was possible because laundry prices had dropped from the astronomical Gold Rush levels.

Husband and wife

Opposite, The Old Mansion House and Mission Dolores

By 1851 merchants looked like merchants as they walked down the street and day laborers and miners looked like day laborers and miners. The city was starting to assume a more settled look, but the new distinctions in men's clothing signaled an end to the egalitarian city of the 49'ers where everyone, regardless of his background, shared the same hardships in everyday life and the same chance for sudden fortune.

In 1849 and 1850, European visitors had been surprised to see that clothing was not the measure of a man. When Frederick Gerstacker returned to San Francisco from the diggings on a steamboat, he thought his clothing was "wild enough to frighten any one." He was still wearing "the 'original costume' of the mountains . . . an old straw hat, which, as it were, from sheer obliging disposition still kept together in two places; a grey woolen blouse, patched and torn all over; and shoes, so completely trodden out of shape, that for the last fortnight I had walked on the side of the soles." Nonetheless, he was permitted to sit in the steamboat's public parlor and eat his meals in the dining room with properly dressed gentlemen and ladies. "In no other country in the world" would such a thing have been allowed, he wrote. "But here, every day, numbers of such figures come from the mountains; and, not only is there no notice taken of their dilapidated appearance, but on the contrary, people generally treat them with marked respect; as one cannot know whether they have not some very decent bags of gold hidden under their rough digger's blouse."

J. D. Borthwick agreed that "appearances, at least as far as dress was concerned, went for nothing at all" when he landed in San Francisco in 1849 and 1850. The well-shaven man with a stove-pipe hat, broadcloth coat, and freshly polished boots was not automatically assumed to be a better man than the plainly dressed individual. "The man standing next him, in the guise of a laboring man, was perhaps his superior in wealth, character, and education."

But this social freedom, as exemplified by such attitudes toward dress, did not last long, and by the mid-1850s a few San Franciscans openly regretted the loss of their city's earlier inno-

cence. "We might have established a sensible society," declared the *Chronicle* in 1856, "but instead of that, instead of a quiet style of home life, a simple style of dress, a reasonable style of living, of house, of furniture, of life before the public, all the vanities of the rotten customs of the older cities have been introduced and doubled."

Another sign that San Francisco's freewheeling Gold Rush days were disappearing was the proliferation of churches. Before the Gold Rush, the only church in San Francisco was the decaying Mission Dolores, and it was several miles from the edge of town. The first Protestant clergyman in town was the Reverend T. Dwight Hunt, who arrived from Hawaii in October, 1848. He was named town chaplain at a salary of $2,500 a year and held a morning and evening service in the schoolhouse on Portsmouth Square. Reverend Hunt had been a missionary trying to save the heathens in Hawaii, and he came to San Francisco with that same calling in mind. Hunt's colleagues in Hawaii thought his mission futile. "The town had then an almost unenviable notoriety for wickedness, and its reputation at the Island was such that any attempt at reforming it was deemed wild and foolish."

But San Francisco's moral condition was not the first problem that clergymen encountered. First they faced the more mundane task of finding a place for services in a town whose residents were living in tents, shacks, and ships anchored in the harbor. Congregations met in tents, schoolhouses, and courtrooms, often staying in one place no more than a few weeks.

On May 20, 1849, half a dozen men and women organized the First Presbyterian Church under Reverend Albert Williams. The congregation worshipped first in the Portsmouth Square schoolhouse, then in the district courthouse on Grant Avenue, between Jackson and Pacific streets, next in a second-floor room of another building on the same block, and then in a tent that had been the marquee for a Boston military company. That made a different location almost every month.

The onset of heavy rains in the winter of 1849–1850 forced the Presbyterians to flee their tent and take refuge with the First

The first First Presbyterian Church

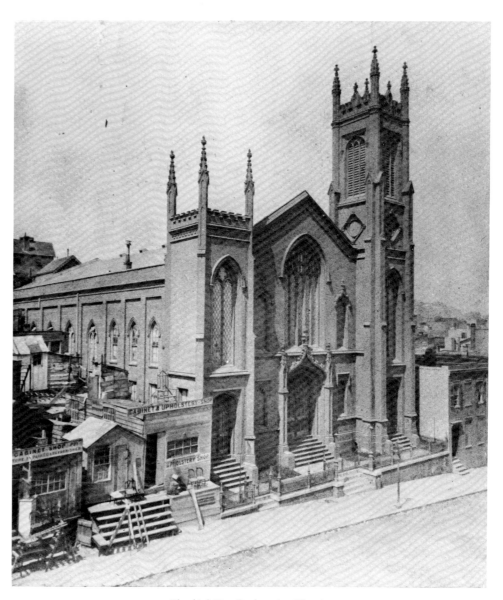

The second First Presbyterian Church

The third First Presbyterian Church

Baptist Church, whose frame building on Washington Street, near Stockton, was the first Protestant house of worship erected in California. A few months later, the Presbyterians were on the move again, to a storeroom in the Custom House, then to the Superior Courtroom, and finally to City Hall.

On January 19, 1851, they moved into their own church, a modest prefabricated structure from New York which stood on Stockton Street between Broadway and Pacific. But the "neat Gothic edifice" burned in the June 22, 1851, fire. In the following months, the Presbyterians worshipped in a courtroom temporarily set up in the Marine Hospital, the Superior Court room at the St. Francis Hotel, and again in the First Baptist Church, the only church to survive that fire. That fall the Presbyterians again occupied their own church, where they worshipped until they built a fine Gothic edifice on Stockton Street near Clay. That church stood until the 1906 earthquake and fire.

The wanderings of the Presbyterians may seem extreme, but most congregations were just as hard pressed to find a place to worship. Nevertheless, most congregations survived those difficult days and prospered. By 1853 San Francisco boasted eighteen churches and two synagogues. By 1860 the number of churches rose to thirty-seven.

Some of the churches were makeshift, odd-looking structures. In 1860 Trinity Episcopal Church worshipped in a building made of iron plates originally intended for a pre-fabricated warehouse, on the north side of Pine Street, between Montgomery and Kearny. Grace Episcopal Church, perhaps the most fashionable congregation in town, met on Powell Street, between Jackson and Pacific, in a frame "carpenter Gothic" building that was just thirty-eight feet wide and sixty-eight feet deep. The tiny church did have a proper sixty-foot-tall spire, but that was more an object of embarrassment than pride to the congregation. It had remained partially built for several years for lack of funds to finish the work.

Other congregations, which were better funded if less fashionable than Grace Episcopal, erected handsome brick churches in the early 1850s. The *Annals* observed in 1853: "The old, small wooden buildings that served the purposes of religious meeting-houses well enough a few years back are being discarded, and magnificent brick structures are rising in their stead." One such building was the First Congregational Church, begun in 1853 at the southwest corner of Grant Avenue and California Street. This church, which combined Greek Revival with the more elaborate Italianate style then coming into vogue, was 60 feet wide and 100 feet deep and held 1,200 worshippers. The 235-foot-tall spire was one of the city's landmarks. The *Annals*, not surprisingly, hailed the $50,000 church as "one of the striking ornaments of the city." The First Congregational Church was a handsome enough building to win similar praise years later. In 1876 B. E. Lloyd thought that the building was "an ornament in church architecture, beautiful and substantial, and finished in great elegance."

Just a week after the Congregationalists began their church, the Roman Catholics laid the cornerstone for St. Mary's Cathedral

Portsmouth Square schoolhouse

diagonally across the street at the northeast corner of Grant Avenue and California Street. By the time the first services were held there at midnight on Christmas Eve, 1854, the archdiocese had spent $140,000 on St. Mary's and had another $35,000 to go. But the money was well spent. St. Mary's seated 1,200 people; it was the largest church in California and one of the most impressive. The brick facade followed the Gothic Revival style, complete with a 200-foot-tall tower, and the interior included spacious galleries, an organ loft, and forty-five-foot-high vaulted ceilings with decorated groined arches.

The organization of a public school system, likewise, showed that San Francisco's mining camp days were over. Late in 1847, a schoolhouse stood at the southwest corner of Portsmouth Square. But once the Gold Rush began, entire families left town for the diggings, "leaving the teacher minus pupils, minus trustees and town council, and minus tuition and salary," according to the *Annals*. Finally, the teacher locked the schoolhouse door and headed for the mines himself. In the next year the building was used as a church, theater, courtroom, police station, and again as a school, until the city demolished it in 1850.

The city government had neither the time nor the money to establish a public school system in the chaos of 1849 and 1850. The few children in town attended classes at churches, one-man or one-woman private schools, or free classes supported by contributions. But the turnover of teachers was frequent, and the schools themselves rarely lasted more than a few months.

On September 25, 1851, the Board of Aldermen ordered free education for all children aged four to eighteen, and divided the city into seven districts, each to have its own school. Men teachers received $150 a month and their women counterparts, $100. Within a year a school was open, in rented quarters, in each of the seven districts, and 791 of the 2,050 school-age children in San Francisco were attending public classes.

The *Annals* enthused: "The school-bell now echoes through the streets of the busy city, and the astonished stranger meets groups of bright and smiling faces merrily trudging to their daily tasks." But the real situation was not actually that cheery. Very few children stayed the entire year at one school, because their families moved around town so frequently or moved to one of the interior mining towns for a while and then back to San Francisco. The Board of Education, moreover, did not devote its full attention to the children and their instruction. The rents for the schoolhouses were ruinous, and the superintendent and his staff devoted much of their time to acquiring land and building a schoolhouse in each district. Not surprisingly, many parents did not want their boys and girls to attend the city schools, and more children went to private than public schools in the early and mid-1850s.

Frame houses began to go up all over San Francisco in 1851 and 1852. Most were modest three- and four-room cottages for working and middle class families. But San Francisco's well-to-do men and their families wanted to live in handsome houses and genteel neighborhoods which, for some, would recall their way of life back East and, for others, would show off the fortunes that they had just won in the West. For those Victorian gentlemen and ladies, the family home meant more than just a financial status symbol. Architect Samuel Sloan declared in the early 1850s: "A man's dwelling at the present day is not only an index of his wealth, but also of his character. The moment he begins to build, his tact for arrangement, his private feelings, the refinement of his taste and the peculiarities of his judgment are all laid bare for public inspection and criticism. And the public makes free use of this prerogative. It expects an effort to be made, and forms opinions upon the result."

The *Elite Directory* of 1879 recalled that "in 1852 society began to crystallize" and "its first efforts at local aggrandizement were on Stockton Street, north of Washington." Stockton Street was far enough uphill to provide a good view of the Bay and to offer an easy walk to the offices and shops on or near Montgomery Street. Some of the finest houses of the 1850s stood there or farther up the slopes of Nob Hill and Russian Hill. But Stockton Street was too close to the saloons, gambling dens, and brothels around Portsmouth Square and the waterfront to please everyone looking

for a fashionable neighborhood. Rich men, therefore, began to build their homes on Rincon Hill, which extended from Folsom to Bryant Street and from Spear to Third Street.

Rincon Hill had good weather, a fine view of the Bay and city, and over half a mile's distance from the city proper and its nuisances. In 1850 Rincon Hill was open land, dotted with small oak trees and underbrush and a few squatters' shacks. In 1851 and 1852 the "steam paddy" leveled the sand hills that hindered travel to the busy streets north of Market Street. By 1853 the houses on Rincon Hill were "numerous" and " elegant," according to the *Annals*. In 1854 enough people lived on Rincon Hill to merit an omnibus running along Third Street every half hour to Portsmouth Square and North Beach.

William Gwin, one of California's first two United States Senators, built one of the first houses on Rincon Hill at 618 Harrison Street, near Hawthorne Street. The two-story frame building sat on a bluff high above the street and was approached by a series of flights of stairs. In 1854 it became the home of Thomas Selby, who built the Selby Shot Tower on Howard Street, near First Street, in 1864 and was Mayor from 1869 to 1871.

Mrs. Selby was a prominent social figure at the time, and in the mid-1860s she added a ballroom to the house which the *Argonaut* later claimed was the first in a private residence in San Francisco. The Selbys gave a grand ball there every year, plus numerous smaller functions. The long flights of stairs leading to the house were canopied for those events and looked like a series of canvas tunnels marching up the hill.

Another early resident of Rincon Hill was William I. Kip, the first Episcopal bishop of California, who lived at 338 Second Street, between Folsom and Harrison. His neighbor at 326 Second Street was Henry W. Halleck, who built the Montgomery Block, the largest and most expensive building on the Pacific Coast when it opened in 1853. Halleck served as General-in-Chief of the Union armies during the Civil War.

The grandest house on Rincon Hill and, for a time, in the entire city was banker John Parrott's mansion at 620 Folsom Street, between Second and Third. As the house neared completion in 1854, Abby M. Parrott wrote her sister-in-law Helen Meagher: "I fear that untiring care and unlimited expense can never produce even the shadow of beauty on these eternal sandhills." Her doubts were unnecessary; their three-story Italianate style brownstone mansion surprised San Francisco with its splendor and accelerated Rincon Hill's emergence as a lovely and stylish spot.

By 1860 Rincon Hill boasted British nobility—Robert Burnett, oldest son and heir of a Scottish Baronet. The tall, red-haired, goodlooking Burnett lived on the bluff at the foot of Beale Street overlooking the cove at the base of Rincon Hill then known as South Beach. Burnett was twenty-six years old and unmarried, but he nonetheless maintained a handsome establishment that included a housekeeper, housemaid, cook, valet, and groom for his horses. He drove one of the first one-horse British dog carts in the city.

Burnett was an innovator in other ways, too. He gave San Francisco one of its first scandals. In 1860 he left the Montgomery Street assay house, where he had been a partner, and joined Charles B. Polhemus as a partner in his California Street mercantile house. Polhemus lived in two rooms above his offices with his wife, who was many years younger and one of the best looking women in town. Burnett spent so much time with Polhemus and his wife that "he was almost a member of the family," recalled the *San Francisco News Letter* years later. But "Burnett's attentions to the wife of the senior partner were more pronounced than compatible with the discretion and prudence of the proverbial Scot." Few people knew what was going on until Polhemus announced in the *Bulletin:* "The interest of Mr. Robert Burnett in our firm ceases on and after this date." Shortly thereafter, Polhemus started to divorce his wife.

Burnett sold his Beale Street house and returned to Europe, with Mrs. Polhemus following him. They were married once the divorce was final. Burnett and his wife later returned to California to raise sheep near Los Angeles but returned to Great Britain permanently once he inherited the family title and estates in

Opposite, John Parrott residence, Folsom Street between Second and Third

Aberdeenshire, Scotland.

By the time Burnett left his Beale Street home in 1861, Rincon Hill was as lovely and settled-looking as the well-to-do neighborhoods of Eastern cities. The houses, which generally sat back from the street in gardens, represented the full variety of architectural styles then in vogue in America. The Greek Revival and Gothic Revival, so fitting for frame houses, were the predominant styles. But other architectural styles were popular, too. W. L. Palmer, owner of the Golden State Foundry, lived in an octagonal house at 329 Second Street, just north of Harrison. John Parrott's home would have fit right in with the brownstone Italianate style mansions which began to rise on New York's Fifth Avenue in the 1850s. And a photograph of four brick bowfront rowhouses along Vernon Place, which led off Second Street, looks just like Beacon Hill in Boston, except for the view of San Francisco Bay in the background.

But the longings which so many San Franciscans of the 1850s felt for their homes back East were most clearly expressed in South Park, where dignified rowhouses surrounded a pretty oval park. In 1852 George Gordon, an Englishman, purchased the six 100-vara lots bounded by Bryant and Brannan streets and Second and Third streets, on the southeast slope of Rincon Hill. He laid out a 75-by-550-foot oval which was fenced and handsomely planted. A windmill pumped water for the garden. Only residents of the surrounding houses had keys to the park gates. It was a private park in the tradition of London's West End or New York's Gramercy Park and St. John's Square, but elliptical in shape like the Boston parks that were all the fashion in the 1850s.

George Gordon wanted his South Park to have the same architectural unity as its Eastern inspirations, and he wrote restrictive covenants into each lot's deed requiring that "the houses must be of brick or stone and occupied exclusively for private dwellings." An advertisement for those lots read: "Parties wanting to build can, for from $2800.00 to $3500.00, have erected comfortable and durable residences, filled with modern conveniences. Gas and water pipe are laid." Gordon, who was a civic booster as well as a businessman, had unbounded optimism for the project. His advertisement continued: "For quiet, economical family residences, free from risk or annoyances of contiguous shops or stores, South Park furnishes the most elegant sites in the City."

In 1854–1855 Gordon built a group of two- and three-story Italianate style rowhouses along South Park's northwest quadrant. The oval park already displayed "floral beauties rarely or never seen outside of a private garden or conservatory," according to the *Alta California* in 1855. That same year, Gordon offered to build another group of houses along the southwest quadrant. The terms were unusual. Buyers paid 8 per cent of the house's cost upon signing the contract, 8 per cent the next year, and then 10 per cent each year until the remaining balance was paid off.

Gordon built the southwest section of houses, but he was beginning to have trouble completing his vision for South Park. One year some of the residents refused to pay the annual assessment for the upkeep of the gardens in the park oval. Gordon still owned the land and had to threaten to build a market on the site before he received all the maintenance payments. All the South Park lots were eventually sold, although it was not until the 1870s, and Gordon's dream "was not so successful as he had hoped pecuniarily," as the *Bulletin* noted in 1869.

The houses which Gordon built do not appear to have been the reason for South Park's slow development. They were as handsome and well-appointed as any in San Francisco at the time. Three of the four houses offered for sale in the southeast quadrant in 1860 contained eleven rooms: two parlors, a dining room, a kitchen, two pantries, five bedrooms, and servants' rooms. The fourth house in this group had nine rooms.

Perhaps Gordon's restrictive covenants put off some would-be buyers who were used to doing exactly as they pleased with their property and home. Back in the early years of the nineteenth century, St. John's Park in New York City had gone nowhere until Trinity Church, its sponsor, loosened its hold on the development of the property. But then again the lots along New York's Gramercy Park and the north side of Washington Square sold

South Park, 1856

quickly and easily, and their deed controls were as strict as the ones that George Gordon added to his South Park lots.

Gordon's covenants had a real purpose. Zoning laws were virtually non-existent in mid-nineteenth-century American cities, New York and San Francisco included, and covenants were one way a family could buy or build a house and know that a tenement, stable, or factory would not rise on a vacant lot nearby.

Maybe Gordon's unhappy personal life impaired his judgment on South Park or led him into more business ventures than he could handle at once. He built one of the city's first wharves, Howison's Pier, in 1850, organized its third iron foundry in 1852, and founded its first sugar refinery in 1857. He founded the Immigration Society in 1855 to make overland and ship travel to California easier and cheaper for settlers from the East. Like so many other San Franciscans, he also proposed bringing boat loads of unmarried women to the city to redress the imbalance between men and women.

The newspapers called Gordon "erratic" as well as a "genius," but few people knew about the tragedy of his marriage and family. That story might be forgotten by now if Gertrude Atherton, who was born Gertrude Horn on Rincon Hill, had not used it as the basis for her first novel, A Daughter of the Vine, published in 1899.

Back in the early 1840s in England, Gordon was the fun-loving son of a comfortable Yorkshire family, according to Gertrude Atherton's account. One morning he awoke from a night of drinking in a local pub to find himself married to the barmaid. Gordon did not try to annul the marriage, but several years later, perhaps appalled at what he had done, he left for California with his wife, Elizabeth Ann.

After living in San Francisco for several years, Mrs. Gordon asked that they return to England. He would hear nothing of the idea. He was already rich and well respected, and almost nobody in San Francisco knew about the unusual circumstances of his marriage. Out of desperation or perhaps spite, Elizabeth Ann Gordon decided to tell him a few things he did not know about her and their marriage. She had arranged that drinking spree ten years earlier in the Yorkshire pub, and, when Gordon was too drunk to know what was happening, she got them married. As if that weren't enough, she also announced that she was an alcoholic and wasn't going to hide it from him any longer.

Gordon's servants cared for his wife while he went on with his business ventures. But Elizabeth Ann Gordon was not through with him yet. She wreaked her vengeance on their only child, the dark-haired, dark-eyed Helen Mae, known as Nellie. Mrs. Gordon hooked the infant Nellie on whiskey by adding a few drops to every meal. When Nellie was sick, Mrs. Gordon put whiskey in her medicine. Soon Nellie would not eat anything unless it contained whiskey.

Almost no one knew about Nellie's craving for alcohol. She was one of the most attractive and sought-after young belles in the city. Her busy father did not learn about her alcoholism until she was seventeen. He thought that Nellie could beat her problem if she were free of her mother's influence, so he sent her to boarding school. But Elizabeth Ann Gordon smuggled bottles of whiskey to Nellie along with her laundry.

George Gordon pleaded with Nellie to stop drinking, and several times she did, only to start again. Nellie's craving for alcohol poisoned her entire life. She lost the man she was to have married, bore his child out of wedlock, married a cousin who was also an alcoholic, and died in 1874 when she was twenty-nine years old. The tragedy of the Gordon family seems too melodramatic to be true, and probably has been embellished with the passing years, but Gertrude Atherton's family were good friends of the Gordons and one family member was at Nellie's bedside when she died.

Nellie Gordon's sad story did not spread much beyond a few neighbors and friends. But Robert Burnett's and Mrs. Charles Polhemus' escapades were well known and helped sustain the reputation for wickedness that San Francisco enjoyed even after the Gold Rush days were over.

San Francisco certainly was not the only city where prostitutes paraded the stylish shopping streets by day and young boys displayed pornographic books and pictures in front of the large hotels. Such sights were a part of most mid-nineteenth-century American cities, even if polite society chose to ignore them. But San Francisco's reputation for wickedness included more divorces per capita than any other place in America. "There are no people in the world who so practically ignore and hold in contempt the legal marital relations as do Californians," reported one New York newspaper in 1874.

An 1851 California divorce law permitted either husband or wife to separate on the grounds of incompatibility and to obtain a divorce from a court-appointed referee rather than going through the expense and publicity of a trial. The state divorce law applied to any California court, "but no court among them all has been more liberal . . . than the District Court of San Francisco," declared the *Chronicle* in 1854. "Marriage among us seems to be regarded as a pleasant farce—a sort of 'laughable afterpiece' to courtship." The *Chronicle* warned that "the divorces which are granted here will exceed in a tenfold ratio the number in any other part of the Union of equal population."

Statistics do seem to back up the *Chronicle*'s opinion. In 1856 there were 260 marriages in San Francisco and seventy-two applications for divorce. Perhaps the situation had something to do with the partial freedom from Victorian social conventions and attitudes, prevalent in East Coast towns and cities. San Francisco women were hardier and more independent than most women living in settled Eastern towns and cities. Although San Francisco was a city by the early 1850s, in terms of population and economic power, the women still faced much of the hardship and isolation from family and friends that were part of frontier living.

San Francisco women were at the forefront of the feminist stirrings of the 1850s. Women initiated nearly all the seventy-two divorce applications filed in 1856. A group of San Francisco women lobbied the legislature to enact a prohibition law in 1855, and others tried to clean up San Francisco's city government and the town's moral tone. In 1858 two women founded the *Hesperian*, a semi-monthly with literature and fashion news specifically for female readers.

Children on Alcatraz

Other women with entrepreneurial spirit successfully operated in the male business world. One woman friend of attorney John McCrakan speculated in the volatile real estate market of the 1850s and made a lot of money. Another woman "set her husband up in business here, manufacturing Soda," recalled one San Franciscan, "and they are making money fast. She doesn't trust him with the profits 'nary time' but keeps the stuff in her own hands."

But Feminism as a cause, did not do well in San Francisco. The menfolk ridiculed Feminism at every opportunity. The *Era* declared in 1855: Women "never talk of 'women's rights'—never parade the streets in bloomers and high heeled boots—never mount the stump . . . telling of the tyranny of men [and] in this respect are angels in contrast with their strong-minded sisters in the East." A year earlier, the *Alta* had ridiculed women's rights' advocates as more masculine than feminine and said their conventions were events where "woman unsexes herself, disclaims the nursery, maternity, and the delicacy of her nature by her forward, impudent, and brawling conduct in public crowds of rowdies."

Men's laughter did not discourage Feminists back East, and it wasn't the reason for the movement's slow going in San Francisco. The geographic isolation of San Francisco from the rest of the country cut would-be Feminists off from the movement on the East Coast. Furthermore, San Francisco women generally had less time and energy for social causes. Middle class women did many home chores that servants would have taken care of back East. Chastina Rix's diary describes her life in the early 1850s. "Washed and baked and brewed and everything else today. Tired enough," she wrote on August 22, 1853. Ten days later she observed: "I know but very little that is going on here. Stay at home very close. Ironing. I have to work pretty hard. Seven in the family most of the time. I hope I shall not always have to work so hard."

San Francisco women were caught in an awkward social and moral position, too. While the rest of the country thought that these women were adventuresome and perhaps a little morally suspect for living in California, the San Francisco men expected them to bring order and a higher moral tone to the city. But the men did almost nothing to clean up the drinking, prostitution, and violence that gave the town such a bad name. That wasn't surprising. Vice flourished in all East Coast cities as well, and the periodic cleanup campaigns there usually amounted to nothing more than good copy for newspaper editorials and Sunday sermons. But Eastern women were not expected to exercise such a large cleansing effect on the community, and they were reasonably isolated from the seamier side of life.

In San Francisco, women and children who lived along Stockton, Mason, or Powell streets had to walk past brothels and strolling courtesans on their way to the shops along Montgomery Street. The Chinese and Latin American streetwalkers had invaded the Kearny Street and Grant Avenue area, but "the principal offenders and those whose example is the most dangerous to public morals are the Americans, who dwell in splendid houses in the principal streets of the city, and endeavor to attract attention by sitting before their open windows and doors," declared the *Alta* in 1854.

San Francisco women found ways to forget such unpleasant things. Some found comfort in reading, and racy novels were often the favorites. Eugene Sue's *Mysteries of Paris*, a "sensation book" of the late 1840s, reportedly told all about the goings-on in that most wicked of European cities. Bookseller's advertisements for the book promised "Love! Love! Love!" in bold capital letters and a flurry of exclamation points. The *Mysteries of Paris* did thrill its readers with stories of high life and low life in the French capital, but there wasn't anything "explicit," as we say today. Still the newspapers denounced the book as immoral, abominable, and unfit to be read, and that sent even more young men and women into the bookstores.

Some women turned to drugs or alcohol. Drugstores sold opium and morphine over the counter, and, if you were afraid to ask for the real thing, there were patent medicines loaded with the same ingredients. Cordial elixirs were a favorite tonic. One druggist advertised his own concoction as "a palatable remedy for deranged digestion and intermittent fever," but everyone bought it to enjoy the lift from its principal ingredient: cocaine.

Some women found solace in a slavish devotion to fashion. "American women indulge in . . . the love of dress to a greater degree than those of any other country," observed the New York *Herald* in 1857. Things were no different in California. One self-styled "Western gentleman" wrote the *New York Herald* that "a majority of the middle class consider their principal mission on earth to be to dress fine and promenade before each other in order to exhibit their good looks and the merchandise they carry on their backs." No sooner had some dressmakers and dry good shops opened along Montgomery Street in 1851 and 1852 than the town's womenfolk put on their best clothes and strolled up and down the street, peering in the pretty display windows as they dragged their finery in the dust.

Most women, however, devoted themselves to caring for their families. For all her complaining about hard work, Chastina Rix was genuinely fond of her home and family. The baby "Bub's business is to laugh, play in the sand, run after his parents and bawl and eat victuals," she wrote in her diary in 1854. "The old man is Justice of the Peace and spends nearly every hour of the day at his office. . . . Chastina does the house-work, sews and tinkers so as to make, by herself, some $30 per month. She is up and has breakfast every morning before daylight and is perfectly healthy and full of contentment and fun. Clara teaches school at the Mission at $100 per month and rides back and forth every day. Dustan works at Wheelwrighting at $4.50 per day. We are all as happy as crickets and as healthy as pigs."

But even a happy family life could not completely remove a woman's loneliness for friends and familiar places back East or ease the pain of her awkward social and moral position. The passage of time and the maturing of San Francisco would help, as would the continuing influx of women and families. Only 8,000 of San Francisco's 50,000 inhabitants in 1853 were women. Women made up just 8 per cent of California's population at the time, and were only one third of the population in the 1880s. Not until the turn of the century were the numbers of men and women equal in the state and in San Francisco.

P.M. STEAMER
MONTANA.

T.E. HECK
430-35

San Francisco was a man's town from the beginning. There was plenty of work to give a man an identity, a daily routine, and a livelihood. At first the local economy depended almost entirely on mining. Merchandise and men landed in San Francisco on the way to the gold fields, and most of the wealth extracted from the earth ended up in San Francisco banks and businesses, or passed through the city on its way back East. Miners spent their money in San Francisco when they struck it rich, and they returned to the city when they ran out of money for another grubstake to return to the gold fields. And every year thousands of miners flocked to the city to escape the winter's cold and rains.

But San Francisco quickly became more than just the center for the 1849 Gold Rush. It became the economic and social focus for everything west of the Rockies. Throughout the nineteenth century it remained the center for mining companies, engineers, and consultants, the port where equipment arrived from the East Coast; and the place from which ore was sold and shipped to the rest of the world. San Francisco also remained the home base for the thousands of men coming West year after year to dig for gold and silver.

San Francisco became the banking center for the West Coast, too. In 1848 and 1849, merchants and miners usually held on to their money, often in the form of gold dust, or left it in the safekeeping of a saloonkeeper or in a mercantile house strongbox. But the success of such a practice depended upon the honesty of the man holding the money, and it suited only the primitive economy of that time. As more and more gold flowed into San Francisco, banks were clearly needed. The "first regular banking house in San Francisco," according to the *Annals*, was Naglee & Sinton, whose "Exchange and Deposit Office" opened on January 9, 1849 in the Parker House hotel. By the end of 1849 there were four other banking houses in town: Burgoyne & Company; B. Davidson, agent for the Rothschild family; Thomas G. Wells; and James King of William. Those firms received and paid out deposits, lent money, and even issued their own gold coins.

Banking grew as fast as the city and its economy. In 1850 banker James King of William thought that $200,000 was "a fair share of the deposits." Yet "the same banker who in '50 and '51 considered himself tolerably well patronized with $200,000, found himself in '52 with nearly $600,000, far behind Page, Bacon and Company who had three times that amount." In 1853 there were nineteen banks in San Francisco; two years later that number had risen to forty-two.

The bankers operated pretty much as they pleased. The State Constitution prohibited joint stock companies and their printing paper money. But that was all. Several express companies, which had originally shipped gold back East, went into banking—Kohler and Company; Palmer, Cook and Company; Adams and Company; Henry M. Naglee; Lucas Turner and Company; and, of course, Wells, Fargo. Sometimes merchants ended up as bankers, too. Joseph and Jesse Seligman sold mining supplies from their store at Sansome and California streets in 1849 and 1850. The Seligmans made a killing when their building remained standing after the May, 1851 fire destroyed most of the city. Soon after, the Seligmans became bankers, and in 1873 they sold out to the London-based Anglo-California Bank.

In the late 1840s and early 1850s, San Francisco was the center for an enormous trade in imported food. The thousands of 49'ers had to eat, but there were very few farms in the Bay Area or the state. The coastal valleys were thought to be infertile. A few San Franciscans began to raise chickens and vegetables at the outskirts of town, but most food consumed in San Francisco and the gold fields was imported from Oregon and the East Coast.

In 1853 San Francisco imported 100,000,000 pounds of flour, 20,000,000 pounds of butter, 25,000,000 pounds of barley, 12,000 hams, 16,000 barrels of salt beef, 40,000 barrels of refined sugars, more than 400,000 bags of rice, 115,000 bags of coffee and 1,100,000 pounds of tea. Californians hadn't yet started to brew their own whiskey or make wine in great quantities, so that year they also imported 20,000 barrels of whiskey, 4,000 barrels of rum, and nearly 200,000 cases of wine.

Opposite, The steamer Montana

But this reliance on imported food did not last much longer. Land was cheap and did not have to be cleared, and the soil proved quite productive once men adapted to the California climate. "If the success of the miner has been great, how shall we term the unexampled prosperity of the less romantic tiller of the soil?" asked the *Annals*. "The splendid agricultural resources of the country are only beginning to be understood." By the mid-1850s, California farms raised nearly all the livestock, grain, and vegetables consumed in the state. In 1860 there were nearly 20,000 farms in California. Ten years later more men were working on farms than in the mines, and the value of agricultural production exceeded that of mining.

As California became more self-sufficient agriculturally, the food import trade diminished. But it did not vanish entirely. Items like tea and coffee still had to be imported, and San Franciscans were always buying wines and liquors from the East Coast and Europe. Moreover, wholesalers often handled both imported and local food destined for Oregon and the Hawaiian Islands.

Because of California's agricultural bounty, food prices were lower in San Francisco than in East Coast cities. It was quite a change from the $1 an egg days of 1849. In 1862 the *North Pacific Review* compared the cost of living in New York City and San Francisco. Fruits and vegetables, not surprisingly, were much cheaper in San Francisco, and the season far longer, than in New York. "Our almost perpetual Summer keeps us supplied as no Atlantic market can be," reported the magazine. Meat was cheaper in San Francisco, too. "Prime cuts of beef" sold for 11–12¢ a pound compared to 14–16¢ in New York. "Ordinary roasting pieces" went for 8–10¢ in San Francisco versus 11–14¢ in New York. Boiling chicken was cheaper in New York at 50¢ a pair, while San Franciscans paid 75¢–$1 a pair. Game was far cheaper in California. Fish prices were about equal in both places. But Nova Scotia salmon was 75¢–$1 a pound in New York, when it was available. "It is a pity they could not have San Francisco's privilege in that respect," lamented the *North Pacific Review*. Salmon never sold for more than 20¢ a pound in San Francisco, "and for months it [was]

the cheapest fish in the market."

During the Gold Rush years, San Francisco imported nearly all its manufactured goods. But businessmen saw the lack of local industry as another opportunity for investment, and San Francisco soon emerged as the manufacturing center of the West Coast. Industry did not have an easy time getting started. Wages were high, and natural resources like coal and iron were scarce. The local market in the 1850s was limited, and industry had difficulty attracting investment capital away from more glamorous mercantile and real estate ventures. Finding sites for factories was difficult. AlthoughSan Franciscans applauded the rise of manufacturing in their city, nobody wanted the noisy and smelly factories near their homes.

By an 1852 city ordinance, slaughterhouses were excluded from the area east of Larkin and north of Market Street, and two years later they—and stockyards—were forbidden to locate anywhere in the city. Factory owners often avoided such troubles by locating their plants beyond the outskirts of the city.

Happy Valley, the one-time tent encampment just south of Market Street around First and Second streets, was becoming "quite a hive of manufacturing industry" in 1850, according to the *Annals*. But the city rapidly engulfed Happy Valley and other areas that had been countryside. In 1855 several factory owners asked the Board of Aldermen to set aside an area south of Mission Creek for industry. The proposed industrial zone was "so remote from the inhabited part of the city that no legal question would likely arise as to what might constitute nuisances in the district, at least within the period named in the ordinance—January 1st, 1869."

Nothing came of the idea and complaining neighbors plagued local industry throughout the nineteenth century. As if that weren't enough trouble, factory owners paid higher rents and prices for land in San Francisco than in most East Coast cities. But San Francisco offered one advantage that made up for all the difficulties. Eastern competitors had to include the shipping charges to California in the cost of their finished product. San Francisco factories could be less efficient or make more money than their

San Francisco Woolen Mills, Black Point

Furniture factory at San Quentin Prison

Eastern rivals and still undersell their products in the local market.

The leading industry in town was iron foundering. The high price of iron prevented San Franciscans from opening foundries in 1849. But the six fires which devastated the city in 1850 and 1851 left tons of scrap iron in the burnt-out ruins, the remains of safes, stoves, tools, even the walls of the pre-fab metal buildings. The scrap cost three-quarters to one cent a pound, while the finished metal sold for 20ᶜ a pound. The earliest foundry was the Union Iron Works, which started in James and Peter Donohue's blacksmith shop. By 1853 there were five other foundries in town: the Eagle, Alta, Vulcan, Pacific, and Sutter. By then "the whole coast was almost entirely dependent on the foundries of San Francisco for necessary iron work," recalled B. E. Lloyd.

The most exciting work at the foundries was designing and producing mining equipment. The Comstock lode was the supreme test of the foundries' skill. As the mines went deeper and deeper, the engineers faced hoisting and pumping problems that had never come up before, "and what was considered large machinery ten years ago is now looked upon as insignificant," wrote B. E. Lloyd in 1876. "Everything that is ordered is wanted in the greatest hurry possible. The mining companies in particular never make up their minds what they want, until they want, and then it is needed immediately," he declared. "Plenty of jobs have been undertaken and finished by our local works in a space of time which would look preposterous to persons in older communities." By 1875 there were forty-two foundries in San Francisco, and the largest one, the Union Iron Works, employed 500 men.

Food processing became important business as the state's agricultural production increased yearly. The first flour mill opened in San Francisco in 1852, and within a year there were ten others in operation. Ships that had returned to their East Coast or European ports with rock as ballast now loaded their holds with California grain or flour.

Perhaps the largest food processing operation in town was the San Francisco Sugar Refinery, founded by George Gordon in 1857 on Folsom Street about a mile from town. The sugar refinery was a virtually self-contained operation. A fleet of company ships brought the raw sugar from Hawaii and Manila to San Francisco. The three-acre installation had processing buildings, a factory making bone black filtering granules, a barrel works, two artesian wells to furnish the 70,000 to 80,000 gallons consumed every day, and a boardinghouse for employees. Every year the refinery used 4,000 tons of raw sugar, 1,600 tons of coal, 400 tons of bones, 1,100,000 barrel staves, and 1,000,000 hoops.

Hutching's California Magazine, an illustrated monthly published in 1856–1861, described the refining processes, which were "the newest and most improved kind," in an 1859 issue. The raw sugar was dumped into one of several 3,000-gallon iron vats where it was boiled by steam. After reaching just the right liquid state, the molten sugar was run through several strainers, the last one being thick canvas. Then the syrup sat in huge vats filled with granulated ivory black or bone charcoal for the following twenty-four hours. When the syrup was drained from these vats, it was a "pale amber color, perfectly pellucid." Next the sugar was crystallized, first in a vacuum pan under high temperatures and then in five-gallon cones, again under high temperature. The sugar, which was white now and partially hard, was baked in an oven capable of holding 170 tons. Finally, it was milled into the right grade of fineness and packed in barrels.

Local factories were also busy producing consumer goods. B. P. Moore & Company, the "pioneer establishment in the manufacture of fine furniture" in the city, sold its output at the southeast corner of Sansome and Pine streets. In an 1864 advertisement they promised that, "being desirous of pleasing their patrons," they would keep "their prices as low or lower than those of Eastern manufacturers, and, in addition, *they will guarantee satisfaction.*" Apparently San Franciscans had some trouble returning unwanted or defective pieces of furniture to a store 3,000 miles away. But well-to-do San Franciscans were more concerned with a status name on their furniture than low prices, and Moore & Company sold fashionable East Coast furniture in their store as well as their own items. M. E. Hughes, a billiard table manufacturer, avoided the stigma attached to locally made furniture by establishing himself as a branch of Phelan & Collender, the stylish New York firm. After he had done that, no one seemed to mind that his billiard tables were still made in San Francisco.

Carriage stores — or "carriage repositories," as they were called — did a brisk business, too. Californians liked driving around long before the automobile. And speeding was a problem from the outset. "Reckless jukes," as the *Alta* called them, sometimes drove their "fast turnouts" and "fast crabs" down the city streets at a dangerous twenty miles an hour. The Board of Aldermen even enacted laws against speeding, and the newspapers sometimes reported the arrest or fining of men for fast driving.

By 1865 there were four large carriage factories in San Francisco: Black & Miller with a store at 717 Market Street, Folsom & Hiller at 531 California Street, A. Searle & Company at 417 Market Street, and H. W. Bragg at 29–31 Battery Street. George P. Kimball, the fashionable New York City manufacturer, opened a San Francisco branch in 1853 on Market near Fourth Street. Some customers bought their carriage right off the showroom floor. Others ordered one made specifically to their design. Deciding what you wanted could be a bewildering task. First, you had to select the model. Would it be a top, side, or end-spring buggy? A brett, phaeton, or coupee? Or perhaps a light or heavy family rockaway? What kind of wood for the body of the carriage? The usual choices were hickory, oak, ash, maple, or birch. And then there was selection of the color of the paint job. How about trim? What style? And again, what wood?

Although there was money to be made in agriculture and industry, neither business was glamorous or exciting to San Franciscans. Trade with faraway places, as always, had a special appeal. And so did mining, even though the miner's life usually was anything but glamorous. But real estate was one business that intrigued almost everyone. The potential profits were incredible. The *Annals* declared: "The richest men in San Francisco have made the best portion of their wealth by possession of real estate." Furthermore, real estate operators had the satisfaction of helping to

build a city from scratch.

San Franciscans were speculating in real estate several years before the Gold Rush. In 1846 merchant William Heath Davis wrote that "land speculations have been brisk at this place. Most of the lots . . . have been taken up." A year later, fifty-vara parcels that cost $15 in 1844 were selling for $1,000. That was just the beginning of the rise in prices. Just a few months after the discovery of gold in 1848, real estate was ten times higher than it had been a year or two earlier. Some property had risen even more. In December, 1849, Thomas O. Larkin sold eight underwater lots and one above-water lot for $300,000. In 1847 underwater and beach property below Montgomery Street had been selling for $600 to $700 an acre.

Larkin sold those lots just in time. The market crashed at the end of 1849. A reaction to the dizzying rise in prices had been inevitable. The boom had been entirely speculative. San Francisco wasn't even a real town yet; it was still a collection of flimsy frame buildings and thousands of tents inhabited by men who had rushed there to make their fortunes and who might leave just as quickly if the money wasn't there to be made.

But the depressed prices of late 1849 did not last long. Real estate values started rising again early in 1850, and soon everyone seemed to be buying and selling property, usually at a profit. In 1850 artist William S. Jewett purchased a small piece of land at the outskirts of town for $200. Within a few months, he sold half of the parcel for $250. "It was all cash transaction," he wrote, "no sham at all about it except I have never seen the lot nor don't know where it is . . . but it is a certainty that I have $250 on it and that I honestly believe it to be in existence and above water."

By the early 1850s rising prices were not entirely speculative. San Francisco had survived the chaos of that first Gold Rush year. The population was growing steadily, and the two- and three-story buildings and planked sidewalks were giving San Francisco the first semblances of a permanent town. The city government, no doubt pressured by property owners, was doing things to facilitate San Francisco's outward growth and make it easier for people to get around town. Most streets and sidewalks were planked by the early 1850s. But wood planking did not hold up to the rainy season and the continual battering from horseshoes and iron-rimmed wagon wheels. Some downtown streets had to be replanked just two or three years after the job was done the first time. "Planking has served well in the infancy of the city," wrote the *Annals*, "but it is probable that so perishable a material will soon give place to cobble-stones or Macadamized paving, or even square-dressed blocks of granite or whinstone." In fact, as those words were written, portions of Montgomery and Washington streets were already cobblestoned.

The city decided that something should be done about lighting the streets at night, too. Before that, the only light came from theater entrances and gambling dens or from oil lanterns that some merchants hung over their doors. Late in 1851, J. B. M. Crooks, a whale oil dealer, was awarded the contract "to light the city," or at least the portion bounded by Battery, Kearny, Jackson, and California streets. Mr. Crooks went about his work in "true San Francisco style," according to the *Alta*. He did not put up enough lampposts, they did not burn all night long, and they gave off too little light. All the city fathers had accomplished, declared the *Herald*, was to "render the darkness visible."

The city fathers were also busy opening up streets which had previously existed only on surveyors' maps. In 1852, Market Street was laid out between Battery and Kearny streets. But it ended abruptly at First Street until the steam paddy leveled the sand hills between First and Third streets several years later. Even bustling Montgomery Street was not yet complete; as late as 1859 it "lost itself at Sutter Street in a huge sandbank," according to one newspaper account. The real chore, however, was opening up the east-to-west streets like California and Bush which ran into sand dunes and Nob Hill beyond Stockton Street. The city had no choice but to do this work. San Francisco had run out of convenient, easy-to-develop flat land, even though growth was spreading south of Market Street and into North Beach.

As if this excavation work weren't difficult enough in itself, a

Opposite, Russian Hill, 1865, viewed from Telegraph Hill

controversy erupted over the issue of street grades. The surveyors ordered the streets above Stockton Street to be laid out ten to fifty feet lower than the existing topography. Otherwise the streets would be too steep for wagon and carriage traffic. Fortunately, the hills were sand, and the steam paddy was indefatigable. But local property owners were none too happy about what was happening. As J. D. Borthwick wrote:

Some of the streets in the upper part of the city presented a very singular appearance. The houses had been built before the grade of the different streets had been fixed by the corporation, and there were places where the streets, having been cut down through the hills to their proper level, were nothing more than wide trenches, with a perpendicular bank on either side, perhaps forty or fifty feet high, and on the brink of these stood the houses, to which access was gained by ladders and temporary wooden stairs.

Buildings perched high above the streets were more than inconvenient for owners who trudged long flights of stairs to their front doors. They were dangerous, because there was no telling when the sand underneath might give way and the house tumble into the middle of the street. Property owners had the choice of building a wood or stone embankment to hold the land in place or excavating the entire parcel of land down to the new street and moving the house to that level. Either alternative cost a lot of money; and, to make matters worse, the city kept changing the grades. Some landowners excavated their property only to find that another system of grades had been established, and they had to bring their property down another five or ten feet.

Landowners on the slopes of Nob Hill weren't the only ones to suffer. Streets in low-lying areas had to be raised. In these areas, the regraded streets "formed a high embankment, with a row of houses at the foot of it, some nearly buried," wrote Borthwick. Landowners below Montgomery Street were particularly hard hit. The Yerba Buena cove had been filled in so haphazardly that the cellars of most buildings below Montgomery Street were flooded nearly all the time. Most streets below Montgomery Street were raised several feet.

Some people wondered why their city had not grown up on the flat shore across the Bay rather than on a sandy, hilly peninsula. "What with digging out and filling up, piling, capping and planking, grading and regrading the streets, and shifting, and rebuilding, and again rebuilding the houses, to suit the altered levels, millions upon millions of dollars have been spent," observed the *Annals*.

But the house movers weren't complaining. They had more business than they could handle even before the city embarked on its massive street grading projects. San Francisco was growing and changing so rapidly that some residential streets were going commercial before the houses were more than a few years old. So they were usually moved to another site rather than torn down. In 1863 the Rothschild agent, B. Davidson, moved his cottage from Sutter Street, between Powell and Stockton, to Ellis Street, above Mason, and Temple Emanu-El rose on his former lot which faced Union Square.

Raising a building

Relocating a frame building a few blocks away was a simple job. Sometimes the house movers carried frame buildings several miles. John Middleton, a Gold Rush physician turned real estate developer, purchased the Lake House, which sat on a lagoon near Ocean Beach in the late 1850s, and moved it the several miles to Second Street near South Park for his residence.

The house movers could raise, lower, or move brick and stone buildings as well. J. D. Borthwick watched several buildings being raised below Montgomery Street "by means of a most ingenious application of hydraulic pressure. Excavations were made, and under the foundation-walls of the houses were inserted a number of cylinders about two feet in height, so that the building rested entirely on the heads of the pistons. The cylinders were all connected by pipes with a force-pump, worked by a couple of men, who in this way could pump up a five-story brick building three or four inches in the course of the day. As the house grew up, props were inserted in case of accidents; and when it had been raised as far as the length of the pistons would allow, the whole apparatus was readjusted, and the operation was repeated till the required height was obtained."

Borthwick was particularly impressed to see the raising of a five-story-tall brick corner building, sixty feet on each side. "There was no interruption of the business going on in the premises," he declared, "or anything whatever to indicate to the passer-by that the ground was growing under his feet." The slate sidewalk was moved right along with the building. But Borthwick missed the even stranger sight at the French consul Patrice Dillon's house, at the northeast corner of Mason and Jackson streets. The house, according to the 1854 grade tables, sat twenty-five to thirty feet below the projected street level. The building was put on high stilts, and the empty space beneath filled with earth.

The growth of public transportation helped the real estate boom of the early 1850s. The first horse-drawn omnibus linked Portsmouth Square with the Mission Dolores in 1850. Several years later, there were routes linking Portsmouth Square to the Presidio, South Park, and North Beach. Hackney coaches were available for hire, and some "were infinitely superior to those of any other city in the world," according to Borthwick. "The cabs—if cabs they could be called—were large handsome carriages, lined with silk, and brightly painted and polished, drawn by pairs of magnificent horses, in harness, which, like the carriages, was loaded with silver. They would have passed anywhere for showy private equipages, had the drivers only been in livery, instead of being fashionably dressed individuals in kid gloves." But the passengers paid dearly for the privilege of riding in such elegance. "One could not cross the street in them for under five dollars," reported Borthwick.

San Franciscans briefly used boats to get around the city, too. One rowboat line carried passengers from the downtown waterfront to the Mission Dolores by way of the Bay and Mission Creek.

But rowboats and horse-drawn omnibuses were anachronisms by the 1860s. The rowboat route disappeared several years before Mission Creek was filled; the omnibuses were slow and the ride along the rutted streets anything but comfortable. The last word in urban transportation in Eastern cities at the time was the horse-drawn street car, also known as the street railroad, because it ran along the street on rails much like a train. San Francisco was far behind East Coast cities in its public transportation. When the *North Pacific Review* compared the cost of living in New York and San Francisco in 1862, it declared that rents in both cities were the same but that the New Yorkers had more choice of where they lived than San Franciscans. Because of the street railroads in Manhattan, New Yorkers could "live away from the bustle of business, and get homesteads in the accessible suburbs, or rent roomy houses at rates more reasonable than are charged in the thickly settled parts of town."

San Franciscans did not lack street railroads for long. The Market Street and Mission Dolores Railroad Company, which commenced operations in April, 1860, started at Market and California streets and ran along Market Street and then Valencia Street to the Mission Dolores. A branch line left Market Street at

Hayes Street and ran as far as Laguna Street. The North Beach and Mission Railroad, which started in 1861, began at California and Montgomery streets, ran down California to Battery Street, along Battery to Bush Street, across Market Street and down First Street, and out Folsom Street. The Omnibus Railroad Company, which opened in 1861, had an even more complicated route, but it basically ran from the Mission Dolores to Third and Howard streets and from there crosstown to the foot of Powell Street.

San Francisco welcomed the street railroads. "Nature is in league with the hackman and railroad companies," wrote B. E. Lloyd in 1876. "In Summer she drives the pedestrian into the horse-car or hack to escape the tempestuous gale that heralds its coming by billows and clouds of sand and dust that come rolling down the highways. In Winter they fly to the street cars for shelter to escape the drenching rain that comes in torrents flooding sidewalk and street."

The *North Pacific Review* thought that San Francisco's street railroads were every bit as good as those in the East Coast cities. But that just wasn't so. San Francisco's topography created problems that railroad engineers never faced in New York and Boston. The right of way for the Hayes Street line had to be cut through high sand hills, because Hayes Street did not yet exist. Sand slides were always blocking the tracks and delaying the trains. Things were just as bad on the line's downtown tracks near California and Market streets. Because the landfill below Montgomery Street was none too good, the ground often settled beneath the weight and vibration of the streetcars and pulled the track down with it. That part of town often flooded during the heavy winter rains, and the line was known as "McCoppin's Canal," after Frank McCoppin, superintendent of the company.

Despite these troubles, the introduction of street railroads did enable the poor and middle classes to live better by bringing suburban areas within reasonable commuting time of their downtown and waterfront jobs. Moreover, they influenced the shape of the city and its real estate values. "The numerous roads that stretch out in every direction through the city," wrote B. E. Lloyd, "have

leveled the sand-dunes, reclaimed the marshes, filled up the gulches, and instead of a desolate and barren waste that was, there have sprung up blocks and streets of comely residences, the homes of thrifty and industrious citizens."

But the rise in real estate values, which began in 1850, did not go on forever. Late in 1853, following a slump in the local economy, the market fell again. Money suddenly became scarce in San Francisco, and that reduced the capital available for real estate speculation and investment. The city entered a several-years-long period of economic uncertainty, at a time of unparalleled prosperity in the rest of the country.

A decline in gold production led to the shortage of money in San Francisco in 1853. The output from the mines in 1853 was $50,000,000, compared to $81,000,000 the year earlier, and production never returned to its earlier levels. San Francisco's emerging economic base in agriculture, industry, and finance could not fully take up the slack. What little money was around went to pay for merchandise that merchants had ordered from the East Coast in the boom times earlier that year. By the time the goods arrived, nobody wanted to buy them, and they sat around unsold in warehouses or were disposed of at great losses.

Earlier that year a number of handsome brick commercial buildings had been erected downtown, and, in those flush times, had been "in great demand at much increased rates." But "when sales and prices fell off, dealers could no longer afford to pay the raised rents," recalled the *Annals*. "Soon the large number of empty stores forced owners of house property to reduce rents from twenty to thirty *per cent;* at which reduction not many more tenements were occupied than before." The value of buildings fell by that same twenty to thirty per cent. The losses were even greater for other investments. Unimproved lots, whether in town or in the countryside, were "almost unsalable at any price." With so many buildings standing empty for lack of tenants, no one was looking for lots to build on.

Millions of dollars of capital and unrealized paper profits vanished in the late 1853 slump. "Nearly all the prominent operators

Opposite, Merchants Exchange

of 1852–1853 are now bankrupt, and the mass of smaller men are utterly ruined," lamented the *Alta* in 1855. One man caught in the crash was Henry Meiggs, a New York lumber dealer who had come to San Francisco in 1849. Within a year of his arrival, he had 100 men working in his sawmill and was worth half a million dollars. Meiggs built a wharf, not far from today's Fisherman's Wharf, to receive wood from forests across the Bay and up the coast. Henry Meiggs also saw himself as something of a real estate developer, and, more than anything else, he wanted to own and develop large parts of North Beach.

Meiggs wasn't the only one in town predicting a splendid future for the area. In 1850 the city appeared to have nowhere to grow but in that direction. "The deepening water will prevent the city from moving much farther into the bay, while the steep rising grounds in the rear will equally prevent it from climbing and spreading over the sandy, irregular country beyond them," declared the *Annals*. "The city will probably therefore be forced to proceed northward toward North Beach."

Meiggs bought every lot he could in North Beach, and he built a mansion at the northeast corner of Broadway and Montgomery Street. When his own money ran out, he borrowed thousands more from banks. To help his speculations along, he used his position as a member of the Board of Aldermen to get the North Beach streets opened and graded quickly. But things weren't going the way Meiggs and so many others had expected. By the early 1850s, the city was pushing south past Market Street and not into North Beach. Meiggs owed over $1,000,000 on all that vacant land, with the interest accumulating at the rate of $30,000 every month.

By 1854, Meiggs had exhausted his bank credit. Rather than lose any of his beloved North Beach property, he got his hands on some city warrants or promisory notes with the help of his brother John, who had been elected city comptroller. These weren't just any city warrants; they had been signed by the mayor, with the payee, date, and amount to be added later. Meiggs filled in his name and cashed the warrants. Even that wasn't enough money to save his dream. He forged some personal notes in his favor and overissued stock in his lumber company.

These reckless acts merely delayed the final accounting. North Beach property values were still falling, and it was only a matter of time before someone discovered what Meiggs had done. So Meiggs took the last of his money, chartered the ship *America,* and skipped town on October 3, never to return to San Francisco or America again.

The number of people arriving in San Francisco to live fell off in the mid-1850s. Anxious San Franciscans, like George Gordon, the South Park promoter, organized immigration societies to attract more people to the city. But the results of their efforts were mixed, at best. San Francisco had quite a reputation for vice, and its city government was well known for its corruption and spendthrift ways. One reason the Vigilantes cleaned up San Francisco's vice and city government in 1856 was to make the city more appealing for newcomers.

News of the city's economic slump had gotten back East, and men were hesitant to move to California when jobs were scarce. In 1855, the banking firm Page Bacon went bankrupt, and in the ensuing financial chaos hundreds of merchants and firms were ruined. Men were thrown out of work. In September, 1856 the *Alta* estimated that 3,000 men in the city of 50,000 were out of work. Things got even worse in the fall of 1857 when the depression known as the Panic of 1857 hit the national economy. Although California did not feel the full brunt of the crisis, San Franciscans worried about the future of their economically troubled city.

By late 1858 things were looking up again. And in 1859, 13,000 newcomers landed in San Francisco, compared to just 5,000 the year before. The city entered a period of rapid growth. That year, too, miners swarmed to Virginia City and Mount Davidson to seek Comstock Lode riches. Eventually the Comstock Lode would yield more than $400,000,000, much of which would flow into San Francisco, physically transforming the city, strengthening its economy, and raising a new group of multimillionaires, the Bonanza Kings, to prominence.

San Francisco's population rose from 25,000 to 56,802 between 1850 and 1860. Just three years later, in 1863, the population was 115,000. Thousands of Americans moved to California to avoid the agony of the Civil War, and local industry thrived as the rest of the country mobilized to fight the war.

Real estate boomed, as the city reached outward and thousands of houses were built to accommodate the burgeoning population. The assessed valuation of real property in town doubled between 1860 and 1863. Then, as now, people were eager to purchase real estate, fearing that its rapid rise in value would carry it beyond their means.

Contractors and real estate speculators made a lot of money so long as the market held up. But they often disregarded the city's appearance and its amenities in their scramble for money and in their haste to finish one project and go on to the next one. Mid-nineteenth-century houses were well built, but most followed a standard design which disregarded a view, the lay of the lot, or the prevailing sun and wind. The situation was not peculiar to San Francisco; it was the same story in every American city. Middle class housing was "painfully lacking in individuality," declared *Appleton's Magazine* in the 1870s, "built on a plan to suit everyone and all, and no one in particular."

Contractors found their job easier if they built row after row of virtually identical facades, and that was exactly what the public wanted. Everyone furnished their homes in the same safe, predictable styles as their neighbors. A prosperous man's drawing room usually followed just "one out of three or four styles—the style dependent only on the degree of expensiveness," observed Nathaniel Parker Willis, editor of the *Home Journal*. The owner of any house, he continued, "might wake up in thousands of other houses, and not recognize for a half hour that he was not at home. He would sit on just such a sofa in just such a recess—see a piano just so placed—just as many chairs identically in the same position and see nothing . . . but perhaps a little difference in the figure on the carpet . . . or the want of a spot on the wall where his head leans in napping after dinner."

This insensitivity to urban values also meant that San Franciscans would have almost no landmarks to recall their city's earliest times. The newspapers were always running articles headlined: "Going and Gone: Vanishing and Vanished Landmarks of San Francisco." One 1879 article reported that not one building from the city's pre-American Yerba Buena days remained standing. The oldest building left in town dated from 1847. The house that Samuel Brannan built that year near the southeast corner of Washington and Stockton streets was still standing, although it had been moved to the middle of the block on the west side of Spofford Alley. It had become "a shaky, dingy, filthy Chinese den." Another building, also dating from 1847, was the one-time Fremont Hotel, at 907 Battery Street, north of Vallejo Street.

The oldest brick building, which dated from 1849, stood at the northwest corner of Powell and Washington streets. Originally it had been two stories tall. When the street in front was lowered in the early 1850s, two more stories were built underneath, making four stories. Henry Meiggs' mansion, another landmark of the Gold Rush era, suffered the same fate. Three stories were added beneath the original structure when Broadway and Montgomery Street were dug down to the new grade.

San Francisco was losing more than just well-loved old buildings to progress; the original topography was vanishing as well. Open spaces where San Franciscans had walked or hunted disappeared as the city reached outward. The south of Market Street area once had a particularly interesting topography. A pebbly beach had extended along the southern side of Brannan Street from Fourth Street to Mission Creek. By the mid-1870s, the Bay there had been filled in a mile or more. Before the early 1850s, there had been a lake, surrounded by oak trees, in the vicinity of Second and Minna streets, where a group of Frenchmen built and launched a fifty-ton schooner in 1850. The area roughly bounded by Folsom and Mission streets and Fourth and Tenth streets originally had been an "impossible morass," according to an 1875 newspaper article, and "the person venturing to cross would be likely to sink out of sight." Folsom Street itself was an elevated

The Second Street Cut in progress, 1869

wooden causeway running over the swamp. Further out Folsom Street, from Division Street to the Mission Dolores area, was marshy ground thought to have the best duck hunting in the state. Until the early 1860s, recalled one San Franciscan, "it was no unusual thing to bag forty to sixty birds in a morning's work." But this marsh was "a dangerous place for the hunter unacquainted with its eccentricities. It was full of red mud springs, where, although the crust appeared firm, the snipe shooter who pressed his weight on the treacherous clay sank up to his chin in the yielding slime." No wonder so many men instead decided to hunt rabbits which abounded in the sand dunes outside the city.

San Francisco's famed hills did not fare much better than the low-lying marshy areas. The sand hills in Happy Valley, just south of Market Street and west of Stockton Street, were the first to go. The steam paddies leveled them in the early 1850s, dumping the sand into the nearby marshes or into the Bay. The developers even had plans for Telegraph Hill. They blasted tons of rock from its eastern side to open up more flat land along the waterfront.

The attack on Telegraph Hill, as outrageous as it seems today, did not begin to equal the 1869 "Second Street cut" for the destruction of urban grace and the greed of its promoters. In one act, the men behind the cut destroyed the city's most fashionable neighborhood—Rincon Hill, bisected Rincon Hill itself, and flaunted outraged public opinion. Second Street was a fashionable promenade and shopping district for well-to-do Rincon Hill and South Park residents, avoided by traffic because it climbed and then descended 100-foot-high Rincon Hill at one of its highest points. Such a street was picturesque for a stylish residential neighborhood, but it would never do in the increasingly industrial South of Market area.

Bringing Second Street down to a level grade meant cutting a chasm up to seventy-five feet deep through Rincon Hill, which had remained fashionable despite the influx of industry and working class dwellings in the level ground on all sides. The Second Street cut, according to the plan's boosters, would facilitate pedestrian and wagon traffic among the foundries, mills, and wharves around Market Street and the waterfront, and the growing industry south of Rincon Hill, like Butchertown and the new Pacific Mail Docks at Second and Brannan streets. The earth removed by the cut would fill in the South Beach cove at the foot of Rincon Hill.

John Middleton, the real estate developer, proposed the cut in 1863. He was already a well-known figure in San Francisco. Just two years earlier, Middleton got into a heated argument on Montgomery Street with Governor John G. Downey over politics and the just-vetoed Bulkhead Bill. The argument ended with the Governor slugging Middleton and the two of them rolling around in the dust before an astonished crowd of several hundred.

Nothing came of Middleton's 1863 proposal until he was elected to the State Assembly in 1868. That year the State Legislature, at Middleton's urging, authorized the Second Street cut. The city government, bowing to the pressure of Rincon Hill residents, one of whom was Mayor Thomas H. Selby, did not act on the law until the State Supreme Court ordered the work to begin.

Between April and November, 1869, 500 men and 250 teams dug a chasm through Rincon Hill, from Folsom Street to Bryant Street. An iron bridge spanned the cut to link the now-bisected Harrison Street. Mayor Selby, who had lived on Harrison Street since the early 1850s, decried the "vandal spirit" among the cut's promoters and called the $90,000 expenditure "a public outrage."

That $90,000 was just the beginning of the costs of this ill-conceived act. The cut turned into a "more stupendous undertaking than was anticipated," according to the 1870 *Directory*. Rincon Hill, it turned out, was composed of alternating layers of sand and rock which "being non-cohesive, bulged downward and inward, like the filling of a swampy piece of land" when exposed on the steep sides of the cut. "The ground. . . would sink . . . thereby endangering the workmen by the caving in of the superincumbent earth."

The landslides became an even worse problem once the wet weather began that fall. So much land eroded that Episcopal Bishop William Kip's mansion slid into the cut. "I called on the Bishop of California one afternoon," recalled a traveling Anglican parson who visited San Francisco in 1869. "The 'Directory' said he lived at 348 Second Street. So I went to Second Street, and found in the part where his house ought to have been a freshly-made cliff, fifty feet high, on either side, and a crowd of navvies carting away stuff. It was impossible to reach the Bishop's nest from the street, so I beat round to get to the back of it. On arriving at the spot, I asked where the Bishop lived. 'The Bishop?' said a jolly-looking gentleman to me; 'why, his house has tumbled down into the street.'"

Bishop Kip moved to a house at the southwest corner of Franklin and Eddy streets. Other families decided that Rincon Hill's days as San Francisco's finest neighborhood were numbered and moved to the other side of Market Street. In 1876 B. E. Lloyd wrote that "Rincon Hill . . . in the earlier history of San Francisco was the most aristocratic residence locality. But when the 'Second Street Cut' was projected, dividing the hill into two half cones, its beauty was endangered, and wealthy persons began to look in other directions for building sites, and the completion of the excavation has rendered it an undesirable place of abode."

Rincon Hill compensated for what it was losing in social caste by attracting interesting, if offbeat and no longer rich, new residents. When an unknown and poor Robert Louis Stevenson lived in San Francisco in 1879–1880, he described Rincon Hill as "a new slum, a place of precarious sandy cliffs, butt-ends of streets.

The Kip residence, Rincon Hill

. . . The city, upon all sides of it, was tightly packed, and growled in traffic . . . but it offered then, within narrow limits, a delightful peace, and (in the morning, when I chiefly went there) a seclusion almost rural."

Here Stevenson met writer Charles Warren Stoddard, part of the tightly knit "Golden Gate Trinity" with Bret Harte and Ina Coolbrith at the *Overland Monthly*. "On a steep sand hill, in this neighborhood, toppled, on the most insecure foundation, a certain row of houses, each with a bit of garden, and all (I have to presume) inhabited," wrote Stevenson. "Thither I used to mount by a crumbling footpath, and in front of the last of the houses, would sit down to sketch. The very first day I saw I was observed, out of the ground-floor window, by a youngish good-looking fellow, prematurely bald, and with an expression both lively and engaging. The second day, as we were still the only figures in the landscape, it was no more than natural that we should nod. The third, he came fairly out from his entrenchments, praised my sketch, and with the impromptu cordiality of artists carried me into his apartment; where I sat presently in the midst of a museum of strange objects — paddles and battle-clubs and baskets, rough-hewn stone images, ornaments of threaded shell, cocoanut bowls, snowy cocoanut plumes — evidences and examples of another earth, another climate, another race, and another (if a ruder) culture."

Here Stevenson picked up the enthusiasm for the Pacific which led him to the leper colony at Molokai and Samoa, where he died in 1894. "You can imagine with what charm he would speak, and with what pleasure I would hear. It was in such talks, which we were both eager to repeat, that I first heard the names — first fell under the spell — of the islands; and it was from one of the first of them that I returned (a happy man) with *Omoo* under one arm, and my friend's own adventures under the other [South Sea Idylls]."

Stoddard lived in the former Pedar Sather residence, which had become a boardinghouse when the Norweigan-born banker moved to Oakland in 1870. Stoddard described the fading mansion and neighborhood in *For the Pleasure of His Company*, published in 1903. "She shone upon a silent street that ran up a moderate hill

Harrison Street, Rincon Hill, c. 1870

between far-scattered corporation gas-lamps — a street having reached the hill top seemed to saunter leisurely across a height which had once been the most aristocratic quarter of the Misty City. The quarter was still pathetically respectable, and for three squares at least its handsome residences stared destiny in the face and stood in the midst of flower-bordered lawns, unmindful of decay.

"She shone on a rude stairway leading up to the bare face of a cliff that topped the hill; and five and forty uncertain steps that had more than once slid down into the street below along with the wreckage of the winter rains. . . . She shone on all that was left of a once beautiful and imposing mansion. It crowned the very brow of the cliff; it proudly overlooked all the neighbors; it was a Gothic ruin girded about with a mantel of ivy and dense creepers, yet not all of the perennial leafage that clothed it, even to the eaves, could disguise the fact that the major portion of the mansion had been razed to the ground lest it should topple and go crashing into that gulf below."

Stoddard somewhat overstates Rincon Hill's decline in his recollection and romanticizes the rigors of his years as a struggling young writer. In 1879 the *Elite Directory* thought that Rincon Hill was still one of the "most genteel neighborhoods" in the city. "Fragments of polite society still linger" there, it noted. The *Directory's* "Calling and Address List" had over eighty names on Rincon Hill that year.

One thing that had not changed over the years was the neighborhood's reputation as a breeding ground for high class scandal. In the late 1870s, another domestic tragedy was unfolding in one of the South Park mansions. This time the personalities were Eadweard Muybridge, a bearded and studiously unkempt photographer, and his wife, Flora Stone. Muybridge was twenty-one years older than Flora; he had been forty-one and she twenty and already once-divorced when they married in 1871. They moved into South Park, but Muybridge was rarely home. He was gone for months at a time on photography expeditions to places like Yosemite and Alaska.

Flora Muybridge had wavy brown hair, blue eyes, and an attractive, if somewhat large, figure. She was not the kind of woman to spend her days wandering around the house in a neighborhood that was so isolated from the city's glamor and excitement. While Muybridge was away once, she met Major Harry Larkyns, a tall, goodlooking adventurer who had lived and fought around the world and was something of a poet and musician. Muybridge's frequent absences gave the two ample opportunity to deepen their friendship.

Flora gave birth to a boy in April, 1874. Muybridge did not think anything amiss until he found a photograph of the child labeled "little Harry." Flora and the child were away visiting relatives in Portland, but the family nurse confirmed Muybridge's worst suspicions. He set off after Harry Larkyns and shot him dead one night on the front porch of a friend's house near Calistoga. A sensational murder trial followed, but Muybridge was acquitted on a defense of justifiable homicide. He returned to San Francisco but left his South Park home and its sad memories.

By then South Park and nearby Rincon Hill were no longer the height of fashion and were definitely in decline. But some gentlemen who could have moved to Nob Hill or the Western Addition went to extraordinary lengths to stay in the neighborhood. When Frederick Macondry's lot started to crumble into the Second Street cut, he moved his large frame house from the southwest corner of Second and Harrison streets to one of the vacant South Park lots. John Oscar Eldridge moved his rambling two-story home from 336 Second Street to 646 Folsom Street, between Second and Third.

The neighborhood remained fashionable enough for handsome new residences to be built there after the completion of the cut. In 1873 Francis Berton, a 49'er who had come from Switzerland, moved from his rooms at the Union Club to a twenty-eight room house he built on two lots facing South Park. The neighborhood managed to retain its appeal; it remained, as Robert Louis Stevenson described it, "a pleasant old spot . . . one of the most San Francisco-y parts of San Francisco."

Despite all the changes from Gold Rush days, San Francisco never changed in its widespread pursuit of entertainment. The one pleasure which continued to be the most talked about was prostitution. But the madams and their "soiled doves," to use one Victorian euphemism, had lost the near respectability they enjoyed in the Gold Rush. The Board of Aldermen, whose members undoubtedly knew what the inside of a brothel looked like, outlawed prostitution in 1854. "This ordinance," reported the *Annals*, "had the effect, for a time, of closing a few of the most notorious Mexican and Chilean brothels. But it was sought to be enforced against fashionable white Cyprians, who had money enough to employ able counsel to show the intrinsically illegal and tyrannous character of its particular provisions; and then it was found to be utterly impracticable in operation." The *Annals* predicted that "mere legislation" would never eliminate prostitution.

The anti-brothel law proved next to meaningless, and prostitution became "the curse-mark of San Francisco's brow," according to B. E. Lloyd. The city fathers could not even confine the brothels and streetwalkers to their Barbary Coast stronghold. Prostitution spread throughout the entire downtown area and into some of the nearby residential districts as well.

From late morning until the late afternoon, saucily dressed streetwalkers, or *nymphs de pave*, if you will, strolled up and down Montgomery and Kearny streets, pausing for a moment outside the entrance to a fashionable hotel or stopping to admire a glittering shop window. Sometimes the young women stepped inside the shops, where they received the warm greeting that befits a regular customer. The dressmaker or jeweler could not ask for a better client than the successful hooker. These women, moreover, influenced feminine fashion. B. E. Lloyd wrote: "Some one has remarked that in Eastern cities the prostitutes tried to imitate in manner and dress the fashionable respectable ladies, but in San Francisco the rule was reversed—the latter copying after the former."

Still, there was no mistaking the women who were available.

Some gave themselves away by their "free and sweeping gait," while others dressed just a bit too richly or wore a little more jewelry than the ladies out on their downtown shopping trips. Some streetwalkers preferred the direct approach. They would glance quickly but searchingly at every man they passed, or walk up to a man and say "How do you do, my dear? Come, won't you go home with me?"

Streetwalkers were as much a part of the downtown scene as the ragged, dirty-faced children who begged for pennies or the men who stumbled along the sidewalks always looking downward and muttering to themselves. They showed up Sunday mornings outside Grace Episcopal Church at California and Stockton streets and at St. Mary's Cathedral just down the hill at the corner of Grant Avenue to try to pick up men as they were leaving services. That stretch of California Street had been a stylish residence area in the 1850s, but it had since become a no man's land between bustling Montgomery Street, Chinatown, and elegant Nob Hill. Brothels and streetwalkers partly filled the void.

By the mid-1870s, stylish brothels or "parlor houses" clustered along the first five or six blocks of Kearny, Stockton and Grant off Market Street, along that part of Market Street itself, and on the first block or two of Third Street. The high class establishments did not venture much beyond Bush and Pine streets. The closer to California Street and Chinatown on Stockton or Grant, the less fashionable the brothel. A few parlor houses even ventured into the well-to-do residential streets on the lower slopes of Nob Hill and beyond Van Ness Avenue. Those places, however, were quite discreet and accommodated regular customers and their referrals only.

By day, the downtown brothels did not give themselves away to the casual observer. The frame houses, which dated from the 1850s when the area had been largely residential, were perhaps a little run down, but respectable looking. Noisy horse and wagon traffic filled the streets, and pedestrians hurried to and fro.

At night, these streets were completely changed. The roar of daytime traffic was gone, as the business wagons and omnibuses all but disappeared from the streets. Now the murmur of voices and occasional drunken songs filled the air. Laughter and music and applause floated out into the street from saloons and theaters. And there were the inevitable sidewalk musicians to entertain crowds at the busier street corners.

The men who arrived in the area on foot or in hired carriages had no trouble picking out which buildings were the brothels. A red light hung over the front door of each. In some places the lights twinkled from one end of the block to the other from dusk until dawn.

The parlor house madams prided themselves on running high-class establishments. A black maid greeted every man at the front door and took him into the front parlor to meet the madam. At this point, some madams might ask a would-be customer to leave, because he did not dress or behave like a gentleman. But that didn't happen very often. She asked the man if he had any particular type of girl in mind. Usually he said no and asked to meet all the inmates of the house. In some parlor houses the women wore fine evening dresses, but the usual outfits were a house dress with nothing underneath, fancy underclothes, or simply stockings and shoes.

The madams spent thousands of dollars furnishing their places to look just right, down to "Old Masters" oil paintings on the walls and bookshelves filled with good books that were never read. B. E. Lloyd believed that "the interior appointments of some of these 'abodes of sin' are rich and costly, and many are furnished in a style superior to the private dwellings of most of the wealthy citizens." Apparently respectable ladies in San Francisco were copying the whores when it came to interior decoration, too.

All this luxury and personal attention did not come cheaply. A man would spend $10 to $30 for a night with the woman of his choice. The inevitable champagne and tipping the musicians who played downstairs all night long added a few more dollars to his bill. But the elegant parlor houses never lacked for clients; they offered a gentleman personal safety and freedom from police interference along with his sexual gratification.

The low-class brothels, on the other hand, were anything but safe, discreet, and elegant. But there was no denying their popularity. Low-class whoring centered around the Barbary Coast, which was bounded by Broadway on the north, the waterfront on the east, Powell Street on the west, and Commercial Street on the south.

The Barbary Coast had been a wicked place since the Gold Rush days. Back in 1848 and 1849 the Latin American whores, who had been the first in town, had pitched their tents near the foot of Broadway and Pacific Street. Then the hundreds of convicts that the British government shipped to San Francisco from penal colonies in Sydney, Australia and Tasmania moved into the area. Within a year or two, the Barbary Coast — which was also known as Sydneytown — was filled with brothels, cheap hotels, pawn shops, saloons, and dance halls.

Respectable San Franciscans avoided the Barbary Coast entirely, and the police entered the area in pairs and then only in the daytime. Known criminals freely walked the streets and boasted of their exploits in the saloons. "It was a grand theatre of crime," recalled B. E. Lloyd. "The glittering stiletto, the long blade bowie knife, the bottle containing the deadly drug, and the audacious navy revolver, were much-used implements in the plays that were there enacted. There was no need of mimic dying groans, and crimson water, for the drawing of warm heart-blood and the ringing of real agonizing moans of death only would be recognized as the true style of enacting tragedy."

Twenty years later, the Barbary Coast still attracted the town's low life. Lloyd described it as "the haunt of the low and vile of every kind. The petty thief, the house burglar, the tramp, the whoremonger, lewd women, cut-throats and murderers, all are found there. Dance-houses and concert saloons, where blear-eyed men and faded women drink vile liquor, smoke offensive tobacco, engage in vulgar conduct, sing obscene songs, and say and do everything to heap upon themselves more degradation, unrest and misery, are numerous." Lloyd must have spent a lot of time exploring the Barbary Coast, because he did not stop there. He went on to describe the gambling dens "thronged with riot-loving rowdies" and opium dens filled with "heathen Chinese and God-forsaken women and men . . . disgustingly drowsy, or completely overcome by inhaling the vapors of the nauseous narcotic." There were some things going on in the Barbary Coast that not even the curious Lloyd dared put into print. Many bars put on shows which featured sex acts between young women and ponies. But one, the Fierce Grizzly, went even further and had a man and a bear in its sex shows.

Despite all these goings-on, the Barbary Coast of the late nineteenth century was not nearly as dangerous as it had been in the 1850s. Lloyd attributed the drop in violent crime to "the restraining power of the law" and to "public sentiment." That may be partly true, even though the city fathers didn't get anywhere passing laws telling San Franciscans not to do what they wanted to do. One thing that definitely curbed violence in the Barbary Coast was the influx of prostitutes and whorehouses into the area. Men were not going to go out for a night of drinking and whoring in the Barbary Coast if they were certain to get hit over the head or slipped knock-out drops in their drinks for their trouble. In the late nineteenth century, the brothel and saloon owners looked after their own interests by maintaining a modicum of order.

Aside from low-class brothels, there were two other places to find whores: the "cribs" and the "cowyards." The cribs were shacks with a front door and a casement window where women sat to display their charms. They usually had two rooms: in front, a six-by-six-foot "reception room" with a chair and sometimes a sofa and, in the rear, the "workshop," with a three-quarter-size iron bed, a wash stand, and a small kerosene stove to keep the room warm and boil water. The women put their street clothes in a trunk in one corner of the room or beneath the bed, because they generally wore a flimsy nightgown, underclothing, or a short skirt and nothing else while working.

The cribs were about as low as a San Francisco whore could sink, and, of course, B. E. Lloyd was there to find out just how bad they were.

At any hour of the day or night, sickly, vice-worn women, abundantly painted and powdered and gaudily attired in the vain attempt to restore their lost charms, may be seen upon the threshholds or lounging by the open windows, half-dead from their excesses, yet perserveringly exerting themselves to win patronage from the vicious and dissipated men that loiter on the walks or straggle through the street. . . . All the surroundings show that the denizens of the place are in the last stages of human

"Beware of Temptation"

degradation—that the days are past when sinning to them had its pleasures; that disease, death, and that dreaded mysterious hereafter will follow respectively, and will come quickly.

Despite Lloyd's lurid words, a few crib women kept their places scrupulously clean and tried to brighten up their grim surroundings with colorful bedspreads and calendars or cheap chromolithographs on the walls. Some women hung a large card above the head of the bed with their name, or whatever they were calling themselves at the moment, in pretty lettering surrounded by a border of flowers. But cribs like these were few and far between. Most were filthy and had furniture in various stages of disrepair. What did a man expect for twenty-five or fifty cents? And the women had no incentive to make him comfortable. Better to get the customer in and out the door as quickly as possible and be ready for the next one. Some crib girls did not even let the men take off their clothes. They laid a piece of oilcloth across the foot of the bed so that the men's shoes and boots wouldn't soil the bedspread. On a busy night, the men lined up outside the cribs, and some women entertained as many as eighty customers before dawn.

"How the San Francisco Police Collect Their Infernal Revenue"

The cribs were not confined to the Barbary Coast. They were scattered throughout the downtown area, particularly in the narrow alleys. The most depraved cribs, according to Herbert Asbury, author of the *Barbary Coast,* lined Morton Street, the two-block-long alley which runs from the east side of Union Square to Kearny Street. Today that street is called Maiden Lane, and it is lined by pleasant shops. B. E. Lloyd thought that the worst cribs were on Waverly Place, a two-block-long alley parallel to and just west of Grant Avenue between Sacramento and Clay streets.

It doesn't matter which alley was the vilest, because the nighttime scene was just about the same on all of them. Men wandered up and down the street, singly or in groups of two and three, laughing and shouting and inspecting the women who sat barechested in the casement windows beneath the glare of red lamps over the doors. Most men had a few drinks before starting their evening foray and shouted compliments or insults at the women they passed. The whores were just as quick to return the insults or to receive the compliments with an invitation to come inside for a better look. Pimps added to the confusion by roaming up and down the street trying to lure men into one of their girls' crib. Some men didn't want to go inside but they could always find plenty of women willing to let them fondle their breasts through the open casement window for ten cents.

The noise and commotion along these alleys on Saturday and Sunday nights was incredible. Men flocked there by the hundreds, because they knew they could find just the kind of woman they wanted among all the sizes and shapes of American women in addition to exotic Japanese, Chinese, and black whores. The crowds of serious fun-seekers, in turn, attracted even greater crowds of voyeurs and men out on the town. Nighttime on the crib alleys became a festival or tribal rite during which men stepped out of Victorian conventions and did exactly what they wanted, if only for a few hours.

The demand for quick and inexpensive sex was all but insatiable in San Francisco, and the much-publicized frolics of the 49'ers palled before the excesses of the 1880s and 1890s. San Francisco had become an adult playground, not just for the local men but also for the tourists who flocked to the city because of its reputation for tolerating loose morals and the unconventional. But there were only so many alleys in the Barbary Coast, in Chinatown, and in the downtown district where the shack-like cribs might flourish. So whoring went high rise. Local entrepreneurs invented the "cowyards," which were a number of cribs under one roof or a several-story-tall building divided into cubicles. The largest cowyards in the 1890s were the Nymphia on Pacific Street near Stockton, the Marsicania on Grant Avenue near Broadway, and the Municipal Brothel on Jackson Street near Kearny.

Of these, the Nymphia was the largest and most imaginative. The U-shaped building was three stories tall and had 150 cubicles on each floor. When the building opened in 1899, the owners, the Twinkling Star Corporation, wanted to call it the Hotel Nymphomania. The police said no to that, but Nymphia was all right. The police were remarkably tolerant of the place. Two patrolmen stood outside the front door every night, not to interfere with the activity inside but to watch the street. They would go inside if there was a shooting or a serious stabbing, but they would have nothing to do with the drunken brawls that were a nightly occurrence.

One floor of the Nymphia was given over to nymphomaniacs, or women who advertised themselves as such, and all the women in the place were naked while in their cubicles. They had to receive every man who wandered in, whatever his race, appearance, or degree of intoxication. And there was no privacy in their rooms. A tall, narrow window had been cut into every door, and the shade which covered the opening raised automatically for a few moments when a dime was put into a nearby slot.

San Francisco whores even advertised their calling. Every woman had business cards with her name and address, at the least. Some cards were quite artistic in appearance, while others spelled out the woman's more desirable physical qualities, lest the customer forget. A black woman working out of the Hinckney Alley cowyards gave out the following message, surrounded by a border of forget-me-nots.

BIG MATILDA
THREE HUNDRED POUNDS OF BLACK PASSION
HOURS: ALL HOURS
RATES: 50¢ EACH: THREE FOR ONE DOLLAR

A few madams decided that the traditional red light over the front door was terribly clichéd, and they hung metal or wood signs on the door or the front of the building. The sign on Madam Gabrielle's Grant Avenue whorehouse, known as the "Lively Flea," showed a large insect relaxing in a bed of flowers, surrounded by a group of fawning cupids. The sign at the Red Rooster on Commercial Street was a large red-painted metal bird with a red light for a beak and in its claws the motto: "At the sign of the red rooster." Once inside the front door, the customer saw another rooster, somewhat smaller, whose claws held a sign with the same words except that "rooster" had been dropped for its familiar, four-letter nickname.

The madams did not stop there. In the mid-1870s, Madam Johanna Werner, keeper of a popular Sacramento Street establishment, decided to go after the tourist trade. She couldn't advertise in local newspapers; even San Francisco wasn't ready for that, yet. So she got mailing lists of out-of-town men who might be interested in her services and sent them advertisements describing the delights of her house and its women. Her first pamphlets included nude photographs of the women and uninhibited discussions of their endearing qualities. For a few years the madams vied to see who could put out the naughtiest advertisements. Eventually they toned down their sales pitches to avoid trouble with the postal inspectors.

Prostitution had become such big business by the turn of the century that literally thousands of San Franciscans depended on it for their livelihood. The streetwalkers, the madams and their girls, the black maids at the front door of the houses, and the musicians in the front parlor profited directly from prostitution. But a lot of people were indirectly involved: the dressmakers who counted the whores among their best customers, the laundries, groceries, and

Men on bicycles, Stockton Street, 1868

liquor stores that catered to the parlor houses, and the carpenters who hastily erected the cribs and cowyards.

What could respectable San Franciscans do about this "social blight" whose "soiled wings . . . hovered over every neighborhood and street?" After all, prostitution flourished in every American city at the time. Most San Franciscans believed that the problem could be traced back to their city's Gold Rush origins. "San Francisco," wrote B. E. Lloyd, "has not yet overcome the immoral habits she contracted in the days when the inhabitants were nearly all males, and they had nothing to restrain them from engaging in the most vicious practices; when there were few mothers to chide their waywardness and say in winning tones 'My son, go not in the way of evil;' and fewer virtuous sisters to welcome brothers home, and by their loving kindness and noble lives, to teach them to cease from sinning."

Occasionally the San Francisco police did close down one of the more obnoxious brothels or cowyards. Several times frenzied mobs invaded the alleys and tore apart several flimsy cribs, sending half-naked whores running screaming down the street. But the women were usually back in business a few days later as if nothing had happened.

The cleverest anti-vice campaign was launched by Abe Reuf, head of the Workingmen's Party, whose machine elected Eugene Schmitz mayor in 1901. Reuf decided to clean up the notorious Morton Street cribs, just below Union Square. Occasionally a respectable woman on a shopping trip wandered into the alley by mistake and was greeted with screams of "Look out, girls, here's some charity competition" and "Get some sense and quit giving it away."

The police closed down every whorehouse on Morton Street and kept them closed. Real estate along the street had little or no value except for prostitution, and property owners began selling out. The buyer, it turned out, was Abe Reuf, and once he bought up nearly the entire street at distress prices, the police left, and Morton Street was back in business.

No wonder San Franciscans didn't know what to do about

prostitution. Maybe B. E. Lloyd, in all his syrupy Victorian sentiment, had the right advice: "We would say to the parents of San Francisco to look closer to their daughters, for they know not the many dangers to which they are exposed—know their associates, guard their virtue—and to mildly counsel their sons, for when upon the street of this gay city they are wandering amid many temptations."

For the men who did not head for the whorehouses during their leisure time, there were always the gambling dens. They had not changed since Gold Rush days, except that the gambling went far beyond the card games that the 49'ers enjoyed. San Franciscans now wagered on horse races, athletic contests, roulette, and dice. And many considered the local stock exchange and real estate market the biggest games of chance in town.

The city fathers had enacted ordinances against gambling in the 1860s and 1870s, but they were no more successful than earlier laws had been in curbing gambling in Gold Rush days. "The law against gambling in San Francisco is a farce," wrote B. E. Lloyd. "It is only a moral morsel that tastes well abroad, but at our own doors, the flavor is too rank to be palatable." The authorities couldn't even enforce the anti-gambling laws that they specially enacted against the Chinese. "Even John Chinaman," continued Lloyd, "chuckles over his heaps of copper coin, that he has gathered from the gaming table, and reflects with evident satisfaction upon the disposition of the municipal authorities to joke."

The gambling laws did have one effect: there were no truly sumptuous gambling dens in San Francisco after the Gold Rush era. With those laws on the books, no one wanted to make the substantial investment in elegant furniture, fine china and silverware, and fancy gaming tables that such an establishment required. Rich men who wanted to gamble in elegant surroundings merely retreated to their clubs, hotel rooms, or home. Nonetheless, B. E. Lloyd thought that there were "numerous gambling houses . . . where much elegance is maintained," along with that all-important "air of gentility." One English journalist, W. F. Rae, was not all that impressed by the place he visited during his stay in

San Francisco in 1869. But his description, which appeared as part of his book, *Westward By Rail*, published in 1871, gives a good idea of what the city's better gambling dens were like.

The visitor rings a bell, and before the door is opened he is generally reconnoitered through a small aperture or grating. As soon as the guardian is satisfied, either from appearances, or from personal knowledge, or from the inspection of a card in the proprietor's handwriting, that no objection exists, the door is opened, the visitor takes a few steps forward, and is brought face to face with the 'Tiger.' He sees what he is told is a Faro table. This table is small, and will not accommodate more than six or eight persons. The dealer occupies one side, and sits with his back to the wall.

In all the hells the costume of the keepers and dealers, or rather the absence of it, was the same, shirt sleeves being their full dress. Those who superintended the games also sat without their coats. The shirts were all spotless. The superintendents, dealers and gamesters all smoked cigars. Nor were their manners more formal than their attire. All the company seemed to be on terms of intimacy; each one not only addressed the others by his Christian name, but as Tom, Dick, or Harry. . . . The losers, who appeared to be in a large majority, took their mishaps most philosophically, while the rare winners did not exult in their good fortune. Indeed, 'Fighting the Tiger' in San Francisco seems to be a pastime which, if neither harmless nor praiseworthy, cannot fairly be denounced as fraught with immediate evil consequences.

In some of the hells a supper is provided, but this is merely what their frequenters can get gratis at nearly every bar-room. A drink may be had for the asking; but this, again, is not a special incentive, but a part of the ordinary social arrangements. Californians do not seem happy unless they are either taking drinks or treating their friends and acquaintances with them. That they should find themselves provided with them in the gaming halls is merely what they consider themselves entitled to expect.

The gambling "mania" even infected as august-sounding an institution as the Mercantile Library. In 1852 it had been founded "to withdraw youths in particular from the haunts of dissipation, and to give to persons of every age and occupation the means of mental improvement, and a suitable place for passing their leisure

hours." In the next fifteen years, the Mercantile Library rented quarters in various spots downtown. But the organization and its growing collection of books and periodicals needed a permanent home, and in 1868 it moved into its own handsome Italianate style building on Bush Street between Montgomery and Kearny. The trustees had raised $20,000 from the sale of life memberships toward the cost of the new building, but that still left the organization nearly $250,000 in debt.

That would never do, and the trustees hit upon a fund-raising plan that no library in any town but San Francisco would have dared think of, much less been able to pull off. The Mercantile Library was going to hold a lottery, and it would be so much fun and

The Mercantile Library, the Ladies Reading Room

the prizes so enticing that the entire city would want to get in on the action. But there was one catch. Lotteries were illegal in California. So the library trustees got a bill introduced in the State Legislature permitting "public entertainments, at which personal property, real estate or other valuables might be disposed of, by chance, raffle, or other scheme of like character." The bill passed at the end of 1870 and was signed by the Governor.

The Mercantile Library was in business. They rented the biggest hall in town, the Mechanics' Pavilion, in the middle of what is now Union Square. The lotteries ran three nights in a row, and every night there was a program of entertainment before the drawing. That satisfied the requirements of the recently enacted lottery law, but everyone was much more interested in the drawings and awarding of prizes that followed. The library trustees chose the prizes well: knick-knacks, various articles of clothing, jewelry, pianos, handsome carriages and horses. Someone even thought to add some books to the list of prizes. But all the loot merely led up to the grand prize at the end of each evening: a house, complete with furniture, in one of the new streets out in the Western Addition. The lottery was a hit, not just for the prize winners but also for the Mercantile Library, which netted $310,000 from the scheme.

Entertainment in San Francisco did go beyond the whoring, the gambling, the drinking, and all the other things that gave the town such a bad name. San Franciscans were eager for some good clean fun, too. In fact, some observers, even back in the Gold Rush period, worried that the preoccupation with money-making and pleasure might lead to a city that lacked the intellectual and cultural vigor of a genuine metropolis. Their fears were understandable. Back in the fall of 1848, one group of citizens proposed forming a temperance society, while another wanted to establish a lyceum. Not now, too premature an idea, declared one of the newspapers; what San Francisco needed instead, according to the editor, was a theater.

The city did not have to wait long. The first entertainment which came remotely close to theater was Rowe's Circus, which opened early in 1849. Night after night hundreds of men filled Rowe's big tent on Kearny Street above Clay and sat on wooden benches, at $3 and $5 a head, to watch men jump horses through hoops and over ropes. Another hit was an act in which men bounded from springboards over one, two, and three horses. Although San Franciscans later remembered these shows as "third rate" and "unworthy of notice," there wasn't much else to do in town those days, and a few months later a man named Foley pitched his colorful tent on Montgomery Street, below California, and yet another circus opened on the west side of Portsmouth Square.

That summer, on June 22, 1849, San Franciscans attended the first concert ever held in their town. It was an evening of song, piano music, and "some comic recitations," performed entirely by ex-New Yorker Stephen C. Massett, who lived in a shack in the sand dunes along one of the roads leading to the Mission Dolores. His program was an ambitious one. He performed several of his own songs, such as "When the Moon on the Lake Is Beaming," "When a Child I Roamed," and "List While I Sing." For his recitations, Mr. Massett did "An imitation of an elderly lady and a German girl, who applied for the situations of soprano and alto singers in one of the churches of Massachusetts" and a Yankee number, "Deacon Jones and Seth Slope."

The evening may well have been the high point of Massett's theatrical career. Every seat in the little schoolhouse on Portsmouth Square was filled that night at $3 and $5 each, and "besides winning many encomiums for his wonderful versatility," as the Annals put it, Mr. Massett was $500 richer for his efforts. Perhaps his only disappointment was that so few ladies showed up for the performance. One line of the concert program read: "Front seats reserved for ladies." Only four ladies were present— "probably all there were in town," declared Charles Warren Stoddard in his account of the event.

The "first real theatrical performance" in town was Sheridan Knowles' "The Wife," given by Messrs. Atwater and Madison's small company on the second floor of Washington Hall on Washington Street opposite Portsmouth Square in January, 1850. It was

an inauspicious beginning for theater in San Francisco. "The most that can be said of the exhibition," sniffed the *Annals*, "is, that the performance was poor and the room well filled." B. E. Lloyd later added that "the tastes of the people were not as crude as their appearances indicated."

But things were looking up. San Franciscans were no longer satisfied with the equestrian circuses, and Rowe converted his Kearny Street tent into a legitimate theater. American and English companies began arriving in San Francisco and theaters were soon opening up one after another—the Eagle, the Tehama, the Pacific, the American, the Dramatic Museum, and the Jenny Lind, which began over Tom Maguire's Parker House Saloon on Kearny Street facing Portsmouth Square. Frederick Gerstacker saw a badly performed "Merchant of Venice" at the Jenny Lind. He did not think the play was worth the $2 price of the ticket but he philosophically added: "You got enough for your money, for while the orchestra before you played one overture, you could plainly hear another from the saloon below."

None of these theaters were open for long. They didn't close for lack of patronage but instead burned down in the fires that swept the city in 1850 and 1851. The Jenny Lind burned down on May 4, 1851 and was rebuilt on the same site within a month. Jenny Lind #2, as San Franciscans called the new theater, had been open no more than a few weeks when it was destroyed in the June 22, 1851 fire. Thomas Maguire, the saloonkeeper-turned-theater-owner, was determined not to lose his theater again. Jenny Lind #3, which opened on October 4 on the same site as #1 and #2, was built of brick and stone. It was one of the grandest buildings in town, a light color stone front three stories tall in a town of frame shacks, with a handsome neo-classical style of architecture. The pink and gold interior had been "fitted up with exquisite taste," according to the *Annals*, and "altogether in size, beauty, and comfort, it rivaled the most noted theaters in the Atlantic States." Jenny Lind #3 seated 2,000 people, and, according to the advertisements, included a gallery appointed "in elegant style for respectable colored people."

Jenny Lind #3 did not last out the year. This time the culprit wasn't fire but the city fathers. City Hall had burned down in the June 22, 1851 fire, and the municipal offices were scattered around town in rented quarters costing more than $400 a month in rent. This drain on the public treasury had to stop, and the Board of Aldermen had to look for another City Hall. Several choice downtown sites were available, and a new City Hall on any of them would not cost more than $200,000, including the cost of the land.

The Board of Aldermen, for reasons known only to them, decided to purchase the Jenny Lind #3 for $200,000. Everybody agreed that it was quite a handsome building and it did face the main public square in town, but it would take another $100,000 to gut and rebuild the interior for city offices. The public was outraged at the thought of spending the extra $100,000 for no apparent practical reason, and crowds gathered in Portsmouth Square, opposite the theater, to protest the proposal. The mayor vetoed the bill approving the purchase, but proponents of the measure had the votes to override him. Finally, the opponents took the matter to the State Supreme Court, which ruled that the city could make the purchase.

What did Maguire do with his $200,000? Three months after selling Jenny Lind #3 to the city, he opened the San Francisco Theater on Washington Street, just above Montgomery. He changed the name to Maguire's Opera House in 1856. Maguire was beginning to enjoy his billing as "the pioneer theatrical manager on the Pacific Coast," and there was hardly a theater on the West Coast in the 1870s of which he had not been the lessee at one time or another. He had also managed many of the theaters in San Francisco.

Maguire couldn't have picked a better town for this calling than San Francisco. Eliza Farnham, the ex-Sing Sing Prison matron who tried to import morally upright women to California during the Gold Rush, thought that San Francisco had more "dramatic and musical entertainment than any other city of its size in America." The newspapers were filled with news of theater openings and mentions of popular plays like "Did You Ever Send

Opposite, City Hall, 1856, formerly the Jenny Lind Theater #3

Gilbert's Melodeon, northeast corner of Clay and Kearny streets

Your Wife to the Mission Dolores" and "All That Glitters Is Not Gold." In 1851 a Chinese theater opened with actors imported from Canton.

The theaters were going up so quickly that they weren't being built properly. The 2,000-seat American Theater, which had been built in thirty-two days, sank nearly two inches on opening night in 1851. The theater stood on Sansome Street, which had been part of Yerba Buena cove, and the contractors had been in such a hurry that they simply put up the building on a layer of sand laid over the soft mud rather than sinking piles for a proper foundation. Somehow the building settled evenly on opening night, and nothing more happened in subsequent days.

Whatever its structural flaws, the American Theater was a handsome place, with thick carpets everywhere, red velvet curtains, red plush seats, paintings on the walls, and a ceiling of "great

gold rayed sun and clouds." The crowds that regularly filled the house apparently felt they were getting their money's worth. When they liked a performance, they wanted the actors on stage and everyone around them to know it, according to Albert Benard de Russailh. He could not bring himself to whistle or cry out during a performance. But after an evening at the American Theater, he decided that "with Americans, whistling is an expression of enthusiasm. The more they like a play, the louder they whistle, and when a San Francisco audience bursts into shrill whistles and savage yells, you may be sure they are in raptures of joy."

Going out to the theater was wonderful fun for adults, but it was not exactly suitable for family entertainment. The theater was morally suspect throughout Victorian America. Some newspapers refused to carry any theater advertisements in their pages, because, as the *New York Daily Tribune* wrote, the "stage, as it is, is more an injury than a benefit to the community — vicious, licentious, degrading, demoralizing." Actors and actresses were a part of the contagion. The *Daily Tribune* considered it a "notorious fact that a large proportion of those connected with the stage are libertines or courtesans — a proportion much larger, we are confident, than can be found in any other tolerated profession." Obviously, a proper mother and father wouldn't expose their children to such a dangerous menace, and some women avoided the theater, too.

With moral standards like those prevalent even in San Francisco, there weren't many places that a family could go together. Furthermore, most men worked ten, or even twelve hours, five or six days a week. The usual thing families did together was to go for Sunday outings in the country.

But first there was the matter of going to church. A few churches had come a long way from the days of worshipping in a drafty tent or a pre-fabricated frame shack sent around the Horn from New York. By the 1860s and 1870s, the services for rich congregations were so elaborately staged and the women so extravagantly dressed that local newspapers complained that the churches lacked only box seats to make them the equal of the theater or opera. "In the more fashionable churches, the display of toilettes is bewildering," observed B. E. Lloyd. "The costliest fabrics, the most delicate tints and shades, the artistic blending of colors, together with the flashing jewels that adorn the persons of the ladies, contrasted with the somber garb of the gentlemen, make a scene of splendor, the attractions of which are sufficient to divert the attention from the most eloquent sermon."

A few churches prided themselves on their Sunday music and hired professional musicians and singers to perform at the services. A musical program like that cost several thousand dollars a year, but many people considered it the high point of the service. Some worshippers left the church once the best of the music was over.

Most San Franciscans did not even bother to go to church. That was one custom they left back East. Instead they slept late on Sunday and, after breakfast, set off for the country. Even in the unsettled years immediately after the Gold Rush, San Francisco had plenty of pleasant places to go for an outing. According to the *Annals*, they "cantered to the presidio or the mission, or scampered among the sand-hills behind the town, or crossed the bay in small steamers to Contra Costa, or formed pic-nic excursions to the fort, or the outer telegraph hill, or on the sea-shore, or somewhere among the lonely and picturesque valleys among the hills."

In the 1860s and 1870s, one of the favorite day trips was to leave San Francisco entirely and catch a ferry across the Bay to Oakland. In 1860 one San Francisco newspaper reported that Oakland was "a very pleasant and thriving village, or town (we are not sure that it is called a *City* now)." San Francisco's feeling of superiority over its neighbors is nothing new.

By 1860 Oakland had "a sizeable collection of well-constructed buildings, mostly frame, including several very good houses of public resort . . . and some handsome private residences." But what drew thousands of San Franciscans to Oakland every Sunday was a plain, "covered with a dense growth of oak of a small species and some shrubbery," extending for miles along the Bay. The soil was "unsurpassed in fertility" and "blessed with an abundance of water among the ravines," while the hills in the distance formed a backdrop to the lovely scene.

In 1854 one ferry line ran two boats to Alameda for the "public who [wish] to attend the camp meeting and the bull fight." What a "laudable disposition to please all parties," cheered the *Alta.* As early as the 1850s, boats were making day trips to Martinez, the Straits of Carquínez, all around the Bay, and even to the Farallones.

In San Francisco itself, throughout most of the nineteenth century, the city was so small that open space was no more than a walk or brief horse car ride from almost everyone's home. The miles of waterfront offered another escape from the city. In 1852 Stephen Woodin wrote his wife that the previous day had been "a very exciting time in our city. . . . We had what the sailors call a Norther. . . . Thousands of people were crowded upon the wharves to witness the rage of the Elements." Wharves had other pleasurable uses, too. In the 1850s and 1860s, Meiggs Wharf was "affected by young lovers, who in the intervals of fog and wind on Summer evenings found it a convenient trysting place," according to the *Elite Directory* for 1879.

San Franciscans appreciated their city's magnificent physical setting from the beginning. "On a clear day the beauty of the Bay of San Francisco, and of the hills and mountains which encompass it, are beyond my powers of description," wrote James Ward in 1847. One newspaper in 1866 advised San Franciscans to worship Nature's wonders. "Every good Californian should make it part of his religion to visit the notable places in the State — that is, so far as his means will permit. If he cannot afford to go to Yosemite, he can at least go to the top of Mission Peak and San Bruno. The city and its surroundings appear in new phases and acquire new interest after being seen from the surrounding mountains; and the mountains themselves become friends."

The rugged splendor of the Bay Area did not meet most Easterners' vision of natural beauty. There were few, if any, grassy meadows, stands of 100-year-old trees, or streams filled with fish. San Francisco had grown up on a windy and fog-swept, treeless peninsula, while "the mountains surrounding the bay of San Francisco were wild and terrible, with naked brown slopes devoid of trees or grass," wrote one observer in the 1870s. "The whole aspect of the harbor was barren, chill, desolate. One felt that one was thousands of miles from civilization — in a land unique; grim, desolate, sufficient unto itself, shut off by sea and mountains from the great world."

In an effort to bring a little of an idealized, gentler nature into their city, families cultivated gardens around their homes and planted trees along the streets, even though skeptics doubted they would ever grow because of the dry summer months and fierce winds off the ocean. Beginning in 1886, Adolph Sutro planted forests on the naked slopes of Twin Peaks and Mount Davidson.

But that was Sutro's private property. San Francisco needed public parks, and the *Chronicle* made that suggestion as early as 1855. The most prominent public space in town, Portsmouth Square, was a mess. At various times the *Alta* described it as "a rag fair or market place," "an eyesore and a disgrace to a city like San Francisco," and a barnyard "for human and other cattle." In 1851 the *Alta* repeatedly asked the city fathers to improve Portsmouth Square, and, when nothing happened, the newspaper asked the owners of the local property to plant trees in the square, suggesting that such a step was in their best interest because it would increase the value of their property. By November of that year the newspaper had collected $1,000 to fence in Portsmouth Square, and, as the fence was going up, money was raised to plant grass and shrubbery.

The effort was in vain. A year or two later, Portsmouth Square was just as big an eyesore as it had always been. "What is here called the plaza, or park . . . now lies before us," wrote Englishman Hinton R. Helper, "but as it is nothing more nor less than a cow-pen, enclosed with unplaned plank, we will say but little about it. In the middle is planted a tall liberty-pole, near which is erected a rude rostrum for lynch-lawyers and noisy politicians. If there is a tree, or a bush, or a shrub, or a sprig of grass, or any thing else in or about it that is green, or that bears the slightest similitude to vegetation, nobody has ever yet seen it; and, as a pleasure-ground, it is used only by the four-footed denizens of the city."

The *Chronicle* believed that "a grand Park within the reach of every citizen would do more in preventing dissipation and vice than half the sermons preached, half the moral lectures and teachings given to children and to men." Apparently nineteenth-century muggers did not hang out in city parks.

There was another reason, which the newspapers usually overlooked, why San Franciscans wanted a park in the late 1850s. Landscape architects Frederick Law Olmsted and Calvert Vaux had just begun work on New York's Central Park, and Boston was planning its lovely Public Garden. San Francisco's pride and its intentions of becoming a great city demanded that a large park be established.

But San Francisco's city fathers were too busy and financially hard-pressed fixing street grades and digging sewers to get around to a park just yet. Work on Golden Gate Park did not begin until 1870. In the meantime, entrepreneurs opened public gardens which combined some of the beauties of idealized nature with the excitement of the amusement park, the restaurant, and the saloon.

Russ' Gardens

Portsmouth Square

State Blind, Deaf, and Dumb Asylum, 15th and Mission streets, 1868

The first was Russ' Gardens, at Sixth and Harrison streets. J. C. Christian Russ had been a successful New York City jeweler in the 1840s. One morning he arrived at his Broadway shop and found that burglars had cleaned him out the night before. He'd had enough of New York, and, with his three oldest sons, he joined Colonel Jonathan D. Stevenson's New York Volunteers to fight in the Mexican War. By the time Russ arrived on the West Coast, the War was almost over. Since his wife and several younger children had accompanied him and his three soldiering sons, they decided to stay in San Francisco. They moved a former ship's cabin to Montgomery and Bush streets, then the edge of town, and converted it into their home.

Russ opened a jewelry shop, got into assaying during the Gold Rush, and finally started speculating in real estate. He was a rich man within a few years, and a ship's cabin no longer seemed like the right place to live. Besides, the sand hill that separated his house from the waterfront and Portsmouth Square was being removed, and the Russes suddenly found themselves living in the middle of the city instead of in the suburbs. So he built a fine house for his family at Sixth and Harrison streets and laid out handsome grounds with paths winding among flower beds, shrubs, ornamental trees, and arbors. The location was "far out in the wilderness," according to California historian Hubert Howe Bancroft, but it was an easy drive to the city on the new plank roads along Folsom and Mission streets.

On May 1, 1853, Russ invited the town's German community to celebrate May Day on his property. More than 1,800 men, women, and children marched out the Mission Road, with bands playing and flags and banners flying in the breeze. Athletic contests were held under the auspices of the Turnverein, and everyone, according to the *Annals*, "danced, sang, drank, smoked and made merry, as only such an enthusiastic race of mortals could." Russ had a good time, too, and thereafter he opened his property to the general public for a modest fee. Russ' Gardens became the place for San Francisco's ethnic groups to celebrate their national holidays—the Germans on May Day, the French on Bastille Day,

the Irish on St. Patrick's Day, and, of course, the Americans on the Fourth of July.

In the late 1850s, another public garden, called The Willows, opened out where the Mission plank road ended. The grounds, which extended from 17th to 19th streets and through to Valencia street, were much grander than Russ' because they had been intended for public use from the beginning. The Willows included hills and meadows, in small scale. The focal point was a hollow with a stream shaded by willows. There was a platform for outdoor dancing, plenty of space for athletics, and tables and chairs beneath the trees for refreshments and snacks. The Willows' beer hall on Mission Street offered a place for serious drinking and merrymaking. Despite its enormous popularity, the Willows closed in 1861 after the winter rains flooded and badly damaged the grounds.

Other countrified playgrounds soon took its place. The City Gardens, which opened on July 21, 1867 at 12th and Folsom streets, occupied the former Shaw estate. Besides the usual lawns and tree-shaded walks, it included a lake with boats to rent, a bowling alley, and croquet grounds. A band played afternoons and evenings, and at night the grounds were lit with lamps and Chinese lanterns. At first the City Gardens was a favorite of the city's *beau monde,* according to one newspaper, but they "seemingly grew tired of it," and "the place became the resort of the working classes."

The largest and most popular place in town, however, was Woodward's Gardens on Mission Street near 14th Street. It was not just a money-making venture. Robert B. Woodward was already quite a rich man and, from all reports, was not obsessed with the idea of piling up an even greater fortune. He was twenty-five years old and a clerk in his father's store in Providence, Rhode Island, when he heard about the California Gold Rush and was seized with "gold fever." He left home with a stock of building materials and $1,000-worth of groceries and provisions. He arrived in San Francisco, by way of Cape Horn, on November 19, 1849.

Woodward opened a grocery store in a two-story frame building, no larger than twenty-by-twenty-five feet, down by the waterfront on Pike Street, between Washington and Clay. He took in two boarders to share his quarters on the second floor. Wood-ward was doing all right with his grocery store, but he realized that there was more money to be made by providing decent room and board at fair prices. Most of the 49'ers were unmarried or had left their wives and families back East. They were living in drafty tents scattered around town, or in hotels four and five to a room, and eating high-priced but ill-prepared restaurant food.

Woodward built a small boardinghouse next to his grocery store. Since it was a great success, he built an addition. He kept expanding his new business until, by 1852, 100 men were living in his various buildings. Then Woodward decided to go into the hotel business. His What Cheer House opened on July 4, 1852, on Sacramento Street, just below Montgomery, and it immediately became one of the most popular and most profitable hotels in town.

Woodward had hit upon an unbeatable formula for success. The What Cheer House offered clean and comfortable, though modest, rooms in respectable surroundings at low prices. Perma-nent lodgers occupied many of the rooms.

In subsequent years, Woodward made several additions to the hotel. By the mid-1860s, the What Cheer House had more than 1,000 rooms, and some went for as little as fifty cents a night. The dining room served more than 3,000 meals a day, many to men working at the nearby banks, countinghouses, and waterfront jobs.

Woodward knew how to make money, and he knew how to enjoy it as well. He brought his family to San Francisco in 1857, and soon thereafter they moved into the four-acre estate he had purchased out on Mission Street. With the help of landscape architects, Woodward reshaped the barren, sandy spot. He added a pond and several gentle hills from which to see the city and the Bay. Thousands of native flowers, shrubs, and trees were planted on the grounds, each with a name tag. Woodward built several conservatories in a vaguely Near Eastern architectural style for his prize specimens. He collected animals, too. While strolling through the grounds, he or members of his family might see a gazelle bounding into the bushes or come upon an ostrich lazily sitting in the sun.

In 1861 Woodward went to Europe for a year and a half. In one sense, it was a buying trip. Woodward and his agents sent back hundreds of boxes of "rare" and "exotic" plants and animals which had not been available in San Francisco.

But the trip, in another sense, was enrichment for Woodward the man. Like so many self-made nineteenth-century American businessmen, Woodward wanted to experience the antiquity and cultural richness of Europe, partly out of curiosity and partly in hopes that its cachet might rub off on him. Like his millionaire contemporaries, he wanted to bring some European culture and status back home with him.

As Woodward visited "all the principal cities" and "all the most remarkable objects on the continent," the *North Pacific Review*, in November, 1862, reported that he was "most deeply impressed with the rare works of art which came under his notice at Rome and Florence, as well as in Holland." He found another thing to collect: paintings. According to the *North Pacific Review*, he was "filled with the laudable project of laying in San Francisco the foundation for a gallery of art which may one day vie with the best collections of the eastern cities."

Woodward didn't waste any time. He asked Virgil Williams, an American painter studying in Rome, to put together a suitable collection. Williams made copies of works described as Aurora of Guido, the Claudian Aqueduct at Rome, Paul and Virginia—"a scene from the French romance of that name," Beatrice Cenci, Tasso reading before Leonora, the Farm of Cincinnatus near Rome, and so on. Williams also sold Woodward quite a few of his own works—some genre pieces taken from street scenes in Rome, a storm on the Campagna, the Alban Mountains taken from the Ponte de Mamello on the road to Vivoli, a farmyard scene with cattle, the Shrine of the Madonna della Febri, and Beppo, King of the Beggers, among others. The prize items were Florentine copies of two Raphael Madonnas.

Woodward wanted some sculpture, and Williams bought a copy of Hiram Powers' bust of California, a female bust, a work called "Indian Girl at the Grave of Her Lover," and another titled

"Rebecca at the Well."

This instant art collection cost Woodward "many thousands of dollars," according to the *North Pacific Review*, but it was well worth the expense. The *North Pacific Review* praised the works as "masterly copies . . . for the most part" and applauded Woodward's public spirit in putting the collection together. "No city can be said to have attained a position without some regard paid to the arts, and it is time San Francisco was redeemed from the old reproach." Woodward's taste in art was a little naive, but it was not much different from that of other rich men on European buying sprees in the 1860s. At least Woodward had the good sense to buy

out-and-out copies of famous works. Two other men back East owned the same Raphael, each believing that his painting was the real thing.

Woodward did not keep all his treasures to himself. In 1860 he opened a museum at the What Cheer House which included over 700 bird specimens, 1,200 eggs, various insects, reptiles, seashells, and minerals, plus ancient coins and Indian war and hunting implements. Guests could use the 2,000-volume library and the reading room with newspapers from leading cities across the country free of charge. Upon his return from Europe in 1862, Woodward hung some of his paintings at the What Cheer House.

But he kept his favorite things and the bulk of his collections at his Mission Street estate. With every year, more and more San Franciscans learned about the idyllic world he had created there. "As the various additions were made, and the gardens grew in beauty," recalled the *Californian* in 1871, "their fame spread far and wide, and many came to see them. The beautiful plants and strange trees, the fine buildings with their novel architecture, the ponds and mossy rocks, the roar of the wild beasts, excited the curiosity of the persons, to the most of whom the picket fence formed an impassable barrier."

Woodward had always been "most hospitable" in letting his friends wander through the grounds around his home. But the sight of men, women, and children trying to catch a glimpse of the estate through the fence led the local newspapers to suggest that he open the grounds to the public. Early in 1866, Woodward did just that, briefly, for the benefit of the Sanitary Fund.

That was the end of any privacy in his home. "Curiosity spread, and persistent sightseers besieged the place weeks after the committee had retired," wrote the San Francisco *Examiner* in 1893. "Woodward realized that it was only a question of being pestered forever or quietly throwing open his place." That May, he opened the property for a modest admission charge and moved to his Oak Knoll farm in Napa Valley north of the city.

Woodward wanted a festive spirit to greet visitors when they arrived at his Gardens. So he removed the formal gateway to the

Woodward's Gardens, main gate

property, which had been suitable for the entrance to a gentle-man's estate, and built new ones, large enough to handle crowds and topped by a row of bears standing on their hind quarters and holding flag poles.

The first thing visitors came upon was Woodward's former residence, now converted into the Museum of Natural Wonders. Woodward decided that the animal and geological items he gathered for himself weren't good enough for public display. He went off to Europe on another buying trip in 1866 and shipped back hundreds of boxes to San Francisco. "Beasts, birds, fish, fossils, antique relics, peculiar animal deformities, in great variety, con-front the visitor at every turn," wrote B. E. Lloyd, "affording the student ample opportunity to increase his knowledge, and at the same time, interesting and instructing to a degree, the most super-ficial observer."

The Museum of Miscellanies, as the collection was also called, included mineral specimens, too. Here Lloyd saw "curious formations of crystals, volcanic debris, petrified animals, serpents, fish and wood, precious stones, showing every shade of color, and every degree of brilliancy."

In 1868 Woodward heard about a natural wonder he couldn't pass up. Several miners had dug up a ninety-seven pound gold nugget in the Sierra Butte mine, and everyone was saying that it was the largest single lump of ore ever found. Woodward bought the nugget for $25,000, and his museum exhibited it for several years to anyone willing to pay an additional twenty-five cents. When the nugget was finally coined, it yielded nearly $23,000 in $20 gold pieces.

Next to Woodward's museum stood his art gallery and the conservatory filled with foreign flowers and plants. Nearby, the "rotary boat" whirled around its circular track on the edge of a pond, while the children on board laughed and screamed with delight. Behind these buildings stretched the grounds where wind-ing gravel paths passed through almost every imaginable landscape scene. "There are sparkling fountains, dashing cascades, murmur-ing brooks, glassy lakes, and trickling rivulets," observed B. E.

Lloyd. "There are mounds and hillocks, grottoes and caverns, lawns and thickets. The broad, natural landscape, with its varied beauties of woodland and prairie, its rolling hills and craggy mountains, its lazy streams and rushing torrents, has been here reproduced in mimic truthfulness." Somehow all this fit into the four-acre confines of Woodward's property.

One of the prettiest spots was the lake, edged by water lilies and filled with swans and ducks. Along the sides stood large globes of colored glass, mounted on posts, and marble statues representing Pandora, Jupiter, Venus, Terpsichore, Psyche, and the "Dancing Girl." A fountain fed the stream before it emptied into the lake, and weary visitors rested on benches and chairs set up beneath the trees.

Woodward was just as thorough in putting together his animal collection as he was with his other attractions. Some tame beasts, like ostriches, deer, and small barnyard animals, roamed the grounds and excited the visitors who suddenly came upon them. There were several ponds where sea lions yelped and sunned themselves on rocks. Bears greedily ate peanuts from the hands of children. Near the main entrance there were miniature carriages for rent, pulled by pairs of white goats. And there were camel rides, rather than pony rides, for the children.

Most of Woodward's animals, however, were part of the Zoological Department on its own piece of land on the other side of 14th Street. An underground passageway connected the zoo to the gardens proper. Woodward's zoo was the largest and most com-prehensive on the West Coast. Here visitors saw "animals of various kinds from all countries and all zones" — California grizzlies, Oregon panthers, Mexican panthers, South American jaguars, Bengal tigers, Arabian camels, Australian kangaroos, plus raccoons, foxes, weasels, opposums, and monkeys.

In 1873 Woodward opened the first salt water aquarium in America. The sixteen tanks, which ranged from 300 to 1,000 gallons, lined both sides of a forty-foot-long hallway, built of stone to look like a subterranean grotto. The only light in the hallway came from the tanks themselves which were lit from above. The tanks were stocked with sharks, cod, perch, flounders, octopi, and other "queer-looking finny curiosities." The public liked the crab, lobster, and crawfish tank the best. These creatures could "be seen in all their grotesqueness," wrote the San Francisco *Illustrated Press*, "crawling and creeping about, now upon the gravelly bottom and now climbing in their awkward manner, up the side of their rough stones, piling themselves upon one another and sometimes bracing themselves up against the glass front as though to take a leisurely view of their curious observers upon the outside." Another hit was the "fish hatching machine."

Woodward, the patron of the arts and the educator, hoped that the crowds would learn something from the exhibits at his Gardens. But Woodward the showman wanted them to have easy, uncomplicated fun, too. He built a bandstand, decorated with hanging baskets of roses and banners streaming in the wind, where a band played every afternoon and evening. On Sunday afternoons there were special concerts. The February 4, 1883 "programme" offered the Grand Duchess quadrille by Offenbach and an aria from Rossini's "Stabat Mater" plus works described as a "Valse Potpourri" and "Fantasia on English Songs."

Over near the Zoological Department, Woodward built an amphitheater with seats for more than 5,000 spectators. Here he put on quite a variety of shows over the years, featuring the Delhi fire eaters; Siberian reindeer; Japanese acrobats; Warm Springs

View of Woodward's Gardens

Indians performing tribal dances; "Split-Nose" Jim, the dancing bear; the first and second international tug-of-war contests; Christal, the Frenchman who wrestled bears; Roman chariot races; Major Burke and his rifle review; Ida Siddons, the rope-jumping dancer; Orndorf and Kidd, the Dutch comedians; and "Yankee Robinson's ballet of Parisian beauties . . . in their marvelous and truly beautiful May 'poie dance.' "

Woodward, however, was something more than a showman; he became known as the "Barnum of the West." Years later, the San Francisco *Examiner* recalled that "any freak that didn't make Barnum gasp Woodward seized on with avidity and plastered the town with highly colored descriptions of its 'remarkableness.' " There was Chang from China, eight-foot-tall, who paraded around Woodward's Gardens in elaborate native garb. A month after loosing Chang on the visitors, Woodward introduced Admiral Dot, a midget twenty-five inches tall, weighing fifteen pounds. "Tom Thumb is a giant in comparison!" and "Even the great Barnum stands amazed! He has offered the Admiral a salary of $12,000 a year!" shouted Woodward's advertising posters and handbills.

Woodward also indulged the public fascination with freaks and deformities. One regular display in the museum was "curiosities and monstrosities of all kinds, alive and dead," including double-tailed, double-headed, and double-bodied calves and horses. At one time, Woodward exhibited a two-headed child, a man with no legs and a woman with no arms. As if that weren't enough, he displayed "real Fiji cannibals, genuine man-eaters," who danced and howled and grinned as they waved bones at the audience.

Woodward's "strangest wonder" was the "headless rooster." His advertising posters showed a rooster standing on two feet while its severed head squawked and blinked on the ground nearby. According to Woodward, a cook in nearby Martinez had been killing chickens by chopping off their heads, but this rooster had not died. After several days, Woodward got word of the phenomenon, and he brought the rooster to his Gardens. For several more days, the headless rooster obligingly walked around for the crowds who paid a special twenty-five-cent admission fee.

There were plenty of souvenirs and things to buy at Woodward's Gardens, too. The Tropical Plant House sold exotic plants and flowers, plus bouquets made to order. Photographs and stereoscopic slides of the Gardens by Eadweard Muybridge and C. E. Watkins were available near the main gate, and the Keeper of the Animals sold tumbler and fantail pigeons, Madagascar rabbits, and Esquimaux [sic] dogs.

About the only thing visitors did not find at Woodward's Gardens was alcoholic beverages in the refreshment rooms. Woodward adhered to strict temperance principles, which he also enforced at his What Cheer House. Woodward's was the only public garden in town not to serve alcoholic beverages, but the rule did not harm its success. Woodward's Gardens was more popular than all its rivals and survived them all; it closed in 1894. Its collections were auctioned off, the hills were leveled and the ponds filled to make way for buildings. It had been open for more than twenty years, and that was a long time for anything to survive in San Francisco. Woodward's Gardens belonged to another, earlier generation by then. San Franciscans had discovered exciting new places for their outings and Sunday excursions.

The well-to-do were the first to desert Woodward's Gardens. They headed for Golden Gate Park and its smooth macadamized roadways which made carriage rides so smooth and so much fun. In 1875, just four years after the park opened, the gatekeeper counted an average of 600 carriages entering the park on weekdays and 1,000 to 1,200 on Sundays. The park roads became the favorite place for the rich to see and be seen; it was their own special world, far away from *hoi polloi* who couldn't afford to own or rent carriages.

B. E. Lloyd described this scene in Golden Gate Park: "Gold-mounted carriages of every approved pattern, drawn by richly caparisoned steeds, driven by uniformed livery-men, whose brilliant buttons are conspicuously numerous, and containing beautiful belles and gallant beaux, are seen whirling swiftly over the open road, now lost behind a curve, now penetrating a thicket — appearing and reappearing, rivaling each other in display, as well as emulating each other in merrymaking and jollity."

All this display began even before the carriages entered the park proper. William Hammond Hall, the park's architect and its first supervisor, set aside a 275-foot-wide and three-quarter-mile-long strip of land, now known as the Panhandle, for the "grand avenue" into the park. The smooth roadway did not run straight into the park, but pleasantly curved to the left and then to the right, and Lloyd thought that this approach was "magnificent in its windings through groves and dense shrubbery, whose perpetual verdure is at all seasons refreshing to the eye."

But Golden Gate Park was far from complete at this point, and it had been quite a struggle even to get the work that far. San Franciscans had always agreed that their city desperately needed a large park, but howls of protest arose when the city actually spent close to $1,000,000 to acquire the 1,007-acre site. "Of all the elephants . . . San Franciscans ever owned," snorted one newspaper, "they now have the largest and heaviest in the shape of Golden Gate Park."

The city fathers, it is true, could hardly have chosen a more unlikely spot for the "Central Park of the Pacific." Sand dunes stretched all the way from Stanyan Street to the ocean. Sand is far from the best soil in which to grow shrubs and trees, and gardening was even more difficult, because the strong ocean winds were always blowing the sand dunes this way and that. "How are they ever going to make a park out there?" asked San Franciscans. "A blade of grass has to be tied down to four stakes or it will blow away!"

Things did look bad for Golden Gate Park for a while. Drifting sand covered the first trees and shrubs and choked the newly laid-out roadways. The only solution was to plant the dunes with a ground-cover with roots dense enough to hold the sand in place. After reading about European sand reclamation projects, Superintendent Hall selected the California lupine for this purpose. The lupine took hold, and the sand problem eased, particularly on the eastern edge of the park. Trees and shrubs, which would have died or been blown away before, thrived because of the ground cover. Hall then dug a well to irrigate all the new plantings and built a fence of tree branches and brush along Ocean Beach, about 100 feet above the high tide line, to keep the sand on the beach and out of the park.

Looking northwest from the vicinity of 14th Avenue and Ortega Street, c. 1898

By 1880 the laughter and snide comments which had first greeted Golden Gate Park vanished, and San Franciscans began to praise their wisdom and foresight for going ahead with the project. But a great deal remained to be done. Only the eastern-most portion looked like a park. Further out little had been planted except for the lupine and other coarse native shrubs, and blowing sand remained troublesome in the windswept portion near the ocean. Things would get better with time, money, and the appointment of John McLaren as Superintendent in 1887.

Golden Gate Park wasn't the only place for countrified carriage rides. By the 1860s the cemeteries just outside town were favorite spots for afternoon jaunts. They had the idealized romantic landscapes and winding paths of the public gardens like Woodward's, but over a much larger area.

Burial customs had come a long way since Gold Rush days. In 1849 the only cemetery in town was at the Mission Dolores. The grounds had been adequate when San Francisco was a village of several hundred people. But shiploads of 49'ers soon began arriving in town, and the number of deaths increased right along with the population.

San Franciscans began burying their dead in several spots much closer to town—on Russian Hill, at Clarke's Point on the eastern side of Telegraph Hill, near First and Clementina streets, and in North Beach near the present-day intersection of Powell and Lombard streets. "No permission had been granted by the authorities for that purpose," reported the Annals, "but after one funeral had taken place, another and another quickly followed to the same quarter, until gradually it became a public cemetery."

The impromptu graveyards received only a portion of the Gold Rush dead. The 49'ers generally buried their dead in open land nearest to where a man had died. Sometimes it was in the backyard of his house, or it might be in the sand dunes behind his tent. The city fathers were too busy with the problems of the living to worry about the dead. They did not bother to keep any records of deaths, and there were no municipal inquests into the causes. "In the bustle of the place, and continual change of the population,

the dead man was not missed, and nobody dreamed of seeking for the absent," wrote the Annals. "He perhaps had gone into the interior, or home, or to the mines—any loose rumor satisfied the few inquisitive acquaintances of the deceased."

Haphazard burials were an obvious menace to public health and community sensibilities. Pierre Charles de Saint-Amant, the French government agent, noted the "pestilent odor" of putrefaction in many places at the edges of town. In 1850 the city finally set aside several acres for Yerba Buena Cemetery at the present-day intersection of Eighth and Market streets. The city fathers had chosen the spot, which was roughly halfway between town and the Mission Dolores, because they did not expect buildings to reach that far for many years. But people complained that it was too far from town and continued to bury their dead wherever they pleased. Moreover, the city hadn't spent any money to make Yerba Buena Cemetery an attractive place. The gravestones and markers "stood in a hollow among miserable-looking sandhills, which are scantily covered with stunted trees, worthless shrubs, and tufted weeds," according to the Annals. The grounds weren't even fenced until 1853, and the graveyard was "among the most dreary and melancholy spots that surround the city."

Yerba Buena Cemetery was a total failure, but, by the mid-1850s, San Franciscans realized that backyard burials weren't the answer either. Workmen were always coming upon the remains of the dead as they graded streets, dug sewers, or excavated building sites. In 1853 several men bought 320 acres a few miles out Bush Street on the slopes of Lone Mountain and planned a proper park-like cemetery much like Boston's famed Mount Auburn or Brooklyn's Green-Wood.

When Lone Mountain Cemetery opened in 1854, the Annals proudly reported that there were already "delightful dells, scooped out among the hills, with the evergreen oaks bordering and fringing their quiet beauty; valleys smiling all over with flowers, of every hue, and knolls covered with shrubs, rejoicing in their crowns of white lilac." More than twenty miles of roads were already laid out, and they were named after East Coast graveyards. The roads followed the lay of the land rather than lines of a rectangular grid, and from many spots pedestrians and carriage passengers had wonderful views of the city and the ocean.

The city closed Yerba Buena Cemetery the same year, but it was not until 1870 that its 3,000 bodies were removed to Golden Gate Cemetery, along with the gravestones and markers. When the move was made, it was carried out "so carelessly," according to one newspaper, "that the memorial tablets were in many instances misplaced, and friends who now go to weep over deceased pioneers often shed their tributary tears above those whom they had never seen in life, or perhaps known and detested."

Once Lone Mountain opened in 1854, San Franciscans had a respectful and beautiful place to bury their dead. The newspapers began to report that leading families were buying lots at Lone Mountain one after another and beginning to build handsome monuments. Other countrified cemeteries opened soon thereafter — Calvary (1860) for Roman Catholics, on forty-eight acres bounded by Geary, Turk, St. Josephs, and Masonic; two Jewish cemeteries, Nevai Shalome (1860) and Gibbath Olom (1861), bounded by Dolores, Church, 18th, and 20th streets, and now Dolores Park; the Masonic Cemetery (1864) on thirty acres bounded by Turk, Fulton, Parker, and Masonic; and the Odd Fellows Cemetery (1865) on thirty acres bounded by Geary, Turk, Parker, and Arguello.

The cemetery processions made their way out of town on Bush Street, which was the only street that had been graded beyond Powell Street in 1860. Smartly turned-out carriages filled with talking and joking men and women crowded the slower-moving hearses and sad mourners.

Lone Mountain Cemetery was renamed Laurel Hill in 1867, and many people, including B. E. Lloyd, were upset by the change. Why? Because Laurel Hill sounded too cheerful! "Lone Mountain is appropriate," he wrote. "There is loneliness in the graveyard! There is loneliness in the silent tomb! The very stones and monuments that boldly rear their heads above the cheerless death-chambers, make mute appeals for silence. Where death is

enthroned, silence reigns; and only in silence is there a perfect realization of loneliness." He went on, "then let San Francisco's burial ground be called by its native name — Lone Mountain. The little warblers whose throats swell with ecstatic trills, that ring out in shrill echoes through the forest, respect the hallowed ground, and warble soft notes of love when perched upon a drooping bough above the graves."

Visitors delighted in all this sugar-coated sadness but did not see the cemeteries as unhappy places. The rural cemeteries, in fact, became "resorts." On pleasant afternoons well-dressed families walked along the paths, with their maps and guidebooks in hand, while the carriages rolled up and down the winding hills. These visitors, however, had their own complaint about the cemeteries. The funeral processions and mourners dressed in black spoiled the festive air of their outings.

Once they had driven this far out of town, many people decided to make a day trip of their outing and headed for the ocean after leaving the cemetery. Back in the 1850s, visiting the ocean and Land's End had been quite a journey. About the only San Franciscans who made the long trek were quail and rabbit hunters and people wanting to see the ocean, the Golden Gate, and Mount Tamalpais. The only building of note on Land's End was Messrs. Sweeny & Baugh's second telegraph station. Their first was built in 1849 on a hill that became known as Telegraph Hill. From an observation deck on its roof men constantly scanned the Golden Gate for arriving ships and used a semaphore to inform waterfront merchants of every vessel's impending arrival and its description. Sweeny & Baugh were so encouraged by the success of their Telegraph Hill station that in 1853 they built another at Land's End, which was also known as Point Lobos. The Inner and Outer Telegraph Stations, as they were called, were in full view of each other, and the men at Land's End could signal those on Telegraph Hill with their semaphore. But the fog often obscured the messages, and Sweeny & Baugh established an electric telegraph, the first in California, to transmit messages from Land's End to Telegraph Hill and the Merchants Exchange on Sacramento Street.

Opposite, Jewish cemetery c. 1870, now Dolores Park

Navigators of the Bay

Land's End's isolation from the rest of the city ended in 1864 with the opening of the Point Lobos toll road along present-day Geary Boulevard. The several-mile-long macadamized roadway was expensive to build. Some 800 kegs of gunpowder had to be exploded just to clear the dunes near the ocean. But the proprietors had great hopes for their roadway. The Mission Street plank road had been a success from the beginning and had helped open up that part of town to development. The Point Lobos toll road caught the public's fancy, too. Now Land's End and the beach were an easy carriage ride from the city, and there was even a mile-and-a-quarter-long clay-surface "speedway" that was constantly rolled to keep it smooth and watered to hold down the dust. Such well-known men as Senator George Hearst, Leland Stanford, Charles Crocker, and James Ben Ali Haggin regularly raced their trotters on the speedway.

Riding to Land's End was half the fun of a visit there. "Everybody knew everybody, so it was a sort of family gathering," recalled Captain Junius H. Foster, proprietor of the Cliff House. "There was a continual nodding and buzzing from one carriage to another, while there was a constant succession of spins on the track between the flyers. These matches were almost always impromptu, and were generally just for the fun of the thing, or for champagne all around for the speeders."

Once at Land's End, there was good food and drink at the Cliff House, which opened October 15, 1863. Captain Foster, who had worked for the Ocean Steamship service, knew all the right people in San Francisco. Cliff House became the "attraction for all the first families of the city," and when Captain Foster added hotel accommodations in the early 1870s, entire families came out to Land's End for days at a time to enjoy the ocean views and sea air.

San Franciscans never tired of visiting Land's End or stopping for a drink or some food at the Cliff House. But in the 1870s they began to complain that these outings weren't as much fun as they had once been. They yearned for the good old days of the 1860s. The reason was obvious to anyone who went to Land's End: Cliff House was crawling with tourists. On some pleasant afternoons

there were 1,200 teams hitched in front of the building, and hundreds more drivers simply turned around and went back to the city or went for a drive along Ocean Beach in hopes of finding an open space when they returned.

The crowds were great for business, but sometimes Captain Foster joined the locals in wishing that the tourists would go home. It was for a far different reason. Some tourists were unbelievably cheap. Foster liked to tell the story of the 340 Massachusetts tourists who spent the day at Cliff House and ordered nothing more than 200 glasses of water and three lemonades!

A few miles to the south of Cliff House, at the end of Ocean Road, stood the Ocean House, opened in 1855. The original structure was reputedly built from timbers of vessels that had run aground on the beach. It was a quiet and respectable enough place until the Ocean View Race Track opened in 1865 on the site now bounded by Ocean Avenue, Sloat Boulevard, 26th and 34th avenues. Then Ocean House became the haunt of hard-living, hard-drinking gamblers and others who attended the races. About a mile up Ocean Road from the beach Cornelius Stagg's Ingleside Inn offered the same freespending, often-boisterous atmosphere.

During the 1860s, Captain Foster did not worry about the competition. He didn't need gamblers at Cliff House, because he had the Society trade and horsey set. But the hard times which hit the local economy in the early 1870s changed all that. Not as many businessmen were buying fancy trotters for themselves or stylish carriages for their families to show off on afternoon rides. Toll receipts on the Point Lobos roadway were down, and the proprietors cut back on maintenance. As the roadway deteriorated, fewer people were willing to pay for the privilege of riding there, and finally, in 1877, the city purchased the Point Lobos roadway for $25,000.

As his genteel clientele disappeared, Captain Foster took in the fast crowd that hung out at Ocean House and Ingleside Inn. He hired pretty young women as waitresses, and he got a little more than he reckoned for in the way of guests. Barbary Coast low life — the whores, pimps, gamblers, and their friends — now passed the night drinking and partying at Cliff House. And what went on in the private rooms upstairs was well-known scandal.

But this naughtiness did not go on for long. Multimillionaire Adolph Sutro lived on the bluff just above Cliff House. Sutro, a quiet and scholarly German Jew, had once been a cigar dealer in San Francisco. In the mid-1860s he put his engineering talents to work and solved the drainage and ventilation problems at the Comstock Lode. He was soon a rich man. Sutro didn't like what was happening one bit. He bought Cliff House in 1883, fired Captain Foster, and installed his own manager to clean up the place.

Sutro's man, Wilkins, did just that, but Cliff House's earlier fashion had disappeared forever. On February 15, 1880, a horse-drawn railroad opened along the old Point Lobos tollroad, and Cliff House was accessible to anyone with the fifty cents fare.

Cliff House, however, didn't need to be fashionable to be a magical place. The sea lions had never left their perch on the rocks offshore. Visitors were delighted to watch their clumsy movements and listen to their loud yelping. Well, almost everyone liked them. When Helen Hunt Jackson, later the author of *Ramona* and *A Century of Dishonor*, visited San Francisco as a young woman in the early 1870s, she did not like the sea lions, which she mistakenly called seals. "It is so much the fashion to be tender, not to say sentimental, over the seals of the Cliff House rocks that I was disappointed not to find myself falling into that line as I looked at them. But the longer I looked the less I felt like it," she admitted. She went on:

It is, of course, a sight which ought to profoundly touch the human heart, to see a colony of anything that lives left unmolested, unharmed by men; and it, perhaps, adds to the picturesqueness and interest of the Cliff House situation to have these licensed warblers disporting themselves, safe and shiny, on the rocks. But when it comes to the seals themselves, I made bold to declare that, if there be in the whole animal kingdom any creature of size and sound less adapted than a seal as a public pet, to adorn public grounds, —I mean waters,—I do not know such creature's name. Shapeless, boneless, limbless, and featureless, neither fish nor flesh; of

the color and consistency of India-rubber diluted with mucilage; slipping, clinging, sticking, like gigantic leeches; flapping, wallowing with unapproachable clumsiness; lying still, lazy, inert, asleep, apparently, till they are baked browner and hotter than they like, then plunging off the rocks, turning once over in the water to wet themselves enough to bear more baking; and all the while making a noise too hideous to be described, —a mixture of bray and squeal and snuff and snort, —old ones, young ones, big ones, little ones, masculine, feminine, and, for aught I know, neuter, by dozens, by scores, —was there ever anything droller in the way of philanthropy, if it be philanthropy, or in the way of public amusement, if it be amusement, than this? Let them be sold, and their skins given to the poor; and let peace and quiet reign along that delicious beach and on those grand old rocks.

After 1883 anyone with ten cents could wander through the grounds of Adolph Sutro's turreted frame mansion from nine in the morning until five in the afternoon. Sutro spent $1,000,000 transforming this rocky crag into an enchanted garden. His gardeners—he employed fifteen at one point—planted rows of cypresses, Norfolk pines, and Australian eucalyptus to break the winds off the ocean. Sutro was particularly interested in his eucalyptus trees, and he brought a boatload of dirt from Australia so that they would feel at home. Once these trees were planted, Sutro's gardeners laid out a formal garden around the mansion, complete with flower beds, fountains, gazebos, and a balustraded terrace overlooking the ocean. But the best-known feature of his gardens were the 100 statues of classical gods and goddesses, nymphs and satyrs, and, inexplicably, some characters from the works of Charles Dickens. Sutro spent a tremendous amount of money for his own and for the public's pleasure, but he had his thrifty side, too. The statues, it turned out, were plaster, not marble, and every spring they were given a fresh coat of white paint.

In the 1860s, tightrope walkers were always talking about stretching a wire from Cliff House to one of the seal rocks, and at least two daredevils, Rose Celeste and James Cooke, actually made their way to the rock and back. Later on, visitors watched Johnnie the Birdman and his canary act, Professor Baldwin who went up in a hot air balloon and came back to earth in a parachute, and Millie Lavelle who slid down a wire to the seal rocks hanging by her teeth.

Probably the most curious event at Land's End wasn't even planned as entertainment. Ralph Starr claimed that he knew how to capture the energy of the tides, thereby providing a limitless supply of cheap power for industry. But Starr had only theories and blueprints for his device. What he needed was money to build the real thing. The idea sounded reasonable, and he received the backing of several San Francisco industrialists. Starr didn't waste any time, and workmen began building an enormous steel device, complete with wheels and cables, on one of the rocks just off Point Lobos.

Only Starr and his backers knew what was happening, and San Franciscans were soon speculating that the mechanism was being built to improve navigation through the Golden Gate or that

Sea Lions

it removed gold from sea water. Starr finally announced that he was building a tide machine and would give the first demonstration on Sunday morning at ten. Hundreds of curious men, women, and children gathered at Land's End that morning, as did Starr's backers. But Starr didn't show up at 10 a.m. When he hadn't appeared by 11 a.m., several backers feared the worst and drove back into town to his house. No one was there, but it looked as if he might return home at any moment. All his furniture and clothing were there, and the breakfast dishes were stacked in the sink. Starr never came home, and no one in San Francisco ever heard from him again. The tide machine sat unused on the rock until it was destroyed bit by bit by the wind and the waves.

Sharing their city with hordes of tourists was a new experience for San Franciscans in the 1870s. Back in the Gold Rush days, San Francisco had been anything but a tourist mecca. A few hardy, inquisitive souls did make the long journey to see the Gold Rush for themselves and the instant city that the whole world was talking about. But once they got there, they had to face the same trying living conditions and high prices that made life so difficult for the 49'ers.

As life for San Franciscans became more comfortable in the 1850s, the city became a more attractive place for tourists. By then San Francisco had matured sufficiently to have all kinds of hotels, restaurants serving foods of every imaginable nationality, and even some sights worth seeing. In 1862 the *North Pacific Review* observed that "the tribe of foreign tourists has been this year unusually large." But visitors had to make their way to San Francisco across the United States or over the Isthmus of Panama or around Cape Horn. Traveling conditions were better than they had been for the 49'ers, but the journey still took an awfully long time.

The completion of the transcontinental railroad in 1869 changed all that forever. Express trains now made the run from New York to the Oakland terminal in seven days, bringing mail, newspapers, clothing, and machinery from the East Coast, along with hordes of excited tourists. "From the time the first train came thundering down the Sacramento Valley with its freight of Eastern passengers, there has been an almost unceasing stream of travel pouring into the city," wrote B. E. Lloyd in 1876.

From first sight, San Francisco was impressive. In those first years, the cross-country trains arrived in Oakland in the evening, and the traveling reporter for the *St. Louis Republican* thought that "the first view gained of the distant city from the windows of the cars, as the train winds through the streets of Oakland down to the water's edge, and thence two and a quarter miles into the very Bay itself [on a ferry], is an exceedingly prepossessing one."

One of San Francisco's most satisfied visitors was Rudyard Kipling, who was twenty-four years old when he stopped in San Francisco on his way from India to England in 1889. He was particularly impressed with the "captivating rush and whirl" of life in San Francisco and "the recklessness . . . in the air. I can't explain where it comes from," he wrote, "but there it is. The roaring wind off the Pacific makes you drunk to begin with. The excessive luxury on all sides helps out the intoxication, and you spin forever 'down the ringing groves of change.' "

Kipling had a good time in San Francisco, and so did Guillermo Prieto, the Mexican author, except that he was always getting lost during his 1877 visit. In the account of his travels in the United States, published in Mexico City the following year, Prieto good humoredly explained how sensibly San Francisco streets had been laid out. How easy it should have been for a stranger, like himself, to get around town.

The streets, with the exception of a few not too catholic diagonals, are very regular; they never suddenly change their names, but lead a person faithfully from one end of town to the other; the system of numbering buildings, odd numbers on one side of the street and even on the other, leaves no room for doubts; in addition to this, at intervals the street lamps bear the name of the street; coachmen, vendors and passers-by are always most willing to assist the stranger in finding his way; and finally, it is the strict duty of the police to lead to his destination anyone who requests it. The streetcars always indicate their direction, and even at night their different colors prevent the dullest person in the world from losing his way.

Then Prieto added: "Now is this flawless system perfectly clear to the reader? And have I mentioned also that many citizens speak Spanish or French or Italian, so that I could never fail to understand them?"

None of this, it seems, was any help to Prieto. "My sojourn in San Francisco was one long repetition of the state of being lost," he admitted. "I would set off toward the south, and loyally as the needle of a compass, end up due north. I would set off for the theater, and find myself horrified at the gateway to the cemetery. Thereupon I would take a streetcar, making every effort to select one I thought I knew. On it would go, and suddenly there would no longer be any streets about me. In a towering rage at my own stupidity I would pull my hat down over my eyes to exaggerate my silly look, take a *peseta* out of my pocket and hand it to the first newsboy who passed, saying only 'Gailhard Hotel' and letting myself be led like a blind man to my very door."

A few tourists didn't like San Francisco at all. Helen Hunt Jackson was among them:

When I first stepped out of the door of the Occidental Hotel, on Montgomery Street, I looked up and down in disappointment.

'Is this all?' I exclaimed. 'It is New York, —a little lower of story, narrower of street, and stiller, perhaps. Have I crossed the continent only to land in Lower Broadway on a dull day?'

I looked into the shop-windows. The identical hats, collars, neckties for men, the identical tortoise-shell and gold ear-rings for women, which I had left behind on the corners of Canal and Broome Streets, stared me in the face. Eager hack-drivers, whip-handles in air, accosted me, —all brothers of the man who drove me to the Erie Railroad station, on the edge of the Atlantic Ocean.

Helen Hunt Jackson was not the all-time spoiled-sport visitor to nineteenth-century San Francisco. That distinction clearly belongs to Anthony Trollope, the successful British journalist and novelist and son of the much-maligned Mrs. Frances Trollope. During an around-the-world tour, Trollope spent several days in San Francisco in the summer of 1875, before going to Yosemite.

Trollope formed some rather definite opinions of the city for so short a stay. He wrote in Liverpool's *Weekly Mercury*, "I do not know that in all my travels I ever visited a city less interesting to the normal tourist, who, as a rule, does not care to investigate the ways of trade or to enjoy himself in ascertaining how the people around him earn their bread." He did not stop there. He had a public in Liverpool hanging on to his every word, and Trollope did not want to let them down. He continued:

There is almost nothing to see in San Francisco that is worth seeing. There is a new park in which you may drive for six or seven miles on a well-made road, and which, as a park for the use of a city, will, when completed, have many excellencies. There is also the biggest hotel in the world, —so the people of San Francisco say, which has cost a million sterling, —5 millions of dollars—and is intended to swallow up all the other hotels. It was just finished but not opened when I was there. There is an inferior menagerie of wild beasts, and a place called the Cliff House to which strangers are taken to hear seals bark. Everything, —except hotel prices, —is dearer here than at any other large town I know; and the ordinary traveler has no peace left him either in public or private by touters who wish to persuade him to take this or the other railroad route into the Eastern States. There is always a perfectly cloudless sky overhead unless when rain is falling in torrents, and perhaps nowhere in the world is there a more sudden change from heat to cold in the same day.

Trollope obviously didn't like the cold summer fogs during his stay. Maybe that's why he was happy to leave. Anyway his parting blast was: "I think I may say that strangers will generally desire to get out of San Francisco as quickly as they can."

Trollope's remarks created a brief stir when they were reported in San Francisco newspapers. But he was long gone by then, and San Franciscans knew better than to take his caustic words seriously. San Francisco may not have become "America's favorite city" yet, but there was plenty to see and do for most visitors. Perhaps Trollope would have had something good to say about San Francisco if the Palace Hotel had been open and he had stayed there. Once the hotel opened, it was near the top of almost every tourist's sightseeing list.

San Franciscans were proud of the Palace Hotel, and rightly so. William Ralston, the flamboyant financier and civic booster, erected the Palace as a monument to himself and to San Francisco more than as an investment. Hotels were the grandest and most expensive buildings in most nineteenth-century American cities, and they usually were among the first things visitors saw in a town. As the *Alta* noted in 1876, "each large city in the Union has vied with the others in striving to keep up with the times in respect to hotels."

Now San Franciscans could boast that their city had the grandest hotel in the entire country. The *Alta* declared: "It is a pleasing fact to note that San Francisco has even gone farther, and surpassed her sisters of the Western Hemisphere, if not the entire globe, by securing the 'Palace Hotel' for an ornament."

Visitors from Great Britain and France, and even the East Coast cities, were impressed by what they saw at the Palace Hotel. Even New Yorkers had to admit that not one hotel in their city was its equal in extravagance or in size. The Palace, however, was not the largest hotel in America, as some people claimed. The United States Hotel, which had opened the same year at Saratoga Springs, New York, had more rooms than the Palace. But that didn't matter much. The United States was part of a summer resort and not nearly as impressive. The Palace was, by far, the largest hotel in any American city.

The very numbers that described its size were staggering. The first thing everyone thought about was the cost: $5,000,000. No other hotel in the country remotely approached that figure. The most-talked-about hotels in New York only cost one or two million. What did that $5,000,000 buy? The Palace stood seven stories tall, and it covered an entire city block running 275 feet along Market Street and 350 feet along New Montgomery Street. The building covered 90,000 square feet—about two and a half acres. The periphery of the outside walls was a quarter mile long, and inside there were two and a half miles of corridors. Guests sometimes lost their way to their rooms, and soon after the hotel opened one man offered this advice to lost guests: "Pretend you

Upper Court, Palace Hotel

are 'full,' let yourself loose and cuss. Someone will come and guide you to your room."

The Palace had 755 rooms, nearly all twenty feet square, with fifteen-foot ceilings. A few rooms were sixteen by sixteen, but they had the same high ceilings. Each room had a private toilet, and every two rooms shared a bath. The toilets were a special pride of the management. The devices, made by Maddock & Sons, had "an arrangement by which the water is carried off without producing the horrid noise one usually hears."

Guests were not expected to spend all their time in their rooms. On the other hand, the Palace had so many public rooms and services that guests could have all their needs met without leaving the hotel. "One can enter its doors," wrote B. E. Lloyd, "dwell therein year after year, and have every want supplied. Everything seems to have been considered. There are amusements, promenades, and every comfort for the mental as well as the physical man."

The Palace included probably the largest lobby in the country, complete with post office, telegraph, book and magazine store, and travel agent; a marble-floored hotel office fifty-five by sixty-five feet, with a twenty-foot-high ceiling; a luxurious bar; a main dining room, fifty-five feet wide and 155 feet long; a breakfast room; a children's dining room; a gentlemen's parlor; a ladies' parlor; a fifty-five by sixty-five-foot ballroom; a music room; a reading room; a barber shop; public baths; separate reception rooms for men and women arrivals; a billiard room with dozens of tables; and several "committee rooms," usually occupied by gamblers. There were eighteen shops on Market and New Montgomery streets. Each store had a show window and door along a promenade within the hotel, in addition to the ones along the street, so that guests did not have to step outside.

All the public rooms were the last word in elegance. Nothing evoked wealth and gentility in Victorian America better than marble, and the Palace had so much marble that one firm could not fill the contractor's orders. In fact, fifteen companies supplied the 804 mantels, 900 wash basins, and 40,000 square feet of marble

flooring. No costs had been spared on the woodwork either. The Palace had mahogany, East India teak, primavera from Mexico, rosewood, and ebony, usually elaborately carved and polished to a mirror finish.

The public rooms were painted a shade of pink, "somewhat resembling the peach blossom," which was "showy in the highest degree, but not at all offensive," one newspaper reassured its readers. The furniture, however, was "peculiar," according to B. E. Lloyd. That didn't mean that it was cheaply made or funny looking. The furniture followed the Eastlake style, then in vogue. What Lloyd thought unusual was Ralston's way of getting the furniture. Rather than going to some fashionable New York or Parisian cabinetmaker, Ralston had most of the furniture made in San Francisco, because he wanted to encourage the growth of local manufacturing. But when it came to some of the other furnishings, the local craftsmen weren't good enough, even for civic booster Ralston. The Palace boasted Irish linens, Bavarian china, French porcelain, and rugs and carpets made to order in France or furnished by the stylish New York shop, W. & J. Sloan. In fact, Sloan's got so much business from the Palace Hotel that they opened a San Francisco branch, which is still here today.

The luxurious furnishings and services were part of the reason the Palace Hotel cost so much money. These items could not be avoided; extravagance was the rule in first-class hotels. Back in the 1850s, the Home Journal had complained that proprietors of big city hotels spent "three times as much as mere comfort requires" on the furniture, that "their tables are spread at three times the expense which health and good digestion crave," and that the buildings were always "situated where ground and rent is highest."

Ralston outspent every other hotel owner on these luxuries, but he also put a lot of money into first-class construction which the public would never see. The brick exterior walls and interior load-bearing walls were two feet thick and rested on foundations twelve feet deep. The mortar between the bricks was unusually hard because of a high proportion of lime to cement. Lastly, there was 3,000 tons of iron bands which were bolted together to form one continuous strip.

Ralston was trying to make the Palace as earthquake-proof as possible. The October 8, 1865 and October 21, 1868 earthquakes had dramatically shown how badly much of the city had been put up. Cornices fell off buildings. Brick walls cracked and tumbled into the streets. Chimneys dropped right through the buildings, and the streets everywhere were littered with broken glass.

Even with all this evidence lying around, the newspapers couldn't decide whether or not prevailing construction practices were safe for an earthquake-prone city. San Franciscans didn't want to think about earthquakes, and, if they did, didn't see them as a serious threat. B. E. Lloyd wrote: "While it would not be very strange if a shock should visit San Francisco, so powerful as to lay much of the city in ruins, and consequently be very destructive to life, yet it is not probable that such an event will transpire."

Fire seemed a much greater danger to a city largely built of wood and buffeted by winds. After his 1872 visit, the correspondent for the *St. Louis Republican* wrote:

With the fearful destruction recently wreaked on Chicago by the dread demon of fire vivid in my mind, it is impossible to walk through the streets of San Francisco without feeling a presentiment of an even more terrible fate in store for this great metropolis. One is forced irresistibly to look upon it as a doomed city and the mind cannot but paint to itself a horrible picture of the lapping flames leaping from one frail tinder-box to another, until not one-third of a thriving, prosperous city is swept from existence, but the whole.

Ralston spent $500,000 to make the Palace fireproof, too. Four artesian wells supplied up to 28,000 gallons an hour, thereby freeing the hotel from dependence on city supplies. A 630,000-gallon storage tank sat beneath the central court, and seven tanks on the roof held another 130,000 gallons. Five miles of pipes, completely separate from the plumbing, carried this water throughout the hotel, and there were 327 outlets along with 15,000 feet of fire hose. Furthermore, there were automatic fire alarms at regular intervals and a fire patrol inspected the entire hotel every thirty minutes all day long.

The Palace was the best known hotel in San Francisco, but there were several other first-class establishments. Baldwin's occupied the triangular 138-by-210-by-275-foot lot bounded by Market, Powell, and Ellis streets. Previously San Franciscans had bought flowers at Lansezeur and Harbert's St. Ann Gardens and children had played in a pond on the site. Baldwin's could not compete with the Palace in terms of size; it had 595 rooms to the Palace's 755. But most San Franciscans thought it was a more luxurious and a more pleasant place to stay than the Palace. When Baldwin's opened in 1876, the *Alta* proclaimed it "San Francisco's *Recherche* Hotel," and went on to say that "for pure elegance and positive magnificence, as well as completeness in every detail, there is not another hotel in the world its superior, and it is almost safe to say, its equal."

E. J. "Lucky" Baldwin, "a successful mining operator of unlimited means," wanted his hotel to be impressive, and he got what he wanted. The hotel's triangular shape, due to the unusual lot, was already an eyecatcher. Then architect John A. Remer selected the French Renaissance style and turned the facade into a profusion of bay windows, Corinthian columns, overhanging cornices, balustrades, and elaborately framed windows. The Baldwin Hotel stood six stories tall. The ground floor was largely given over to shops with expansive plate glass windows. The sixth floor was incorporated into a mansard roof, which evoked images of Second Empire Paris considered so stylish in post-Civil War America.

The Baldwin's architectural *piece de resistance* was a 168-foot-tall hexagonal dome, above the Market and Powell streets angle of the building. The dome, which was five stories high inside, was reserved exclusively for the ladies and included their very own billiard room, a sewing room with a magnificent view of the city, and a conservatory complete with rare flowers, an aquarium, and a fountain!

The hotel facade, elaborate as it was, gave only a hint of the splendors that awaited guests within. E. J. Baldwin ordered the finest furniture and appointments that his "unlimited means" could buy. Apparently he wanted everyone to know how much he had spent; he didn't leave the price tags on, but the store labels which delighted Victorian status seekers were everywhere. The dining room silverware came from Tiffany, the chandeliers from Michael & Vance, carpets from W. & J. Sloan, and linen and more carpeting from A. T. Stewart & Company in New York City, the nation's most fashionable department store.

Even the items that lacked such instantly impressive names were quite special. The grand staircase had a five-foot-four-inch-tall newel post, "composed of the choicest woods . . . moulded and carved, and mounted with bronze masks," which was topped by a bronze female figure, holding a cluster of crystal lights. This newel post arrangement was "certainly the most beautiful object of its kind ever made," gushed the *Alta*, "and the proprietor has spared no money on its construction." The guests' check-in counter, likewise, was a "work of art," made of the purest white marble, paneled in onyx, by Fisher Brothers of New York City. The counter was "executed in a style never before attempted because of its great cost." Baldwin even saw to it that the ten-ton office safe from Herring & Company was "the best of its kind the firm ever sold," and the office clock, which cost $2,500 from Tiffany, was, naturally, "without peer in America."

Baldwin's Hotel was more than just a showcase for expensive furniture and knick-knacks; it included some features, like the ladies' dome, that were unusual even in a hotel of this quality. There were three different kinds of elevators. The smallest ones, which were similar to dumbwaiters and run by electricity, carried cards and packages from the first floor to the service rooms on each of the floors upstairs. Another elevator, larger and powered by a steam engine, carried the guests' luggage upstairs. The real delight, however, was the steam-powered passenger elevator, which ran from the basement to the top of the dome, in the center well of the grand stairway. "Its design," reported the *Alta*, had been "taken from the latest Parisian novelty—an open car." Its walls were a combination of plate glass, etched glass, and mirrors, with ornamental hardwood trim, "the intention and design being to allow the passengers to see and be seen in their ascent and descent."

The main dining room had a surprise, too. Previously, most hotel dining rooms were located in the middle or the rear of the building, and their windows looked out on an air shaft or courtyard. Guests had often eaten their meals, even in the daytime, beneath the glare of gas light. That had once been considered the height of fashion. But it was no longer so in the 1870s. The dining room in the Baldwin faced Ellis Street and in the daytime received all its light and air from the windows. The room was quite lovely, or, as the *Alta* would say, it "has not its equal in any hotel in the United States." The dining room was thirty-two feet wide and 138 feet long, but it had been divided into three areas by clusters of columns and statuary. The floors were encaustic tiles, in a mosaic pattern, imported from England, and the walls and ceilings were frescoed in various floral patterns.

The Palace and the Baldwin are nineteenth-century San Francisco's best-remembered hotels. (The Baldwin burned in 1898, and its uninsured $3,000,000 loss ruined "Lucky Baldwin.") But there were more than 100 other hotels in town in the 1870s and 1880s. If boardinghouses, "many of which are large and commodious, and some extremely 'high toned,' " according to B. E. Lloyd, were included in the list of travelers' accommodations, the number of hotels would be more than 1,000.

Only three other hotels, besides the Palace and Baldwin's, were considered first-class at the time. The Grand Hotel, which opened on the southeast corner of Market and New Montgomery streets in 1870, had been the finest and largest in town, "until the shadow of the Palace fell upon it." That statement was no exaggeration; the Palace stood just across New Montgomery Street. Ralston was a part owner in the Grand Hotel, too. It stood three stories tall, with a mansard roof, and had 400 rooms.

Another favorite was the Lick House, at the southwest corner of Sutter and Montgomery streets. How times had changed between the completion of Lick House in 1862 and the opening of the Palace and Baldwin's in the mid-1870s! Although the Lick House contained 204 rooms, it was just three stories tall. Originally it did not have an elevator, and the height was kept low so that

guests did not have to walk flight after flight of stairs to reach their rooms. Consequently, the Lick House extended 200 feet along Montgomery Street and 160 feet up Sutter Street. Land prices in such choice locations had risen so much by the 1870s that no investor would have put a three-story building on that site.

In the early 1860s, Alstrom & Johnson, the managers, advertised the Lick House as "*the* first class hotel of San Francisco," and, to back up that boast, they pointed out that there were baths on every floor. That would have been inadequate fifteen years later. By then, the standard was a toilet for every room and a bath for every other room.

Lick House advertisements also pointed out that "its interior is finished with a degree of excellence unsurpassed by any hotel in the United States." The Lick House, however, had little of the white marble and rare hardwoods that were *de rigeur* for later first-class hotels. In fact, the Lick House was one material after another masquerading as a more expensive one. The building was brick, but the exterior walls were stuccoed and painted white to look like marble. The baseboards, pilasters, and cornices in the lobby were redwood painted to look like Sienna marble, and all the woodwork in the upstairs halls and the public rooms and bedrooms was redwood painted to look like oak. One newspaper complimented the painters, Frost & Richards, on their work, saying, "their imitations are so perfect that it is difficult to tell the genuine from the counterfeit."

All that sham didn't bother San Franciscans in 1862. The Lick House was the best hotel in town, and, what's more, it introduced to San Francisco that sensation known as the "bridal chambers." New York City's Irving House invented the bridal suite in 1848, and soon it was a standard feature of the most fashionable East Coast hotels. The bridal chambers, in theory, were so sumptuously done up that "Eve might have whispered love to Adam after she was expelled from Paradise without regretting the change."

The bridal chambers at Lick House apparently met this criteria. According to one newspaper reporter, they were "the most attractive feature of the house — at least have been so far considered by lady visitors." The suite consisted of a parlor, bedroom, and bathroom. The parlor furniture was richly carved rosewood, covered in blue and gold brocatelle, and the wall-to-wall carpeting was the same colors in a medallion pattern. The windows, which faced Sutter Street, had two sets of curtains, one in richly embroidered lace, the other in blue and gold brocatelle. The parlor included a fireplace with white marble mantel, a pier mirror in a gilt rococo-style frame, and two chandeliers appropriately decorated with cupids and "all the little 'fixins.'" When the reporter described the bedroom, he didn't even mention what the curtains or carpeting looked like. He got right to the point. "The bedsteads [are] large and roomy, the mattresses soft and downy, and the linen of virgin whiteness."

The Lick House could not match the hotels of the 1870s and 1880s in size or architectural treatment, but the proprietors knew they had an unbeatable Montgomery Street location and did not let the place run downhill. They were always redecorating the rooms, buying new furniture, and installing the latest mechanical conveniences. But the true strength of the Lick House over the years was its dining room, which served such good food in such a handsome setting that well-to-do San Franciscans often ate there rather than going to one of the fashionable restaurants. The dining room was oval in shape, and Corinthian pilasters divided the walls into a series of panels decorated with large mirrors and paintings of Eastern scenery. The man from the *St. Louis Republican* thought that the Lick House "justly" had "the finest dining hall in this country. It is not unlike that of the Fifth Avenue Hotel, New York, though its elegance more nearly resembles that of the Grand Hotel, Paris." What greater accolade could the Lick House have received?

The last first-class hotel was the Occidental, which filled the east blockfront of Montgomery Street between Sutter and Bush. The Occidental opened on January 1, 1863, and, in many ways, it looked much like the Lick House diagonally across the street. The stucco facade displayed the same style as its neighbor — what we now call the Italianate but what the newspapers then described as

Opposite, Occidental Hotel, Montgomery Street, 1866

"Renaissance—a mixture of Italian, Greek, Corinthian, and other orders combined." The interior of the Occidental, however, showed some of the grandeur that was fully realized in later hotels. All the woodwork was solid mahogany. The doorknobs and even some of the plumbing fixtures were silver plate. The main dining room was thought to be particularly impressive, because the doors,

windows, and ornamental plasterwork were overscaled. The windows, for instance, were six feet wide and fifteen feet tall, with interior mahogany shutters. The ceiling rosettes were six and a half feet wide, and the newspapers reported that "under the stucco ornaments . . . the coloring is scarlet, which relieves the dread appearance of so much white, and produces a beautiful effect."

For all its luxury, the Occidental upset many San Franciscans when it went up. It was a high-rise building, and people didn't like that. The Occidental Hotel was an "extraordinarily high" four stories. It looked quite imposing and, because it loomed over its neighbors, guests got "a magnificent view" of the city and the Bay from the upper floor rooms.

Hotels like the Lick House and the Occidental, which retained their fashion year after year, were the exception rather than the rule in San Francisco. Hotels which had once been all the rage lost their desirability ten or fifteen years after they opened. Sometimes the proprietor did not spend enough money to keep the place up-to-date in conveniences or furnishings. Occasionally the surrounding neighborhood went downhill and pulled the hotel down with it. Sometimes the once-special hotel lost the lure of novelty in the public eye, and fickle travelers went elsewhere. The American Exchange, Brooklyn, Cosmopolitan, and Russ were all one-time favorites which became distinctly second rate by the 1870s and 1880s.

B. E. Lloyd, who so carefully pointed out these distinctions, declared that the second-rate establishments were hardly as bad as their name implied. These hotels "have all the conveniences of suites, baths, reading-rooms, hotel coaches, etc., that the better houses maintain." He thought that the second-class hotels of San Francisco were superior, in many ways, to first-class hotels in many Eastern cities. What San Francisco's second-class hotels lacked, he believed, were those things "that apply to the aesthetic tastes— elegant mirrors, rich furniture, and various ornamentation that is for 'effect' more than for use."

Not only travelers occupied the hotels. Thousands of San Franciscans made their homes in every kind of hotel in all parts of

Hotel Pleasanton, 1890

town. Hotel living was a tradition in San Francisco stretching back to Gold Rush days. At that time, housing was scarce, and men who were unmarried or had left their families back East thought themselves lucky to find a hotel room somewhere. But hotel living remained popular long after things had gotten easier in the 1850s. A disproportionate share of the city's population was always single men or couples newly arrived in town or planning to stay for only a short while.

These people could not rent an apartment, because there weren't any. Apartment buildings, as we know them today, were all but unknown in most cities until the 1880s. Respectable families would not think of living under the same roof with other people, and real estate investors were afraid to give anything a try that was so unpopular. When apartment buildings were first introduced in New York City around 1870, they were an immediate success. But they were known as "French flats," which implied the loose morality as well as the elegance of nineteenth century Paris.

The single family house remained the American ideal. Occupying an entire house, however, was an expensive proposition, and it trapped the single man or the childless couple in all the housekeeping duties. One alternative for these San Franciscans was moving into a boardinghouse where the landlady cooked all the meals and performed all the household duties. B. E. Lloyd knew that "a man of domestic habits is a rarity; and women have come to regard family cares and duties as a sort of drudgery without their province." The boardinghouse, however, created as many problems as it solved. Privacy was almost nonexistant, and residents were at the mercy of the landlady when it came to what they ate or how often the linen was changed. Boardinghouses, moreover, were socially suspect in some circles. "Some of the up-town boarding-houses rival in elegance the best hotels," remarked B. E. Lloyd, "though, as a rule, to live at a boarding-house is to be on the social decline, requiring only a little push to send you down the grade."

Most unmarried men, widows, and childless couples had no choice but to live in a boardinghouse. But hotels offered a far better living arrangement for those with some money. Hotels provided freedom from all household responsibilities yet gave much of the privacy of a home. By the 1870s, hotel living had become quite the fashion in San Francisco, and men and women and sometimes even families that could have bought and staffed a Nob Hill or Western Addition mansion were happily ensconced in a suite at the Palace or Baldwin's.

Obviously the hotels of different ranks attracted different kinds of residents. Even the finest establishments quickly gained reputations regarding the type of people living there. The Occidental was especially popular for a residence, according to Lloyd. "Many of the California Street speculators luxuriate there; capitalists; lawyers 'up in the profession,' with large incomes; wealthy, retired merchants; favorite employees with large salaries; rich widows; and 'ladies' and 'gentlemen,' are among the resident guests." The "more modest-appearing" Cosmopolitan, on the other hand, had "not so much of the society *ton* as the Occidental, yet it reposes on an elegant dignity, very much in accord with the tastes of gentlemen inclined to the old school style." Lloyd was quick to add that "a residence at the Cosmopolitan, however, does not detract from one's reputation, but rather indicates a retiring disposition."

All these hotels had dining rooms. Some of them, like Baldwin's, Lick House, or the Palace, were justly famous for their cuisine as well as the elegant surroundings and attentive service. Others like the What Cheer House served simple, well-prepared food and plenty of it at workingman's prices. The hotels which were patronized by French, German, or Spanish travelers and residents served the food reminiscent of their homeland.

Some tourists were quite content to take all their meals in the hotel dining rooms. Often they did not have much choice, because they had paid for three meals a day along with their room rate if the hotel operated under the American plan. Taking every meal at the hotel certainly made traveling easier. The stranger did not have to search out a place to eat every time he was hungry.

Some tourists didn't mind that inconvenience, because they

were curious to see how San Franciscans lived, and they had heard so much about the city's restaurants. "San Francisco is famed for its restaurants," wrote New York State born Samuel Williams who worked for the *San Francisco Evening Bulletin* and wrote an article on the city for *Scribner's Monthly* in 1875.

In no city in America are these establishments so numerous in proportion to the population. They number between two and three hundred, and it is safe to say that at least thirty thousand people take their meals at them. They are of all grades and prices—from the "Poodle Dog," Martin's and the Maison Dorée, where a meal costs from $1.50 to $20—down to the Miners' Restaurant, where it costs only forty cents. Between these extremes are a large number of French, German, and Italian restaurants were one may get a royal breakfast for half a dollar, a lunch for twenty-five cents, and a dinner, including claret, for seventy-five cents, *a la carte*. A tenderloin steak (and there is no better beef in the world than here), potatoes, bread and butter, and coffee will cost fifty cents; a lamb chop, potatoes, bread and butter, and coffee, twenty-five cents; an omelet or eggs boiled, scrambled or fried, with coffee, and bread and butter, thirty-five cents. A grade lower down, but in places cleanly and entirely respectable, one gets three dishes for twenty-five cents, and may find quite a decent meal for twenty to thirty cents.

Writing just a year later in his *Lights & Shades of San Francisco*, B. E. Lloyd thought that the most fashionable restaurant in town was the Maison Dorée at 217 Kearny Street. The food was French, the appointments the extreme of Victorian elegance, and the company a cross section of San Francisco's *beau monde:* well-to-do uptown ladies and their daughters out for an afternoon of shopping, Montgomery Street financiers enjoying some of their money on a long lunch, and "high-toned young gentlemen who sport delicate canes, glossy hats, spotless kids and unruffled linen."

Equally elegant, though a shade less respectable, was the Poodle Dog at Grant Avenue and Bush Street. Although the Poodle Dog had been around since 1849 next to the site of the first St. Francis Hotel at Grant Avenue and Clay Street, it did not come into its stylish own until it moved to new quarters at Grant Avenue

and Bush Street in 1868. Apparently Lloyd was quite fond of the place. "There is no question as to the excellence of the *cuisine*," he wrote in 1876. "The pastry is the most delicate, and the wines the finest flavored. The tables are artistically ornamented, and the cutlery and ware have the 'real' ring."

With his eye for scandal, Lloyd was probably much more interested in the clientele than in the food itself. The first floor dining room was frequented by the same respectable folk as the Maison Dorée and other high-toned restaurants. The second floor was banquet rooms. But it was the private rooms on the third, fourth, and fifth floors that San Franciscans whispered about. Lloyd wrote: "If a registry were kept of all the after-dark patrons, giving also their companions, the publicity of it would be a startling disclosure to the social world." Every private room had sofas and locks on the door as well as dining tables, and there were even suites that included a parlor, bedroom, and bathroom so that the men and their lady friends might spend the night.

San Francisco women, like women in every city, had their favorite shopping promenade. In the 1870s and 1880s, a six-block-long stroll, known as "the Line," started at Baldwin's Hotel at Market and Powell streets, went down the north side of Market to Kearny, and down Kearny to Bush. Visitors weren't all that interested in buying the same goods that were sold or actually produced in their home towns. They wanted to see something different and to experience the things that made San Francisco such an unusual place.

For the quaint and different, nothing surpassed a visit to Meiggs Wharf, near the foot of Powell Street, now the site of Fisherman's Wharf and Pier 45. The surrounding North Beach was picturesque, because it slumbered after the speculative boom of the early 1850s. Ramshackle frame buildings lined the streets and clung to the hillsides, much as they had twenty or thirty years earlier, except now they were just a little more run-down looking. "It has an age," wrote one newspaper in 1872, "and in a new city anything that can boast or even remind us of the past is relished in the garishness of fresh buildings and fresh paint."

Warner's Cobweb Palace

Interior, Warner's Cobweb Palace

Meiggs Wharf hadn't changed much since the 1850s except that the last 300 feet had blown away during a gale in 1864. Nautical and "curiosity-shop-like" establishments clustered around the land end of the wharf, and visitors found a "quaintness" here "that would not be amiss in the ancient quarters of London itself." Meiggs Wharf was a "lounging place" for "a few specimens of ancient mariners," according to one newspaper. "There is a cherished association for them in those relics that strew the locality. Sitting on an old figurehead that lies ignominiously on the ground, those fossilized seamen, surrounded by souvenirs of the lands and seas of their wanderings, smoke their black clay pipes and tell many wonderful stories of scenes and adventures some of which date back half a century. And they never lack an audience," be it neighborhood children or tourists in search of just that sort of atmosphere.

The best-known spot on Meiggs Wharf was old Abe Warner's Cobweb Palace. Abe Warner was quite a sight with his unruly white hair, long beard, and butcher's top hat. He had once been a butcher in New York City's Fulton Market. His saloon was as unusual looking as he was. The three rooms looked like some aged sailor's attic, covered with years of dust. Everywhere there were seafaring souvenirs — South Sea Island warclubs, an Eskimo canoe and totem pole, masks and screens from the Orient. There was always something going on at the Cobweb Palace. Cats and dogs wandered in and out of the place and screeching parrots, magpies, and parakeets flew around at will. Just outside the front door Warner had cages with monkeys and two California cinnamon bears. Warner liked spiders, too, and the saloon ceiling was festooned with years' and years' accumulation of spider webs.

Warner's was more than just the picture of studied chaos. The seafood was good. The specialties were clam chowder, cracked crab, and mussels Bordelaise. But Warner was running a drinking establishment as well as a restaurant and informal museum. His bar served some of the finest wines, brandies, and liquors to be found in San Francisco. The place closed in 1897 when Warner retired at the age of eighty.

Nob Hill was another sight that visitors were sure to talk about back home. San Francisco could not boast a broad Parisian-style boulevard, with a handsome mall running down the center, such as Boston's impressive Commonwealth Avenue. Nor had San Francisco's millionaires found one street on which to build their mansions one after another in a parade of wealth, like New York's far-famed Fifth Avenue. San Francisco's richest men instead had selected the very top of Nob Hill as their city's most fashionable address.

What other city in America had such a spectacular setting for its finest mansions? Long before the Big Four and Bonanza Kings had fixed upon this spot or even made their fortunes in railroading and mining, San Franciscans were climbing Fern Hill or the Clay Street Hill, as it was known, to enjoy a view of the city and its environs that was "unsurpassed for life and variety." A favorite destination was the corner of Mason and Sacramento streets. Here "you command the business portion of the city," wrote one reporter, "while turning toward the right the eye follows the scattering

Opposite, The California Street cable car

Mark Hopkins mansion

houses until they are lost at the foot of Twin Peaks and in the hazy horizon of San Mateo. The sweep of the Bay can be seen from the mouth of the Sacramento River to the distant point where the sea and sky meet. . . . On the city side the irregular outline of the wharves is concealed by a forest of masts, while here and there a cloud of dense, black smoke shows that a river or ocean steamer is preparing to go out. Across the Bay, the nine miles on clear days looking to be not more than three stretch away the houses and suburban villas of Oakland, Alameda, and Berkeley."

Nob Hill was too steep for horse-drawn omnibuses or street railroad cars. Without public transportation, it had remained reasonably open for so central a location. The beginning of cable car service on Clay Street in 1873 and on California Street in 1878 made Nob Hill instantly accessible and fashionable.

The first mansion was the James Ben Ali Haggin residence, completed in 1873 at the southeast corner of Taylor and Washington streets. Haggin and his family had been living in the modest frame building that Grace Church had erected in 1850 at the southwest corner of Powell and John streets. If Haggin suffered any deprivation while living in the ex-church, he more than made up for it when he moved to Nob Hill.

Haggin's mansion was the "equal, if not superior, to any residences previously celebrated . . . in design, beauty, finish, and size," according to one newspaper. The Parrot residence on Folsom Street and the other Rincon Hill mansions had finally met their match. Haggin's mansion would "materially add to the architectural renown of San Francisco, as well as furnish additional proof of the great wealth and aesthetical tastes of our moneyed men."

The Haggin house was ninety feet square, and with its high basement, two full floors, and stylish mansard roof it added up to fifty feet in height. The facade displayed the Italianate style, but Messrs. Kenitzer & Raun, the architects, had not let their imaginations run wild. "There is no extravagance in column or balustrade," observed one critic, "and on the other hand there is nothing severely plain. A happy medium has been struck between lavish ornament and niggardly simplicity."

The interior more than made up for whatever ostentation the facade lacked. There were sixty-one rooms, not including three conservatories and numerous bathrooms and room-sized closets. The rooms were huge — a parlor thirty-four by twenty-seven feet, a sitting room twenty-five by eighteen, a library twenty-four by twenty-one, and a dining room thirty-five by twenty-one. All the appointments were properly lavish, but the most-noticed part was the plasterwork, which was reputedly "superior to everything of the sort that has been attempted on this coast." The plaster for the walls was as hard as cement and three coats thick. The ceiling cornices, moldings, and centerpieces were "bold and elaborate, the designs in every instance being new and beautiful."

The house stood at the corner of Taylor and Washington streets, but its grounds extended down the rest of the block to Clay Street. Haggin was one of the leading horsemen in town, and he built a two-story-tall stable and carriage house measuring twenty-eight by 127 feet, on the other corner of the property. The facade was redwood and cedar oiled and varnished, and the interior was as "commodious and perfectly appointed as a gentleman can desire."

Haggin did more than build the first mansion on Nob Hill; he kicked off a mansion building spree among the town's millionaires. In 1879 the *Elite Directory* observed that "the rage for splendid houses began with the costly country seats at Menlo and the building of the Haggin house. . . . Since then it has seemed to be the aim to make each new private residence finer, more artistic, costlier than its predecessor."

General David Colton, who was so involved with the Big Four that some newspapers jokingly referred to the "Big Four and a Half," built an Italianate-style mansion at California and Taylor streets, with a thirty-three-by-sixty-three-foot music room and art gallery, which boasted a domed twenty-four-foot ceiling. Collis P. Huntington, one of the Big Four, later bought the house.

For all its grandeur, the Colton house was overshadowed by Leland Stanford's $2,000,000 mansion at California and Powell streets and Charles Crocker's residence which filled the block now occupied by Grace Cathedral. Even before these mansions were completed, San Franciscans knew that they would soon be surpassed by Mark Hopkin's improbable-looking $3,000,000 castellated mansion. People rarely bothered to stop and look any more at the Haggin mansion which had started it all. In 1894 the *San Francisco News Letter* declared that the "house, although charmingly appointed, [was] not commodious enough for larger gatherings."

The Nob Hill mansions were more than architectural wonders. They were symbols of their owners' wealth, success, and personal worth. The massive bank buildings on Montgomery Street, impressive as they were, did not excite onlookers in the same way. The money and power of these institutions was abstract and remote, but sightseers could readily identify with another man's achievements and even dream that someday they might live in just such a house.

Nob Hill was an unabashed show of extravagance and *nouveau riche* vulgarity. But, "this profuse display of individual wealth has been attended with a corresponding development of taste," declared the *Elite Directory* of 1879. "Many of them have been filled with pictures from home or foreign easels selected with a discretion that indicates a growing culture. This passion for tasteful decoration has extended through society."

No matter how rich or how big San Francisco was becoming, plenty of people always worried that the city was culturally inferior to the East Coast. A mansion or hotel or bank building, no matter how grand, could not be praised merely on its own merits. It always had to be compared to similar buildings elsewhere in the country and judged their superior, whether it was or not. One San Francisco newspaper described the Leland Stanford mansion in room-by-room detail, as it neared completion in 1876, and not unexpectedly pronounced it "the finest private residence in America." The newspaper could not let the statement go at that. The Stanford mansion had to be evaluated alongside others around the country. "Compared with the solid elegance here seen, the country residence of Jay Cooke, over which the Eastern newspapers became delirious, was a mere shell. Many houses in New York show more elaborate work in detail, but they are cramped out of proportion by

the value of the ground on which they stand, and their beauties seem dwarfed and insignificant." The reporter went on, "A. T. Stewart's $3,000,000 white marble Fifth Avenue mansion and Le Grand Lockwood's Norwalk, Connecticut villa, likewise, were inferior to Stanford's residence." Then the critic got tangled up in all his rhetoric and cast doubt on his earlier evaluations. The only residence in the entire country equal to Stanford's, it seemed, was the Fargo mansion in Buffalo, New York.

San Franciscans need not have been so defensive about the city or their taste. The Nob Hill mansions may have been more than a little overblown, even by the permissive architectural standards of the 1870s and 1880s, but so were rich men's homes everywhere. San Franciscans were sometimes embarrassed that this domestic grandeur was only built of redwood, with the exception of James Flood's incongruous-looking brownstone pile. But redwood, the local building material, was appropriate to local buildings. What's more, redwood allowed the Big Four and Bonanza Kings to act out their wildest architectural fantasies, which would have been out of the question with the brick or stone employed in the rest of the country.

The Mark Hopkins mansion best epitomized the brash architectural spirit of Nob Hill. Amelia Ransome Neville, who had moved to San Francisco from Ohio in 1856 at the age of nineteen, recalled this turreted redwood castle in her reminiscences of San Francisco, *The Fantastic City.*

Diagonally across California Street from the Flood house stood the Hopkins castle, whose gray towers could be seen from the bay and far south of the city. Terraced gardens fell away on the steep hillside at the back, and surrounding them was a mighty stone wall, forty feet high against the terrace of the lower level along Pine Street. There, massive oak doors swung on iron hinges to permit the entrance, not of armored knights on horseback, but of basket phaetons, the family barouche, rockaways, and broughams. A long looped "S" of a driveway led upward to the house, and when lamps along its way shone at night, with the castle windows alight, the effect from the city below was enchanting.

Within, the house was a mass of anachronisms. One entered portals of a feudal castle into a court of a doge's palace, all carved Italian walnut with a gallery around the second story where murals of Venetian scenes were set between the arches.

They were the work of Jules Tavenier, French artist, who stopped in California after a trip to the South Seas, where he painted long before Gauguin.

A beautiful place in itself was this central court, as were many individual rooms in these anachronistic mansions filled with rare inlaid woods, marble mosaics, and rich furnishings. It is said that the architects measured shelves in the libraries of some of them and ordered yards of books from dealers to fill the spaces, as they would order fixtures. Of the truth of this I am not certain, but astonishing effects in servants' liveries I well remember. The Negro coachman of one new millionaire wore a suit of white cloth with black velvet buttons as large as butter-dishes, and orange-topped boots—his own taste, I fancy.

In spite of its absurdities, the Hopkins house achieved a general effect of stately magnificence, a sort of Mrs. Malaprop dignity. And it looked enduring. But alas, this feudal castle was built of wood painted the color of stone, and it burned like any shanty in 1906—as did all the Nob Hill palaces.

Nob Hill was completely transformed in the ten years after the Clay Street cable car line started running. A few San Franciscans, however, remembered the days when it had been what one newspaper called "a Sahara of desolation." In the 1850s and 1860s, "sand was everywhere, with nothing to relieve it but clumps of live oak, low, gnarled and bushy, which seemed to flourish where even the hardy lupine failed to gain a foothold." The houses were few and far between, and the largest was the Tillinghast place, a large, square house, with Southern-style verandahs on all four sides, at the northeast corner of Pine and Mason streets. The very top of the hill was a shantytown where several large families lived in shacks made from scrap lumber and tin they had scrounged around town. Their chickens, ducks, cows, and pigs roamed around the highest barnyard in San Francisco.

Another long-vanished part of Nob Hill was Julia Dean's cottage, which stood on California Street on the future site of the

Remains of early Nob Hill, view from Hopkins mansion looking north

Leland Stanford mansion. Julia Dean was an actress, and she bought the house in 1859, hoping to retire in San Francisco and live out her days tending the flower garden and ornamental shrubs surrounding the cottage. Soon after she bought the house her career foundered, and she had trouble paying the loan she had taken to acquire the property. She went to England to revive her career. "The venture proved disasterous," recalled one newspaper, "and she returned brokenhearted only to see her home sold, her furniture and pictures scattered, and to die several years after — long before her prime — in the hopeless struggle to retrieve her waning fortune."

Banker Erwin Davis bought Julia Dean's cottage but never lived in it. He had his own ideas for the property. He demolished her home, except for its framework, which became the nucleus for his own sprawling house, topped with a cupola. The spot was further transformed when the city graded California Street and left the houses on the north side as much as sixty feet in the air. Davis found himself twenty feet above the new street level, and he built a stone retaining wall around his property. He also built a grandiose four-story-tall stable on the rear of his lot facing Pine Street.

The property, however, seemed to be cursed. One rainy winter night a section of Davis' wall collapsed and fell into the street. The pressure from all that damp soil had been too great. Davis repaired the breach, but the wall was thought to be unsafe thereafter. His home wasn't quite right either. "Though the house dominated everything in the neighborhood," wrote one newspaper, "and gave a vantage from which one could survey the city and the bay, yet the effect was marred by its great height from the street." Then Davis lost his money in a number of ill-advised speculations, and he left San Francisco for London.

Leland Stanford bought the property, and "the whirligig of time now brought in its revenges," according to one newspaper. "The banker had effaced every trace of the actress' hands. Now, in turn, with the grotesque irony of circumstances, his own costly efforts in architecture and landscape gardening were swept away by the Railroad King. The magnificent stable was removed; the ele-

gant mansion followed; the wall, with its fine iron gates, was demolished; the ornamental trees uprooted; the carefully shorn terraces were plowed up and scraped down and carried away."

Around 1880 a few landmarks of the past still survived among the mansions of the Big Four and the Bonanza Kings. Millionaire Nicholas Luning's one-time home at Pine and Powell streets was almost unchanged, although the flower garden had not been tended since his death. A combination grocery store and residence, with sharply peaked roof, at the southwest corner of Clay and Powell streets was an even stranger relic. Its framework had been brought around the Horn in the early 1850s, and the building had originally stood at Pine and Powell streets.

Chinatown was a favorite sight the tourists never missed. All late nineteenth-century American cities had districts given over to Blacks and one European ethnic group or another. But the Chinese were a totally exotic and even strange race to most Americans. Nowhere in the country were their numbers greater or more visible than in San Francisco. Chinatown was a world unto itself, and San Francisco guidebooks declared, "the few white stragglers that are met upon the streets are scarcely more numerous than would be found in any open seaport town in China, and they gaze about them with the same curiosity as do those who are visiting for the first time the cities of the Celestial Empire."

The first Chinese to arrive in California were two men and one woman who landed in San Francisco in the summer of 1848 and set out for the gold fields. Thereafter the Chinese immigration turned into a flood. The *Annals* estimated that 10,000 Chinese arrived in San Francisco in 1852 alone. At first they tried their luck panning for gold but, like other 49'ers, began to return to San Francisco when the mining life proved more arduous and less profitable than they expected.

By the beginning of 1850 there were 800 Chinese in town, and the number had risen to 3,000 a year later. In the Gold Rush years, most San Franciscans were a uniformly motley group, dressing the same, enduring similar daily hardships, and having the same dreams, even though they had come from all over America

Chinese laundry

and the world. The Chinese stood out, even then, because of their race and their native garb. "Go where he [the visitor] will," wrote the *San Francisco Herald* in 1852, and "he meets natives of the Celestial Empire, and subjects of the uncle to the moon, with their long plaited queues or tails, very wide pantaloons bagging behind, and curiously formed head coverings—some resembling inverted soup plates, and others fitting as close to the scalp as the scalp does to the Celestial cranium it covers."

The Chinese settled along Sacramento Street, around Kearny and Grant. But that area had not yet turned into an exclusively Chinese district. In 1852 the *Herald* observed: "They are not confined to any particular street or locality, but are scattered over the city and suburbs." Some men were farming at the outskirts of town, while 150 Chinese were living in a picturesque fishing village, complete with twenty-five boats, where Mission Creek emptied into the Bay south of Rincon Point.

More and more Chinese immigrants, however, began to live and work around Sacramento Street, and by the mid-1850s it was

known as Little China. Around 1860 San Franciscans began calling the area Chinatown. By the mid-1870s, Chinatown had spread out to nine square blocks: Clay, Washington, Jackson, and Pacific streets for the two blocks between Kearny and Stockton, and the four blocks of Grant Avenue from Sacramento to Pacific.

The Chinese had easily taken over the area, because white tenants and landlords fled at the sight of the first Chinese on their block. B. E. Lloyd explained how it happened. "Any building adjacent to one occupied by Chinese is rendered undesirable to white folks, and although the landlord may hold out inducements to white tenants and refuse any and all offers from Chinese, heavy taxes and no income from the property will soon convince him that John's money is preferable to no money at all, and he finally succumbs to the pressure." Once the Chinese occupied a building, they seldom moved out. Again Lloyd told why this happened and displayed the prejudice of the times.

They simply make the building uninhabitable for decent white folk. Their manner of living accomplishes this, without any extra precaution on their part. They will divide the rooms into numerous diminutive compartments by unsightly partitions, and the smoke and rank odor from their open fires and opium pipes discolors the ceilings and walls and renders the whole building offensive, both to sight and smell, so that the expense of renovating it would not be offset by the rental receipts of six months or a year.

Though most San Franciscans found the Chinese strange, and even offensive, they were pleased to hire them to do their laundry and housework. Their unusual customs made a visit to Chinatown all the more exciting. Visitors were disappointed if they expected the streets and buildings to look like those in China. Almost all the buildings were built by American carpenters and were originally intended for American occupants. The changes that the Chinese made in the buildings, wrote Lloyd, "together with the signs, placards, and various gaudy ornaments with which the outer walls, windows, and doors are bedizened, almost conceal the architectural style of the buildings; but when the attention is called to it, the handiwork of the Caucasian mechanic is discovered through

Chinatown grocery store

the semi-transformation, and the delusion that this is an oriental city, *in the Orient,* is dispelled." The Chinese used these buildings much differently than their previous American inhabitants. Not one square foot went to waste in living or working arrangements. A family of six often lived in a single room no larger than eight by ten feet and sometimes worked there as well. Their shops and business places were just as cramped, according to Lloyd.

They are all crowded with goods, from floor to ceiling; narrow counters, with scarce room enough for the salesman to pass to and fro behind them, are the rule, and rude shelves suspended from the ceilings, loaded with all manner of merchandise, obstruct the view and render the whole incommodious. But yet there is much order in the arrangements. Every article is kept in its particular place, and in all the apparent confusion there is complete system. Whatever is desired from package or shelf is readily found—each attendant knowing just where to put hands upon it.

The Chinese spilled out of the buildings and into the streets, too. "The side-walks are monopolized by them, with their little tables of fruits, nuts, and cigars," observed Lloyd. "The cobbler, tinner, chair-mender, and jack-of-all-trades, claim, by squatter right, a seat upon a box or door-sill, where to ply their trades; the alleys, lanes, and by-ways give forth dense clouds of smoke from the open fires, where cooking is performed, and the house-tops are white with drying garments, fluttering from the network of clothes-lines that are placed thereon by enterprising laundrymen. Even across narrow streets lines are thrown upon which are placed to dry all manner of wearing apparel."

The more adventuresome tourists in Chinatown could stop at one of the restaurants known to welcome Westerners. The guidebooks, however, warned that "everything pertaining to the banquet is cast in the Oriental mold. There is no apparent attempt to imitate American customs or style, either in table etiquette or in the preparation of food." The only concessions that Americans could expect were a host who could speak English and knives and forks instead of chopsticks. Some of the food, according to contemporary accounts, seems quite similar to that served in Chinatown restaurants today—boned duck with grated nuts and mushrooms, chicken stewed with chestnuts, and shrimp with leek and bamboo shoots. But guidebooks also warned that some food would be "insipid or offensive to the American taste." Those dishes, undoubtedly, included nineteenth-century specialties like brochettes of chicken hearts or shark fins fried in batter.

Chinatown was most attractive to tourists during its festivals. The most colorful, of course, was New Year's. "The Chinese quarter . . . is a scene of gay life and heathen revelry, that surpasses description," wrote Lloyd.

The streets are all aglow with fantastic holiday trappings. . . . Much fantastic-colored bunting is displayed from windows and house-tops, and depending over the walks are Chinese lanterns of every size, color, and design; while the doors, windows, and walls of the houses, both inside and out, are decked with placards bearing all sorts of strange characters, wrought in gilt, black, and bright red. . . .

When their use is not prohibited by a city ordinance, the roar of fire-crackers and Chinese bombs is incessant, and deafening as the noise of battle. . . . Squeaking Chinese fiddles and kettledrums add their harsh tones to the general discord. To those unaccustomed to the habits of this people, the scene is one of utmost disorder and confusion. . . .

The sidewalks, and even the middle of the streets, are thronged with eager life. Wealthy merchants, clothed in long priestly robes of purple silk or satin, pass to and fro, busy in conducting some particular parts of the ceremonies of the celebration, and women and children, dressed in most peculiar and brilliant attire, their faces painted till they look more like dolls or toys than humans, mingle in the motley throng.

This was the image of Chinatown most visitors carried home. But the New Year's celebrations and restaurants had very little to do with life in Chinatown. The predominant, inescapable fact of life for the Chinese was terrible overcrowding. In 1885 a committee appointed by the Board of Supervisors declared that a "safe minimum estimate of the population is about 30,000 Chinese living in twelve blocks." Another survey of Chinatown, four years later, counted 45,000 residents within the same area.

Tourists and San Franciscans who wandered into Chinatown could see the cramped shops, the laundry flapping in the breeze in alleys and on rooftops, and the craftsmen who had no place to work except in doorways along the sidewalks. But these sights merely looked unusual, even quaint, to the casual observer. Anyone who explored Chinatown thoroughly or really thought about what they observed on the streets, would have seen the misery and squalid living conditions that most Chinese endured. In 1870 a reporter from the *Alta* accompanied the city health inspectors as they made their rounds in Chinatown. His story showed how bad things really were.

Rooms, which would be considered close quarters for a single white man, were occupied by shelves a foot and a half wide, placed one above the other on all sides of the room, and on these from twenty to forty Chinamen are stowed away to sleep. In many of these places there is scarcely a chance for even a breath of fresh air to creep in, and the occupants are obliged to breathe over and over again the limited allowance. How life can exist in such a place is a mystery. Besides being crowded in the manner above stated, in many of the lodginghouses filth has been allowed to accumulate to the depth of several inches and in a number of instances the moisture, leech-like, was found dripping from rooms above. In the cellars and underground coops, which frequently extended half a block, there is no way to obtain a circulation of air—all that does creep in being by the narrow door of the street. Here they burn oil lamps and cook their food, the smoke from which fills the air, and curls lazily up out of the door when it chances to be open.

A public outcry followed this article, and the Board of Supervisors passed a law which became known as the "Cubic Air" act. According to its provisions, rooms could not be rented out as sleeping quarters unless there were 500 cubic feet of air for each person. This law did not help the Chinese. It didn't offer any way to alleviate the poverty and overcrowding within Chinatown which led to these conditions, and it was enforced only in Chinatown and not in the rest of the city.

The Chinese had never been really welcome in San Francisco, except as low-paid servants in middle class households and as workmen in the mines and for the railroads. In fact, San Franciscans were downright hostile to the "heathen Chinee" since Gold Rush days. "The manners and habits of the Chinese are very repugnant to Americans in California," declared the *Annals* in the early 1850s. "Of different language, blood, religion and character, inferior in most mental and bodily qualities, the Chinaman is looked upon by some as only a little superior to the Negro, and by others as somewhat inferior." San Franciscans, furthermore, saw all sorts of unpleasant characteristics in the Chinese. " 'John's' person," wrote the *Annals*, "does not smell very sweetly; his color and the features of his face are unusual; his penuriousness is extreme; his lying, knavery, and natural cowardice are proverbial; he dwells apart from white persons, herding only with countrymen."

The Chinese did indeed live together in their own communities, which was understandable, given the prevailing prejudices. But this clannishness was an unpardonable sin to most Americans. "Indians, Spaniards of many provinces, Hawaiians, Japanese, Chinese, Malays, Tartars and Russians, must all give place to the resistless flood of Anglo-Saxon or American progress," declared the *Annals*. "These peoples need not, and most of them probably cannot be swept from the face of the earth; but undoubtedly their national characteristics and opposing qualities and customs must be materially modified, and closely assimilated to those of the civilizing and dominant race."

The Chinese resisted American values and society, and there was "a strong feeling—prejudice it may be—existing in California against all Chinaman," continued the *Annals*, "and they are nicknamed, cuffed about and treated very unceremoniously by every other class." Legal harassment went back to the Gold Rush days. There was a $20 a month mining license charge for all foreigners enacted in 1850. That fee was reduced to $3 and $4 a month in 1852 and 1853, and it was the largest revenue source for the state until it was repealed in 1870. Even though the license fees paid by the Chinese generated one quarter of the state's income, Governor John Bigler asked the Legislature in 1852 to ban the immigration of "coolies" into California. The proposal was fiercely debated in the Legislature and in San Francisco but nothing came of it.

Other laws made life difficult for the Chinese and denied them their civil rights. There was the 1855 act forbidding the testimony of Chinese in court cases involving whites. The Chinese could not become citizens and, therefore, had no vote. They were turned away from the San Francisco County Hospital in the 1860s and 1870s. The Board of Supervisors passed special taxes for laundry owners, fishermen, and vegetable sellers, all jobs dominated by the Chinese. Another ordinance outlawed the yeo-ho poles with which they carried laundry and vegetables around town. But the most insulting law was the "queue ordinance." No prisoner in a city jail could wear his hair longer than one inch. That meant Chinese prisoners would lose their queues, which were so important to their dignity.

San Franciscans relished rumors about dark doings in Chinatown. Of course, the Chinese were godless heathens in the eyes of Roman Catholics and Protestants, and churches all over the country dispatched missionaries to save them. Then there were the stories about rampant prostitution in Chinatown. That was true, just as it was in many other parts of town. But apparently the Chinese whores were more devious than their white sisters; they were said to be luring innocent young white men into wicked ways and giving them all sorts of diseases.

Dr. C. C. O'Donnell came up with one of the most outrageous accusations against the Chinese. He was the city coroner and, in his annual report for 1885–86, he blamed the Chinese for thirteen of the eighty-six suicides in the previous year. In order to protect public health, he suggested that all Chinese be sent from the city and Chinatown be demolished.

These proposals were ridiculous, but there was a sad element of truth in Dr. O'Donnell's report. It was not that the Chinese were directly driving white men to suicide, just that cheap Chinese labor was denying white men jobs. "Inability to obtain work actuated thirteen of our noble citizens to sacrifice their lives rather than lead a life of crime," wrote Dr. O'Donnell. "[They] were crowded out of every avenue of employment by the base Coolie slaves of Asia."

Hard times had befallen San Francisco and all California in the 1870s. The prosperity of the 1850s and 1860s was only a memory. The transcontinental railroad, which everyone had expected to bring even greater wealth to California, turned out to do just the opposite when it opened in 1869. Local factories were no longer protected from the full brunt of East Coast competition by the time and expense of shipping goods around Cape Horn. And San Francisco lost its economic influence over the interior, because East Coast merchandise could now be shipped directly to other cities. To make matters worse, thousands of Easterners flocked to California on the railroad. The Panic of 1873, which crippled the national economy until the late 1870s, sent even more people out West in search of jobs and a better life. But jobs were already scarce in California, and the oversupply of men wanting to work depressed wages.

Workingmen needed someone or something to blame for their troubles, and property owners, the railroads, and the Nob Hill millionaires were frequent targets for their orators and parades. But those men had the money and power to fight back.

The Chinese, however, were defenseless, disenfranchised, and already the target of prejudice. So the insults to the Chinese and the discriminatory laws continued into the early twentieth century, even as the courts were striking down earlier "anti-coolie" ordinances as violations of the federal Civil Rights Act of 1870 and the due process and equal protection clauses of the Fourteenth Amendment.

The hostility toward the Chinese turned to violence. The situation in San Francisco never got as bad as it did in Los Angeles, where mobs killed twenty Chinese in 1871. But things did get out of hand in San Francisco in 1877. After a sand-lot political rally in front of the half-finished City Hall on July 23, hundreds of men headed for Chinatown, beating up any Chinese they found along the way and looting and burning laundries and shops in Chinatown. The mobs even tried to cut the firemen's water hoses when they arrived to put out the fires. The violence lasted three days until the militia, police, and a hastily formed volunteer Committee of Safety restored order.

Casual observers of the San Francisco scene overlooked the poverty and desperation which drove some men to these acts just as they failed to see what life in Chinatown was really like. According to conventional thought, San Francisco was a good place to live if you were unwilling or unable to find work. "San Francisco is the Elysium of 'bummers,' " wrote Samuel Williams in his 1875 *Scribner's Monthly* article. "Nowhere else can a worthless fellow, too lazy to work, too cowardly to steal, get on so well. The climate befriends him, for he can sleep out of doors four fifths of the year, and the free lunch [in saloons] opens to him boundless vistas of carnal delights."

If any of these "bummers" read *Scribner's Monthly*, they must have laughed bitterly at the suggestion that their lives were "vistas of carnal delights." Many of them were living in rooming houses or flophouse hotels south of Market Street where open cesspools and inadequate sewers bred diptheria and typhoid. But they at least had a roof over their heads. Hundreds of men, perhaps thousands, slept in the haybunks along the Vallejo Street wharf or in the sails of ships anchored in the harbor. Others lived in the sprawling lumber yards east of Beale Street or in tin and scrap wood shacks in the city dumps. So many indigent men lived in the dump just south of Townsend Street, on land reclaimed from Mission Bay, that the newspapers gave the area the name "Ragtown."

Private charities did not help the "down and out." The Sailors Home, which occupied the former United States Marine Hospital at Rincon Point, had a noble-sounding name and purpose, but it turned out to be one of the leading crimp joints in town. Men who unwittingly sought aid there often found themselves shanghaied and forced into service on ships against their will. Yet the State Legislature appropriated funds for the Home every year.

City institutions did not do much better by the people they were supposed to help. In the early 1890s, William Randolph Hearst sent one of his reporters, a young woman named Winifred Sweet, out on an unusual assignment for the *Examiner*. In the middle of a weekday afternoon, she put on some soiled old clothes and headed for Market Street. There she pretended to be sick and collapsed to the sidewalk to see what would happen. A crowd quickly formed, and the police arrived and hustled her away to a city hospital in a police van, which shook and jolted as it ran over the cobblestone streets. Winifred Sweet's travails had only begun. Once she got to the hospital, no medical treatment was forthcoming. Instead "one by one every person present stopped near me and sniffed my breath. The policeman was the last of all. 'No, I can't smell any whiskey,' said he. 'I wish to heaven I could say as much for you,' thought I." Finally a doctor examined her. She was given an emetic of hot water and mustard, and sent on her way, back to the *Examiner*, in this case, to write her article on the appalling treatment she had received.

San Francisco had more than its share of insanity and suicides. These problems had been around since the Gold Rush days. Many 49'ers had arrived in San Francisco exhausted in body and spirit. Their despondency was aggravated by the difficult living conditions and the distance from home. The state was quick to organize an Asylum for the Insane, but its doctors apparently were more interested in improving the inmates' moral behavior than in getting to the source of their troubles. Nearly two thirds of the inmates were unmarried men, which is not surprising considering the lack of women and families in San Francisco in the 1850s. The Resident Physician's report for 1854 concluded that "celibacy tends to augment the number of lunatics from the restraints which it imposes and the vices to which unmarried persons are more or less exposed."

What exactly were these vices which led to insanity and hospitalization? "Intemperance of spirits" was the leading cause, rather than a symptom, according to the report. The second cause was masturbation. "The perversion of this propensity [for sex] is the source of innumerable evils," declared the Resident Physician, "and the only remedy is the suggestion and recommendation of Spurzheim: 'that of instructing young persons in the terrible and fatal consequences of improper gratification of this passion, as preferable and better than keeping and permitting them to grow up in a state of ignorance, compromising and, in the end, destroying their own bodily and mental constitutions, and that of their descendants.' "

Although the Resident Physician adhered to Victorian morality, he offered some advice for the psychologically troubled that sounds surprisingly up to date. "Individuals thus afflicted should arouse themselves and strive against every feeling of despair and despondency; should seek active employment, industrious toil, manual labor, and ardently engage in the duties of life," he declared. "Then, with sensible, moderate and rational habits of life, and fortified with pure and correct principles of morality and religion, if trouble and misfortune come, the mind and feelings will not be enfeebled or crushed, but purified and strengthened." And he had some good advice for those who overindulged in food and drink. "Our manner of living . . . requires, and health demands, a less quantity of food, and drinks of a different and milder nature."

This advice did not alleviate the problem of insanity and suicide in San Francisco. In 1874, 58 people killed themselves, according to city records, and in 1875 that number had risen to 64 people. Suicide "is confined to no particular class of individuals, or no condition or circumstance in life," observed B. E. Lloyd. "Wealth and poverty, sick and well, American, European, Asiatic, male and female, contribute alike to the list of those who willfully commit self-murder."

Lloyd, like everyone else, attributed these suicides to such things as business reverses, family problems, and separation from home. But he realized that the type of person who would pull up stakes back home and come all the way to San Francisco had something to do with the high suicide rate. "The population is not a fair average of the human family," he declared. "The most excitable and unsettled people have been attracted hither from all parts of the world, bringing with them a temperament favorable to the development of insanity. And then the circumstances to which they are exposed are inimical to the exercise of self control."

Gertrude Atherton thought that San Francisco's isolation from the rest of the world was responsible for the problem. She found San Francisco a depressing place, particularly after she returned in the mid-1890s after living in Europe for several years. "I used to walk past those long rows of houses, drab, with box-windows, as alike as a row of lead pencils in a box, visualizing the dull, eventless lives of those who lived in them, depressing my spirits to zero," she recalled years later. "I doubted if anywhere on earth could one feel so isolated, so blue, so stranded, as in San Francisco. Well had it been called the Jumping-Off Place. In the nineties, despite the sentimentalists, it was gray and ugly and depressing."

Crime was another unpleasant fact of life that went back as far as the Gold Rush period. The first money appropriated by the *ayuntamiento*, the town council, organized in July, 1849, purchased the brig *Euphemia* so that it could be converted into a floating

Prison ship Euphemia

prison. But the city fathers were almost powerless to stop violence and crime in those unsettled years. They didn't have the money to hire more than a handful of policemen. Anyway, it would have been almost impossible to restrain the high-spirited 49'ers even with an adequate police force.

Even if the police apprehended a criminal, getting the culprit behind bars was a feat. The courts were a mess. One of the more unusual judges was William B. Almond, who presided over a civil court in 1849 and 1850 in the Portsmouth Square schoolhouse. "The novel and summary manner in which he conducted business and disposed of sometimes very important cases was a source of as much merriment to some and mortification to others as anything else then transpiring in the town," recalled the *Annals*. His Honor sat in an old chair, resting his feet on a fireplace mantel, "paring his corns, or scraping his nails, while the 'learned counsel' briefly presented the case." Judge Almond was not one to listen to flowery speeches, legal precedents, or rambling testimony. There were too many cases awaiting trial for those formalities. As the *Annals* declared: "He was a man of quick discernment and clear judgment; and his opinion once formed, and that sometimes occurred before even the first witness was fully heard, his decision was made."

The prisons were just as casual as the courts. The *Euphemia* did not serve as a prison for long; a creditor of the city repossessed it. But that was not much of a loss. In 1850 the *Courier* had described the *Euphemia* as a "regular Calcutta hole." In 1851 the city built a jail, on dry land this time, but it, too, was badly overcrowded.

Security at the new jail was so bad that eight men escaped during one month in 1851. The building had not even been finished before the first prisoners arrived, and it might have stayed that way for years if Sheriff Jack Hays had not spent some of his own money for its completion. The city hadn't come up with the funds, and he had failed in his attempt to raise the necessary money through public subscription.

Conditions were awful. In 1853 a Grand Jury counted six men in each eight-by-twelve-foot cell, and, not surprisingly, the sanitation problem was appalling. The rules were lax in the early 1850s.

Prisoners were sometimes let out for a night on the town, and one criminal, Mrs. Biddy Gilligan, got even better treatment. She was incarcerated only when there was room for her. On July 17, 1851, the *Alta* reported that she had been arrested fifty times in the previous three months but was always set free because the jails were so badly overcrowded. On August 13, she was in court again for another offense, and the judge actually sent her to jail. But the prison was full by September 12, and Mrs. Gilligan was released. The *Alta* reported that she "went on a bender as soon as she got out yesterday. She ought to be provided for."

Things were no better in the detention cells at the police station in the basement of City Hall. Conditions there were "a disgrace to any civilized city," reported the Grand Jury. At times, thirty to forty men occupied a single room that should have held one quarter that number. There were no sanitary facilities, and the diet was bread and water.

In 1850 the *Annals* had reported "the boldness and number of criminals [were] very alarming. All manner of burglaries, robberies, and thefts were of daily occurrence. So were personal assaults of an aggravated nature; while murders were repeatedly taking place." And don't forget the men who tried to burn down the town several times in 1850 and 1851.

The crime problem had "not sensibly diminished" in 1852, and San Franciscans began to look for ways they could protect their persons and property. Like most men of the Western frontier, San Franciscans carried weapons for their own protection. J. D. Borthwick attended a masquerade ball where no weapons were to be admitted. He didn't like the ball much. There were almost no women there. "But it was worthwhile to go, if only to watch the company arrive, and to see the practical enforcement of the weapon clause in the announcements," he recalled.

Several doorkeepers were in attendance, to whom each man as he entered delivered up his knife or his pistol, receiving a check for it, just as one does for his cane or umbrella at the door of a picture-gallery. Most men drew a pistol from behind their back, and very often a knife along with it; some carried their bowie-knife down the back of their neck, or in their breast;

demure, pious-looking men, in white neckcloths, lifted up the bottom of their waistcoat, and revealed the butt of a revolver; others, after having already disgorged a pistol, pulled up the leg of their trousers, and abstracted a huge bowie-knife from their boot; and there were men, terrible fellows, no doubt, but who were more likely to frighten themselves than anyone else, who produced a revolver from each trouser-pocket, and a bowie-knife from their belt. If any man declared that he had no weapon, the statement was so incredible that he had to submit to be searched; an operation which was performed by the doorkeepers, who, I observed, were occasionally rewarded for their diligence by the discovery of a pistol secreted in some unusual part of the dress.

Walking the streets at night was particularly dangerous. On July 28, 1851 the *Alta* suggested that every person living at the outskirts of town pick up two bricks before he set off on his way. The article did not say whether the bricks were in addition to or in place of the knife or pistol men were supposed to carry at all times.

Crime and violence diminished later in the 1850s and 1860s as San Francisco and the daily lives of the people assumed some semblance of normalcy. But the newspapers were still filled with stories of "garrotings" or muggings on the city streets, murders, and homes and stores being burglarized. It was still unwise to walk alone at the edge of town at night. Around 1860 the city more or less ended at Larkin Street, and one newspaper recalled: "Beyond that point it was venturesome to ramble, as the hills were the haunts of predatory Mexicans, who, by assiduous practice, had reduced the national talent for theft to a fine art."

Still, despite its national reputation for high living and naughtiness, San Francisco was the home of thousands of quite respectable working and middle class families. Husbands went off to jobs six days a week; wives cared for the house and made sure that the children went off to school every morning. In fact, by one important measure, San Francisco was the most domestic, most family-oriented of all large American cities. According to several estimates, a greater percentage of permanent residents owned their own homes in San Francisco than in any other big city in the nation.

John Wesley Probasco residence, 616 Taylor Street

Few neighborhoods in town were more solidly middle class than the Western Addition, beyond Van Ness Avenue. "The houses are nearly all large and handsome, and the great, bare spaces which still disfigure the blocks out on Post and Geary streets are conspicuous by their absence," observed one newspaper in 1879. "In fact, this is one of the handsomest portions of the city, and it shows better than any statistics can do the marvelous strides that the city has taken in the last ten years."

In the 1850s, the Western Addition had been rolling sand dunes, covered with the hardy California lupine, "with only the occasional shanty of a squatter to render the desolation more complete." The only significant house belonged to Henry Perrin Coon, mayor from 1863 to 1867, in the vicinity of Sacramento and Scott streets. Only Bush Street had been graded beyond Larkin Street, and its traffic was mainly funeral processions on the way to rural cemeteries and people leaving town for a country outing. Bush Street, however, offered a way to and from the downtown area, and, one by one, well-to-do men built country houses among the sand dunes. C. J. Hullyer built one of the handsomest in the mid-1860s, an Italianate villa at the corner of Sutter and Gough streets. Bishop William I. Kip moved to the corner of Franklin and Eddy streets when his Rincon Hill home tumbled into the Second Street cut in 1869.

The building boom of middle class row houses swept the Western Addition in the mid-1870s when the outermost edge of city growth reached Van Ness Avenue and pushed beyond. Van Ness Avenue itself was becoming quite a stylish address, and San Franciscans expected that it would soon rival Nob Hill in the wealth of its residents and the architectural display of its homes. In 1876 a group of Van Ness Avenue property owners met to discuss what, if any, special improvements should be made to the street. G. H. Thompson, a civil engineer, recommended that an eighteen-foot-wide strip down the middle of the street be set aside for gardens and a promenade. Unfortunately, nothing came of this idea which would have given San Francisco an ornamental boulevard much like Boston's Commonwealth Avenue or New York City's Park Avenue. Instead the property owners planted a double line of trees on each side of the street. Such a step "will not only be a great embellishment to the city, but enhance the value of property there," declared one newspaper. Furthermore, it said, Van Ness Avenue would "present somewhat the appearance of the Champs Elysees of Paris when the work is done." That fashionable association, in itself, made the plan go through.

No single street in the Western Addition ever equaled Van Ness Avenue. Individual mansions, scattered here and there, were as grand, but the Western Addition was not destined for extravagance. The typical block was lined with the homes of the middle class and well-to-do, each one looking remarkably like its neighbors in scale and ornamentation. The sameness of the houses on each block and the similarity of one street with another was typical of late nineteenth-century middle class urban neighborhoods across the country, developed quickly and on speculation.

Although all Western Addition streets were more or less equal, some were "more equal than others." California Street had more than its share of large and distinctive homes, and the *Elite Directory* of 1879 singled it out as one of the six "most genteel neighborhoods" in town. The only other street beyond Van Ness Avenue to win that recognition was Pacific Avenue. Although only a few homes had been built in Pacific Heights by 1880, the main question in most San Franciscans' minds then was just how desirable the location would become. By 1894 the answer was clear. That year the *San Francisco News Letter* informed its readers that the finest mansions in town, other than the Nob Hill palaces, were being built along Pacific Avenue.

San Francisco's population was 56,802 in 1860. It jumped to 149,473 by 1870, to 233,959 by 1880, and to 298,997 by 1890. The demand for housing pushed city streets and blocks of elaborately ornamented dwellings and flats far into the Mission district. Woodward's Gardens had been in a country setting when it opened in 1866; ten years later its rolling hills and ponds were an anomaly in the midst of the densely built-up city. The Mission was another middle class neighborhood, but with some extraordinary homes on

Pacific Avenue, looking west from Franklin Street

Haley & O'Neill Tract Homestead Association in the Mission

the higher elevations of Dolores and Guerrero streets and even in the flats, along Folsom Street and South Van Ness Avenue between roughly 20th and 26th streets.

In the 1870s, the city pushed out Market Street toward Twin Peaks. Growth had been slow in the area, because a rocky outcropping completely blocked the line of Market Street near today's U.S. Mint. Once workmen cleared away the obstruction in the early 1870s, the land beyond became easily accessible to the downtown shopping and business district, and homestead associations began selling lots to families wishing to live in the suburbs. As early as 1870, houses were being built on the former Hillside Homestead grounds, bounded by Noe, Beaver, Fourteenth, and Castro streets. The Flint Tract Homestead Association, adjacent to the Hillside property, ran along Castro Street and up the hill toward Buena Vista Park. These lots were particularly desirable, according to one newspaper, because "a splendid view of the city is obtained, and a large strip of the bay is seen."

The houses going up all over town in the late nineteenth century were far more comfortable than the dwelling houses of the 1850s and 1860s. They had hot and cold running water, gas lighting, fully equipped kitchens and bathrooms, and fireplaces in many of the rooms to take the chill off a foggy or rainy day. The city outside their front doors had matured considerably since the 1850s. Now the streets were properly graded and regularly sprinkled with water in dry weather to keep down the dust. Some streets were even paved or macadamized. Except for outlying districts, most streets had sidewalks, usually of wood plank, and there were gas lights to offer some illumination on moonless or foggy nights.

By the 1880s and 1890s, middle class San Franciscans were living as well as their Eastern peers. But San Francisco houses had some important differences. "There seems to be a passion for bay windows—'they are all the rage.' The smallest cottage and the grandest mansion have their bay or oriel windows," observed B. E. Lloyd. Bay windows came into fashion, so the story goes, to catch every bit of available sunlight in the often foggy and overcast San Francisco climate. That is true. But San Franciscans were not the

only Americans enamored of bay windows in the late nineteenth century. The bay window had come into fashion in East Coast cities after the Civil War, because it offered a way to break the visual monotony of long stretches of flat-fronted row houses. The bay window, in theory, lent some individuality to a house. But every city house had to have its bay window, and the rows of bay-windowed houses looked just as monotonous as the long stretches of flat fronts.

The bay window was more popular in San Francisco than in any other city, and it became the trademark for the city's Victorian residential architecture just as brownstone was the only acceptable facade material in New York and the "bow front" was the last word in Boston.

San Francisco houses, furthermore, were "more ornamental" than those on the East Coast, according to Lloyd. Architectural taste was freer and less traditional in San Francisco. But the reason that the houses were more elaborately decorated in San Francisco than on the East Coast had more to do with available building materials than differences in taste. Redwood was the local building material, and it was much easier to carve than the traditional brick or stone. Even the humblest cottage had its gingerbread ornament around doors and windows and at the roofline. All this ornament was a mixed blessing, according to Lloyd. "There is a picturesqueness about it that is pleasing, but there is also, unfortunately, a great deal of sameness, as if everything was done by mill-work and by the same pattern." That was to be expected when most houses were erected on speculation and their architectural embellishment was mass produced in factories.

Some of Lloyd's contemporaries did not view the town's architecture as a mixture of good and bad. They thought it was downright awful, which must come as a shock to Victorian-loving San Franciscans today. One of the problems, in these people's eyes, was the architectural eclecticism in vogue in the 1880s and 1890s. They were much happier with the predictable and restrained Greek Revival and Italianate styles. In 1886 one newspaper pointed to the "mania for curiously shaped dwellings" that "raged principally

in the western part of town. Not only has their configuration been a marvel to eyes accustomed to straight lines and even surfaces, but the painting and exterior embellishment has been done in a miraculously slapdash manner."

The real villain, according to one newspaper, was the Eastlake style. The craze for Eastlake houses began in San Francisco about 1880. "The Eastlake designs look very pretty when they are planned . . . but most of the so-called Eastlake architecture in this city does not deserve the name." In fact, Eastlake was not a style in the true sense of the word, and Charles Eastlake wasn't even an architect. He wrote a book, *Hints on Household Taste*, on interior decoration and sensible, honest furniture styles. Architects latched onto some features of his furniture designs and in the eclectic spirit of the age started applying them to buildings. There were no rules as to what did or did not constitute an Eastlake design, but the term became a fashionable, readily marketable catchword for the frenzied architecture of the 1880s and 1890s.

Not surprisingly, some San Franciscans were unhappy with these houses. One newspaper described them as "carpenters' frenzies" and "saw and hatchet artistry." Helen Hunt Jackson, it turned out, didn't like any of the local residential architecture dating back to the 1850s or the way the houses were perched on hills.

Some of the houses were almost incredibly small, square, one story high, with a door in the middle, between two small windows. Others were two stories high, or even two and a half, with little dormer or balconied windows jutting out in the second story; but there was none large, none in the least elegant, all of wood, painted in light shades of buff, yellow or brown, the yellow predominating. . . . These were evidently the homes of the comfortable middle class of San Francisco.

Many of the houses on the highest seaward streets are handsome, and have pleasant grounds about them. But going only a few steps further seaward, you come to or look down on crowded lanes of dingy, tumbling, forlorn buildings, which seem as if they must be forever slipping into the water. As you look up at the city from the harbor, this is the most noticeable thing. The hills rise so sharply and the houses are set on them at such incredible angles that it wouldn't surprise you, any day when you

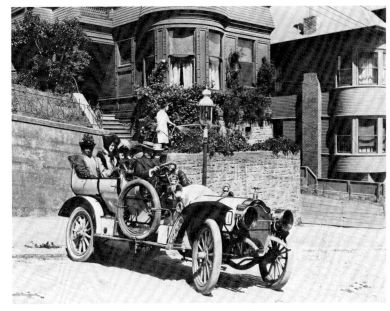

2323 Franklin Street, 1906

are watching it, to see the city slide down whole streets at a time. If San Francisco had known it was to be a city, and if (poor, luckless place that it is, in spite of all its luck) it had not burned down almost faster than it could build up, it might have set on its myriad hills a city which the world could hardly equal. But, as it is, it is hopelessly crowded and mixed, and can never look from the water [like] anything but a toppling town.

Some San Franciscans even feared that their town lacked any style or beauty. "San Francisco is not now architecturally handsome. Perhaps it will never be," declared one newspaper in 1875. Three years earlier, a *St. Louis Republican* reporter had written: "San Francisco is not a beautiful city in daylight, view it from any point you may. Striking it is, but certainly never beautiful."

In terms of domestic architecture, the buildings were actually no better and no worse than those in other American cities. And San Francisco houses did enjoy the handsome hillside settings,

Opposite, 19th Avenue, 1905

with spectacular views, which were unavailable in much of the rest of the country. But many San Franciscans suffered from an inferiority complex regarding their taste and culture and were unsettled by the enormous changes sweeping their city. Trade engulfed once-quiet residential streets, while prostitution swept into other once-respectable districts. Some neighborhoods, like North Beach, boomed briefly and then slumbered for decades.

Typical of the changes that troubled old time residents was what happened on Stockton Street. Back in the 1850s, Stockton Street, between Clay and Union, was a stylish residential area, the rival of Rincon Hill and South Park. In 1852 the *Annals* reported that Stockton Street was "being ornamented with many handsome brick tenements which were intended for private residences of the wealthier citizens.

Stockton Street began to run downhill in the 1860s as the Chinese moved into the area. Very few of the old houses were actually torn down. They were turned into rooming houses or business buildings. In 1905 the San Francisco *Argonaut* wrote that "a visit there today is a painful shock," because of the "examples of dilapidation and ruin wrought by the coming of the Chinese." On the block of Stockton Street between Jackson and Pacific, the former homes of Thomas O. Larkin, Judge M. Hall McAllister, Judge J. P. Hoge, real estate developer John Middleton, and Dr. J. P. Whitney were still standing, but they were sadly run down and every room was occupied by at least one Chinese family. Banker F. L. A. Pioche's residence on the block between Sacramento and Clay streets had become the Chinese consulate. The grocery store at the southwest corner of Powell and John streets had been Grace Church in the 1850s and later the J. B. Haggin residence. Around the corner on John Street, then "the head center of the Negro colony," stood the one-time James C. Flood house.

A few houses retained their old time appearance and dignity. In 1905 shipping prince Martin R. Roberts' house still stood at the northwest corner of Stockton and Washington streets behind its handsomely planted gardens and cast-iron fence. Next door, to the north, stood the one-time home of Captain F. W. Macondray, the

tea merchant. Lawyer John Benson's cottage survived on Stockton Street, near California, "looking much as it ever did, save for lack of paint."

The passing years were also cruel to Rincon Hill. Most Rincon Hill houses were still standing at the turn of the century, but they usually were being used as boardinghouses. Only a few were as elegantly maintained as ever and occupied by well-to-do families, often the descendants of the original builders. George Gordon's tasteful Italianate row houses still surrounded South Park, but many of them were shuttered and looked to be empty or had a "Rooms To Let" sign on the front door. The South Park oval was still there, but it was untended and the pretty flower beds had given way to weeds and overgrown geraniums.

The decline of ex-Governor and U.S. Senator Milton S. Latham's mansion at 630 Folsom Street paralleled the fate of the neighborhood. Latham had lost his fortune and moved to New York City in the late 1870s. The mansion and its grounds were so grand that only a rich family could afford to live there in proper style. Such families no longer wanted to live on Folsom Street by the 1880s, no matter how handsome the residence. The house had several owners in quick succession after Latham, and, by the 1890s, had become a boardinghouse.

Jack London, who was born in 1876 near Third and Brannan streets, around the corner from South Park, described the neighborhood of his youth in his story, "South of the Slot." "Old San Francisco . . . was divided by the Slot . . . North of the Slot were the theaters, hotels, and shopping district, the banks and the staid, respectable business houses. South of the Slot were the factories, slums, laundries, machine shops, boiler works, and the abodes of the working class."

Remnants of Rincon Hill's genteel past still lingered around the turn of the century. One local landmark that had not changed much over the decades was John Parrott's mansion at 620 Folsom Street, next door to Latham's mansion. When Parrott died in 1884, his widow, Abby, sold the property to the Wieland family who owned the nearby brewery. They did not seem to mind the

M. R. Roberts residence, northwest corner of Washington and Stockton streets, 1863

increasingly noisy and commercial world just beyond their carefully trimmed lawns and old-fashioned gates.

The finest remaining home on Rincon Hill was the forty-room Peter Donahue residence at 454 Bryant Street, at the northeast corner of Second Street. Just before the turn of the century, the *Morning Call* described it as "one of the few houses in this locality which has improved with age." Several photographs taken in 1894 show its grandeur. The three-story mansion had a mansard roof, elaborate carved ornaments, and a central entrance that was approached by a long flight of steps and sheltered by a Corinthian-columned front porch. The grounds occupied the 300-foot-wide Bryant Street blockfront between Second Street and Stanley Place and included a carriage house, servants' quarters, palm trees, a fountain, urns on pedestals, and even a statue of a deer. A broad white and black marble tile sidewalk led from the front gate to the stairway that reached the front door.

The photographs of the Donahue mansion in 1894 include the surrounding neighborhood, and it doesn't look all that run down. Industry and workingmen's boardinghouses moved into the southern slope of Rincon Hill more slowly than into the northern slope. In the photograph a pleasant row of two-story Italianate houses, much like those going up in the Western Addition, stand on Stanley Place (now Sterling Street) facing the side of the Donahue mansion grounds. All this vanished in the 1906 earthquake and fire.

The story of the April 18, 1906 earthquake is so well known that it has entered the national folklore, along with the Chicago Fire of 1871 and the Johnstown Flood of 1889, as a great natural disaster and test of man's heroism and resiliency. Even today, most Americans think of earthquake when they think of San Francisco.

The damage caused by the earthquake showed San Franciscans how carelessly much of their city had been built. The Palace Hotel suffered broken glass, cracked marble floors, and fallen plaster. But the hundreds of thousands of dollars that Ralston had poured into the hotel to make it earthquake resistant had been well spent. No important structural damage occurred, and the proprietors expected things to be back to normal within a week.

Many buildings around town were not that fortunate. Real estate speculators and builders had ignored the lessons of the 1865 and 1868 earthquakes. Hundreds of buildings collapsed outright or fell over on their neighbors. Damage was particularly severe in the landfill areas along the waterfront, south of Market Street, and in the Mission district. Stone and brick facades tumbled into the streets in piles of rubble, leaving the rooms and furniture open to everyone's view on the street.

Perhaps the greatest shock of the earthquake was what happened to the new $6,000,000 City Hall. The building had been under construction for twenty years and was an impressive, though ungainly, symbol of civic pride. But its grandeur was only superficial. Entire walls crumbled and massive stone columns fell into the street, leaving the relatively intact dome oddly perched above the twisted debris. City Hall, one man observed, was "now a ruin, noble with a beauty that it had lacked when entire."

The real destruction came from the fire that broke out immediately after the earthquake. Only seven months before, in October, 1905, the National Board of Fire Underwriters announced that San Francisco's water system, which had a 36,000,000-gallons-a-day capacity, was unsafe in event of a major fire. Fire Chief Dennis Sullivan agreed with the assessment. For several years, he had tried to get the Board of Supervisors to build a backup salt water system and to put the old cisterns buried beneath the streets back into operation again. But he had gotten nowhere.

Once the 1906 fire got started, it is doubtful that even those measures would have saved the city. The Fire Department's alarm station on Brenham Place in Chinatown had been virtually destroyed in the earthquake. Many firehouses were badly damaged, and, even if the men could calm the horses enough to harness them to the fire engines, it was difficult to get through the broken and rubble-choked streets. Once the men reached the scene of a fire, there was almost no water to fight it. The water mains had been broken in the twisting of the earth, and the hydrants delivered only a feeble stream before running dry.

At first, San Franciscans did not realize what danger their city was in. They expected the fire department to put out all the fires. They rescued the people trapped in the rubble of fallen buildings, talked with their friends and relatives about the calamity they had just lived through, and went downtown to see what had happened to their offices or businesses. General Frederick Funston, leaving his apartment at Washington near Jones Street for downtown, surveyed the city from Nob Hill. "There came not a single sound, no shrieking of whistles, no clanging of bells," he wrote later. "The terrific roar of the conflagration, the crash of falling walls, and the dynamite explosions that were to make the next day hideous, had not yet begun."

By the time the fire was extinguished on April 21, some 490 square blocks and 28,000 buildings lay in ruins. The business district and three-fifths of the entire city were gone. An estimated 450 San Franciscans were dead; 250,000 people were homeless. San Francisco was virtually destroyed, but its spirit wasn't broken. It would rise again—as yet another instant city.

Chronology of an Instant City

1776

June 29
Presidio of San Francisco founded.

October 9
Mission Dolores founded.

1835

June 25
First building in Yerba Buena pueblo erected.

October
William Richardson draws first official plan of Yerba Buena.

1846

City Hotel, the first hotel in Yerba Buena, built at the southwest corner of Clay and Kearny streets.

July 9
Captain John Montgomery and men from the *U.S.S. Portsmouth* seize Yerba Buena without a struggle.

1847

January 30
Yerba Buena renamed San Francisco.

late
Portsmouth Square schoolhouse, the first in San Francisco, erected.

1848

San Francisco's estimated population at the beginning of the year is 1000.

January 11
First anti-gambling law enacted.

January 24
Gold discovered on the American River.

February 2
First Chinese arrive in San Francisco.

May
San Francisco is nearly deserted as many people leave town for the gold fields.

Summer–Fall
San Francisco booms. The first Gold Rush crowds begin arriving from the East Coast.

Fall
Latin American prostitutes set up their tents on the south slope of Telegraph Hill.

October
T. Dwight Hunt, the first Protestant clergyman in town, arrives from Hawaii.

November
Post Office opens at Clay and Pike streets.

1849

January 9
The "first regular banking house," Naglee & Sinton's Exchange and Deposit Office, opens.

May 20
First Presbyterian Church organized.

June 22
First concert in San Francisco: Stephen C. Massett's songs and piano music performed in the Portsmouth Square schoolhouse.

July
Brig *Euphemia* converted into a floating prison.

August
Reporter Bayard Taylor arrives to cover the Gold Rush for the *New York Daily Tribune*.

October
Rainy season begins. Fifty inches of rain reportedly fall in the Winter of 1849–1850.

December 24
The first fire.

December
Real estate values drop. Prices begin to rise again early in 1850.

1850

San Francisco's estimated population is 20,000 to 25,000 by the end of 1850.

January 3
Sale of beach and water lots.

February
City sets aside several acres near Eighth and Market streets for Yerba Buena Cemetery.

March 18
All land titles that have been granted or sold by any person other than the elected Alcalde or Town Council are declared illegal by the Town Council.

April 1
Government established for San Francisco County.

April 15
San Francisco incorporated as a city.

May
City begins planking streets to avoid a repeat of the 1849–1850 Winter "mud plague." Seventeen streets planked, in part, by the onset of the 1850–1851 rainy season.

May 4
The second fire.

May 11
Construction begins on San Francisco's first brick building, at Montgomery and Merchant streets.

June 14
The third fire.

August 14
Rowe's New Olympic Ampitheatre opens on Montgomery Street, between California and Sacramento streets.

September
Charles P. Kimball publishes the first San Francisco City Directory.

September 17
The fourth fire.

September 25
Board of Aldermen orders free education for all children ages four to eighteen.

October–November
Cholera epidemic strikes the city.

October 30
Jenny Lind Theater opens.

November 18
Charles L. Wilson given right to build a toll plank road from San Francisco to the Mission Dolores.

1851

An estimated 3,000 Chinese live in San Francisco.

January
The first steam paddy arrives in San Francisco, speeding up the cutting down of hills and filling of swamps. Yerba Buena cove is being filled in quickly.

January 19
The First Presbyterian congregation moves into its prefabricated church on Stockton Street between Broadway and Pacific streets. They had originally worshipped in a tent.

March 26
The State gives up title to all land below the high water mark within the city limits of San Francisco.

May 4
The fifth fire, which comes on the first anniversary of the third one, destroys eighteen square blocks, nearly three quarters of the city. $12,000,000 in damages.

June 9
First Committee of Vigilance formed.

June 13
Jenny Lind Theater reopens on Kearny Street, near Washington Street.

June 22
The sixth fire.

July
Winn's Fountain Head restaurant opens.

October 4
Jenny Lind Theater reopens again.

October 20
The American Theater, the first brick building erected on the landfill below Montgomery Street, opens on Sansome Street, between California and Sacramento streets.

1852

May 22
The Board of Aldermen fixes a fire district, the first law to reduce the danger of fire in San Francisco.

July 4
Woodward's What Cheer House hotel opens on Sacramento Street.

December
Parrott Block is finished at the northwest corner of Montgomery and California streets.

December
Fourteen volunteer fire companies in town.

December
By the end of this year, handsome houses have been built on Stockton Street. Growth has begun on Rincon Hill, too.

December 6
The Board of Aldermen enacts a building code intended to bring about fire resistant construction.

1853

San Francisco's estimated population is 50,000, of whom 8,000 are women.

January
Winn's Branch opens.

May 1
Russ' Gardens opens.

July 17
Construction begins on St. Mary's Church at California and Grant streets.

September 11
First telegraph connects Point Lobos with the Merchants Exchange.

October 22
The St. Francis Hotel burns.

November 17
Street signs ordered by the Board of Aldermen.

December
The Montgomery Block completed by the end of the year.

December
Real estate values drop. Beginning of several years' hard times for San Francisco.

1854

April 12
U.S. Bonded Warehouse at Battery and Union streets collapses.

May 30
Lone Mountain Cemetery dedicated.

October 5
Meiggs skips town.

November 2
First cobblestone paving: Washington Street, between Grant and Kearny streets.

1855

Enough Chinese immigrants have settled in the vicinity of Sacramento and Grant streets that the newspapers are beginning to call the area "Little China."

June 20
The Board of Aldermen order the surveying of the area west of Larkin Street.

October
Custom House on Battery Street completed at the cost of $850,000.

1856

November 29
Maguire's Opera House opens.

1857

June 15
San Francisco Water Works organized.

December 15
Johnson's Melodeon opens.

1858

Local economy picks up after several years of stagnation. A boom period is beginning for San Francisco.

1859

December 5
Gilbert's Melodeon opens.

December 19
Work begins on the Market Street Railroad.

1860

Federal census counts 56,802 people in San Francisco.

The city's built-up area ends around Larkin Street.

July 1
The San Francisco and Mission Railroad finished. Service begins three days later.

July 25
Nevai Shalome Cemetery opens.

November 8
Calvary Cemetery dedicated.

1861

February 26
Gibbath Olom Cemetery opens.

April 4
Spring Valley Water Company is filling the Potrero Hill reservoir.

July 1
Mason Street Schoolhouse opens at Washington and Mason streets.

July 3
Arrival of the first Pony Express shipment.

1862

Lick House hotel opens.

Occidental Hotel opens.

Russ House hotel opens.

September 4
North Beach and Mission Railroad organized.

November
North Pacific Review reports that Robert Woodward is putting together a collection of Italian paintings, including some copies of the Old Masters. This collection will form the first public art gallery in San Francisco.

November 6
Direct telegraphic link opens between New York and San Francisco.

1863

San Francisco's population is estimated to be 115,000, quite a jump over the 56,802 counted in the 1860 federal census.

July 2
Spring Valley water first enters San Francisco from Lake Honda.

September 1
Travel between San Francisco and Oakland simplified with the start of railroad and ferry connections.

1864

Point Lobos Toll Road opens, along the route of Geary Boulevard.

January 26
Masonic Cemetery Association organized.

May 18
Maguire's Academy of Music opens.

June 11
The end 300 feet of Meiggs Wharf blown away in a storm.

August 31
Cosmopolitan Hotel opens.

1865

September 24
James Cooke walks from Cliff House to the Seal Rocks on a tightwire.

October 8
Earthquake.

1866

Robert Woodward returns to Europe to enlarge his collections.

March 23
Temple Emanu-El on Sutter Street consecrated.

May 4
Woodward's Gardens opens.

December 3
Paid fire department starts.

1867

Lone Mountain Cemetery renamed Laurel Hill Cemetery.

July 21
City Gardens opens at 12th and Folsom streets.

July 31
New California Market opens.

November 4
Blasting at Telegraph Hill.

1868

October 21
Earthquake.

1869

April–November
Second Street "cut" completed.

1870

Federal census counts 149,473 people in San Francisco, up from 56,802 in 1860.

Bodies in Yerba Cemetery removed to Golden Gate Cemetery.

City growth pushing out Market Street, past Mint Hill, toward Buena Vista Hill and Castro Street.

1871

December 28
First stone laid for new City Hall, rising on site of Yerba Buena Cemetery.

1873

J. B. A. Haggin residence completed; it is the first mansion on Nob Hill.

Salt water aquarium, the first in America, opens at Woodward's Gardens.

August 2
Andrew Hallidie makes the first trial run of his cable car on Clay Street, between Kearny and Jones streets.

1875

City growth is extending beyond Van Ness Avenue, into the Western Addition.

Summer
Anthony Trollope visits San Francisco; he doesn't like anything he sees.

October 5
Palace Hotel opens.

1876

January 17
Wade's Opera House opens.

March 6
Baldwin Hotel opens.

June 3
Anti-queue ordinance enacted.

1877

Point Lobos Toll Road sold to
the city.

July 15
Work starts on California Street
Railroad.

July 24
First "sandlot riot" shows the depth
of anti-Chinese feelings in
San Francisco.

1880

Federal census counts 233,959
people in San Francisco, up from
149,473 in 1870.

City growth is pushing into
Pacific Heights.

1883

Adolph Sutro opens the grounds of
his Land's End mansion to the public.

1884

John Parrott dies. His widow,
Abby, sells their Folsom Street
mansion to the Wieland family.

1885

A report made to the Board of
Supervisors documents the overcrowding in Chinatown.

1886

Adolph Sutro begins planting trees
on barren hills like Twin Peaks and
Mount Davidson.

1890

Federal census counts 298,997
people in San Francisco, up from
233,959 in 1880.

1893

Woodward's Gardens closes.

1898

November 23
Baldwin's Hotel destroyed in a fire.

1900

Federal census counts 342,782
people in San Francisco, up from
298,997 in 1890.

March 26
The Board of Supervisors prohibits
the burial of the dead in San
Francisco after August 1, 1901.

1905

October
The National Board of Fire Underwriters judges San Francisco's water
system possibly inadequate in event
of a major fire.

1906

April 18
Earthquake. The fire starts which
will burn down much of the city.

Bibliography

Schaeffer, L. M.
    York, 1860.
Shaw, Pringle. R
Shumate, Albert.
Soulé, Frank, Jol
    New York, 18
Starr, Kevin. Am
Stillwell's San F

Abandone
Alta Califo
  72, 79,
  128, 12
American
Angelique,
Annals of S
  24, 25,
  35, 37,
  51, 53,
  76, 79,
  103, 1(
  150, 1!
Apartmen
Appollo, 1!
Arson, 44
Asbury, H
Atherton,
Ayres, Jan

Baldwin, I
Baldwin's
Banking,
Barbers, 5
Battery St
Bay Wind
Beale Stre
Big Four,
Blacks, 11
Boardingh
Bonanza k
Bootblack
Borthwick
  35, 36,
  58, 62,
Broadway,
Brown, Jo
Bryant Str
Buena Vis

A partic
Amelia Ran:
Historical Sc
the turn of t
zine and new
people. Unfc
librarian. Ma

Aidala, Thor
  1974.
Asbury, Herl
Atherton, G
Bancroft, Hu
  1890.
Barth, Gunth
Borthwick, J.
Bronson, Wi
  1959.
California His
  Portsmouth
  An Hour's
    pp. 29(
  The Makin
    pp. 32:
  The Makin
    pp, 65-
  Vanished W
    June, 1
  San Franci
    ber, 19
  Paradox To
    pp. 30-
  Food Habit:
    1958, p
  Food Habit
    1958, p
  Eldorado G
    1959, p
Camp, Willian

Grid Street Plan, 23
Growth, 16, 39–40, 81, 83–84, 87
Gwin, William, 67

Haggin, James Ben Ali, 139
Hall, William Hammond, 115
Halleck, Henry W., 51, 67
Happy Valley, 17, 28, 51, 76, 89
Harrison Street, 67, 89, 109
Hayes Street, 85
Helper, Hinton R., 31, 35, 58, 106
Hillman's Temperance Hotel, 58
Hills, 15, 40, 86, 89, 105, 157
Holinski, Alexandre, 55
Home Journal, 87,127
Hopkins, Mark, 140–141
Hospitals, 148
Hotels, 16, 19, 53–56, 110,
  124–133
Houses,16,17, 19, 20, 21, 23, 33,
  65–70, 82–83, 87, 151–160
Hullyer, C. J., 152
Hunt, Rev. T. Dwight, 62
Huntington, Collis P., 139
Huntley, Sir Henry Vere, 55
Hutching's California Magazine, 79

Illustrated London News, 21, 39
Indians, 27
Industry, 51, 70, 76, 78–79, 147
Ingleside Inn, 121
Iron Foundries, 78

Jackson, Helen Hunt, 122, 124, 157
Jackson Street, 44
Jackson's Restaurant, 57
Jenny Lind Theaters, 103

Jewett, William S., 23, 81
Jones' Hotel, 53, 55

Kearney Street, 53, 93, 103, 134
King, James, of William, 75
Kip, Bishop William I., 67, 89, 152
Kipling, Rudyard, 124

Lammot, Robert, 60
Lamson, J., 34
Landfill, 40, 42, 82, 89
Landmarks, 46, 87
Land's End, 118, 121
Larkin Street, 51, 76, 151
Larkyns, Major Harry, 92
Latham, Milton S., 158
Laundry, 29
Laurel Hill Cemetery—see
  Lone Mountain
Le Count and Strong's Directory,
  1854, 51
Leidesdorff, William A., 15, 16
"Leg Preserving Ordinance," 42
Lick House, 129, 131
Lights and Shades in San Francisco—
  see B. E. Lloyd
Little Chile, 33
Lloyd, B. E., 24, 32, 64, 78, 85,
  90, 93, 94, 95, 96, 99, 103, 105,
  112, 115, 118, 124, 127, 128,
  129, 132, 133, 134, 143, 145,
  149, 155
London, Jack, 158
Lone Mountain Cemetery, 117–118
Loneliness, 25, 73, 149
Long Wharf, 31

McCoppin's Canal, 85
McCraken, John, 32, 45, 71

McLaren, John, 117
Macondry, Frederick, 92
Maguire, Thomas, 103
Maison Doreé, 134
Market Street, 17, 48, 53, 76, 79,
  85, 93, 117, 128, 129, 134,
  148, 155
Markets, 56, 76
Marryat, Frank, 44, 57, 59
Mason, Richard B., 12
Massett, Stephen C., 101
Masturbation, 148–149
Meiggs, Henry, 86
Meiggs Wharf, 105, 134, 136
Mercantile Library, 100–101
Mexican War, 11
Middleton, John, 83, 89
Mission Creek, 51, 76, 87, 143
Mission District, 109, 110, 152,
  155, 160
Mission Dolores, 11, 48, 56, 62, 83,
  85, 117
Mission Road/Street, 109, 110
Montgomery, Captain John, 11
Montgomery Block, 51–52
Montgomery Street, 16, 24, 34, 40,
  43, 44, 46, 51, 53, 72, 73, 81,
  93, 124
Morton Street (now Maiden Lane),
  96
Moving Buildings, 82–83
Muybridge, Eadweard, 92
Muybridge, Flora, 92

Naylor, Peter, 21
Neville, Amelia Ransome, 140–141
New York Daily Tribune, 12, 32, 104
New York Evening Post, 23
New York Herald, 12, 72

Niantic, 19–20
Nob Hill, 12, 17, 40, 51, 65, 82, 93,
  136, 139–142
North Beach, 81, 83, 86, 117, 134
North Pacific Review, 76, 85, 110,
  123
Nymphia, 97

O'Donnell, C. C., 147
O'Farrell, Jasper, 11
Oakland, 95, 105, 123
Occidental Hotel, 131–132
Ocean House, 121
Office Buildings, 51–52
Oriental Hotel, 53

Pacific Heights, 152
Palace Hotel, 125–128, 160
Palmer, W. L., 68
Panama, 12, 19
Panhandle, 115
Parker's Building, 46
Parker House, 15, 16, 20
Parks, 68, 106, 116–117
Parrott, Abby M., 67, 158
Parrott, John, 20, 51, 67, 68, 139,
  158
Parrott Block, 20, 51
Permissiveness, 36–37, 62, 71, 86
Phinney, J. B., 43
Plummer, Charles G., 55
Point Lobos Turnpike, 121
Polhemus, Charles B., 67
Poodle Dog, 134
Population, 39, 43, 73, 87, 142, 152
Pornography, 70–71
Portsmouth Square,16, 27, 33, 35,
  43, 46, 62, 83, 106, 150

Post Office, 52
Powell Street, 64, 72, 134, 139
Prefabricated Buildings, 20–23, 53, 64
Presidio, 11, 29, 56, 83
Prevaux, Lydia Rowell, 24
Prieto, Guillermo, 124
Prison, 149–150
Prostitution, 33–35, 60, 72, 93–99, 121, 147
Public Health, 24, 43, 145–146, 148
Public Transportation, 67, 83, 85

"Queue Ordinance," 147

Racism, 27, 146–147
Rae, W. F., 99–100
Rain, 17, 19, 21, 23–24, 40
Ralston, William, 125, 127
Rats, 24, 57
Real Estate, 17, 71, 79, 81, 83, 85–89
Rents, 17
Restaurants, 17, 19, 21, 55–58, 110, 133–136, 145
Reuf, Abe, 99
Rincon Hill, 12, 28, 67–68, 89–90, 158, 160
Rix, Chastina, 72–73
Roberts, Martin, 158
Royce, Sarah, 60
Russ' Gardens, 109
Russian Hill, 12, 17, 65, 117
de Russailh, Albert Benard, 31, 33, 34, 60, 104
Ryan, William, 17

de Saint Amant, Pierre Charles, 58, 117
St. Francis Hotel, 53, 64
St. Louis Republican, 124, 128, 131, 157
St. Mary's Cathedral, 64–65, 93
Sacramento River, 11, 12
Sacramento Street, 23, 57, 110, 136, 139, 143, 152
Sailors Home, 148
Saloons, 58, 59, 65, 136
San Francisco Argonaut, 67, 158
San Francisco Bulletin, 67, 68
San Francisco Chronicle, 62, 71, 106
San Francisco Courier, 150
San Francisco Examiner, 111, 114, 148
San Francisco Herald, 81, 143
San Francisco Morning Call, 160
San Francisco News Letter, 140, 152
San Francisco Sugar Refinery, 78–79
Sather, Pedar, 90, 92
Schaeffer, L. M., 29, 58
Schliemann, Heinrich, 21
Schools, 65
Schoolhouse on Portsmouth Square, 62, 65, 101
Scribner's Monthly, 134, 148
Sea Lions, 122
Second Street, 67, 68, 83, 87, 89–90, 92
Selby, Thomas, 67, 89
Sheet Metal, 21, 23
Sidewalks, 24, 40, 155
Sloan, Samuel, 65
South Beach, 67, 89
South Park, 68, 70, 83, 92, 158
South Van Ness Avenue, 155
Stanford, Leland, 139–140
Starr, Ralph, 123

Steam Paddy, 40, 42, 67, 89
Stevenson, Robert Louis, 90
Stockton Street, 23, 48, 64, 65, 72, 82, 93, 123, 158
Stoddard, Charles Warren, 90, 92, 101
Street Grades, 24, 82, 155
Street Planking/Paving, 23, 24, 40, 81, 155
Street Railroads, 83, 85
Suicide, 31, 147, 148
Sutro, Adolph, 106, 122
Sweeny & Baugh, 118
Sydam, J. 17
Synagogues, 83

Taylor, Bayard, 15, 17, 19, 21, 23, 27, 29, 31, 40, 51, 53
Telegraph Hill, 12, 17, 33, 52, 89, 117, 118
Tents, 17, 19, 35
Theaters, 101–104
Third Street, 67, 93
Tightrope Walkers, 122
Toilets, 24, 155
Tourists, 121, 123
Trade, 40, 43, 52, 75, 79
Transcontinental Railroad, 123–124, 147
Trinity Episcopal Church, 64
Trollope, Anthony, 124–125

Union Hotel, 53
Union Square, 82, 96
U.S. Bonded Warehouse, 43
U.S. Exchange Hotel, 43
U.S.S. Portsmouth, 11

Valencia Street, 109
Vallejo Street, 28, 148
Van Ness Avenue, 152
Vernon Place, 68

Ward House, 53
Warehouses, 19, 21, 40, 42, 43, 44, 51
Warner, Abe, 136
Washerwoman's Lagoon, 29
Washington Street, 44, 64, 81, 139
Water Supply, 12, 24, 48, 51, 68
Western Addition, 92, 152, 160
Weston, William, 45
Wharves, 11, 15, 44, 148
What Cheer House, 57, 110–111, 114, 133
Wiley, Reverend Samuel H., 45
Williams, Samuel, 134, 148
Willis, Nathaniel Parker, 87
Willows, 109
Winn's Branch/Fountain Head, 58
Winter of 1849–1850, 23, 24, 40, 62
Women, 27, 31–35, 39, 58, 59, 71–73, 101, 134
Woodin, Stephen, 105
Woodward, Robert B., 57, 109–114
Woodward's Gardens, 109–114, 115
Work, 39, 71, 72, 73
Wyld's Guide, 17, 21, 29, 32, 39, 43

Yerba Buena, 11, 87
Yerba Buena Cemetery, 117, 118
Yerba Buena Cove, 12, 15, 40, 42, 43, 82

Zoning, 70, 76